BUILDING

YOUR

DREAM
HOUSE

BUILDING
YOUR
DREAM
HOUSE

WILLIAM P. SPENCE

STERLING PUBLISHING CO., INC.
NEW YORK

DISCLAIMER

The author has made every attempt to present safe and sound building practices, but he makes no claim that the information in this book is complete or complies with every local building code.

The publisher does not warrant or guarantee any of the products described herein or perform any independent analysis in connection with any of the product information contained herein. The publisher does not assume, and expressly disclaims, any obligation to obtain and include information other than that provided by the manufacturer.

The reader is expressly warned to consider and adopt safety precautions that might be indicated by the activities herein and to avoid all potential hazards. By following the instructions contained herein, the reader willingly assumes all risks in connection with such instructions.

The author and publisher make no representation or warranties of any kind, including but not limited to the warranties of fitness for a particular purpose or merchantability, nor are any such representations implied with respect to the material set forth herein, and the publisher takes no responsibility with respect to such material. The publisher shall not be liable for any special, consequential, or exemplary damage resulting, in whole or part, from the reader's use of, or reliance upon, this material.

Library of Congress Cataloging-In-Publication Data

Spence, William Perkins, 1925–
  Building your dream house / William P. Spence.
    p. cm.
  ISBN 1-4027-0086-5
  1. House construction—Amateurs' manuals. 2. Dwellings—Designs and plans. I. Title.
  TH4815 .S677 2003
  690'.837—dc21

                                    2002010865

BOOK DESIGN: RENATO STANISIC
EDITOR: RODMAN PILGRIM NEUMANN

10 9 8 7 6 5 4 3 2 1

Published by Sterling Publishing Co., Inc.
387 Park Avenue South, New York, NY 10016
© 2003 by William P. Spence
Distributed in Canada by Sterling Publishing
c/o Canadian Manda Group, One Atlantic Avenue, Suite 105
Toronto, Ontario, Canada M6K 3E7
Distributed in Great Britain and Europe by Chrysalis Books
64 Brewery Road, London N7 9NT, England
Distributed in Australia by Capricorn Link (Australia) Pty. Ltd.
P.O. Box 704, Windsor, NSW 2756 Australia
Printed in Hong Kong
All rights reserved

Sterling ISBN 1-4027-0086-5

CONTENTS

INTRODUCTION 8

SECTION ONE: SOME ARCHITECTURAL STYLES

1 GALLERY OF HOMES 13

SECTION TWO: PLANNING THE HOME

2 PLANNING THE ROOMS 118

3 PLANNING THE FOYER, LIVING ROOM, FAMILY ROOM, DEN, RECREATION ROOM, HOME OFFICE & BASEMENT 122

4 PLANNING KITCHENS & DINING ROOMS 144

5 PLANNING BEDROOMS, LAUNDRY ROOMS, STORAGE FACILITIES & UTILITY ROOMS 173

INTRODUCTION

The demands placed on the American home today have changed considerably from those of past generations. The use of the computer, the Internet, and various methods of telecommuting from the home have made significant changes. More families have both husband and wife working and there are more single parents. This hectic pace of life influences the facilities and design of kitchen areas and dining spaces. More people are working from a home office. The explosion of electronic entertainment devices and the expansion of television sources is a factor to be considered. The need for rooms to be flexible to meet changing requirements as children get older or the parents retire is a major consideration. The busy home needs space for family activities and hobbies that today are many and are part of the beauty of family life.

This book is designed to help those planning a new home or undertaking a remodeling project to make the best use of the space available and develop a flexible floor plan providing for the multiple uses of today's home. It will help with planning individual rooms and the relationships between these rooms. Information on the process of selecting a building site and concluding the purchase without ending up with legal problems is presented. And finally, a general story of how a typical house is built will help conceive a structure, which will be your dream house.

As you work on the plan, more detailed information about the technical aspects of the house become more important. In order to explore these in detail, consider the information in the following publications.

Additional Information

Other books by William P. Spence published by Sterling Publishing Co., Inc. provide detailed information about the many aspects of building a house.

Carpentry & Building Construction, 1999
Constructing Bathrooms, 2001
Constructing Kitchens, 2001
*Constructing Stairs, Balustrades
    & Landings, 2000*

Doors & Entryways, 2001
*Encyclopedia of Construction Methods &
    Materials, 2000*
*Encyclopedia of Home Maintenance
    & Repair, 2000*
Finish Carpentry, 1995
Installing & Finishing Drywall, 1998
Installing & Finishing Flooring, 2003
Residential Framing, 1993
Windows & Skylights, 2001

SECTION ONE:

SOME ARCHITECTURAL STYLES

A GALLERY OF HOMES

The concept of a home has changed dramatically over the last several decades. The lifestyle of the family has changed due to many technical developments and the pressures on the members of a family. The infusion of computers, the Internet, multimedia products, and other developments have changed the way the family lives in a house. Two working parent families and parents working full time at home have created a need for revised use of space. The rapid development of new materials and construction techniques require consideration of factors not available just a few years ago. Life is on a faster pace and planning is necessary to accommodate the needs of the individual family members.

OPPOSITE PAGE: *Courtesy California Redwood Association, Novato, CA*

The way some people look at a house has changed. Some prefer quality design and materials even if the size of the living area is a bit smaller. They also are interested in the character of the house and a location and design that provides efficient and relaxed living. They want a house that reflects them—not a mass produced cookie-cutter dwelling. Privacy both inside the building as well as from the exterior is widely desired.

Designers are giving more attention to providing living spaces where the entire family can relate to each other—such as an integrated living, dining, and kitchen space—yet provide privacy areas for children to study and play as well as the home office now so widely required.

As the home is designed, attention must

ABOVE: *Courtesy California Redwood Association, Novato, CA*

also be focused on other important aspects, including building codes, a buildable site, future maintenance and repairs, the possibility of expanding the house in the future as family needs change, construction costs, financing, quality construction, and availability of utilities.

The family home is often the major financial asset and deserves careful planning, design, and material selection. In addition to meeting the multiple needs of today's busy family, thought must be given to providing value so it becomes a stable asset in the family financial situation. One additional factor to maintaining value over the years is location. The old cliché that the three most important things when selling a house are location, location, and location is true today.

This first chapter presents a series of fine homes ranging from cottages through homes of various sizes and designs. The designs vary somewhat depending upon the section of the country in which they have been built. Others represent variations of classic designs that have been widely used over several centuries. Study these homes and use ideas you see as you develop your dream home.

REDWOOD HOMES—STRUCTURES OF GREAT BEAUTY

LEFT: *The dramatic roof enhanced by dormers and a two-story window presents a house with a pleasing mass and proportions. The redwood siding blends with the darker roofing material forming a pleasant, unified building.*

BELOW: *The beauty of the redwood siding blends this house into the surrounding water and vegetation. The whole scene is a house in harmony with its environment.*

Courtesy California Redwood Association, Novato, CA

ABOVE: *This redwood paneling on the walls and ceiling form a warm, secluded atmosphere that is enhanced by multiple sources of light.*

RIGHT: *This raised bathtub has redwood steps and platform and is surrounded by walls covered with redwood paneling. The warmth of the walls provides sharp contrast with the white ceiling.*

Courtesy California Redwood Association, Novato, CA

LEFT: *Redwood paneling frames the fireplace forming the focal point of the room.*

BELOW: *The beauty of the exterior glazing is framed by the warm redwood paneling. The light color ceiling provides a pleasant contrast and reflects the natural light across the room. The white sofa provides a prominent focal point of the sitting area.*

Courtesy California Redwood Association, Novato, CA

A CLASSIC COLONIAL

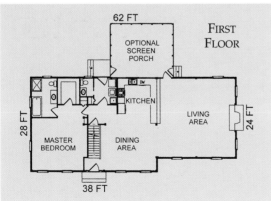

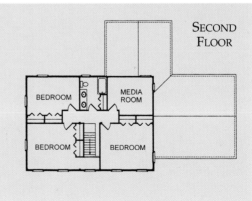

ABOVE: *This classic two-story colonial has two fireplaces, custom brickwork with quoins on the corners, and the typical symmetrical front elevation. The post and beam framing, beamed ceilings, and rustic fireplace establish the colonial appearance typical of this era.*

Courtesy Habitat Post & Beam, Inc., 800.992.0121

ABOVE: *The dining room has a large fireplace typical of American colonial homes. The beamed ceiling and natural wood balustrade add to the atmosphere.*

LEFT: *This view is from the second floor down the stair to the front door. One side is open to the dining room.*

Courtesy Habitat Post & Beam, Inc., 800.992.0121

The large living room has a beamed vaulted ceiling with natural, exposed wood decking providing a warm, rustic atmosphere. Double hung windows are typical. The walls are finished with gypsum wallboard.

Courtesy Habitat Post & Beam, Inc., 800.992.0121

A EUROPEAN/AMERICAN COUNTRY HOME

ABOVE & LEFT: *General and Mrs. Hodges spent many years in Europe. Upon retiring they designed this home using many of the architectural features from European residences. It has stucco exterior finish. Notice the wide, dark framing around the windows and the small panes of glass.*

Courtesy Major General (Ret.) and Mrs. Paul Hodges

ABOVE TOP: *The living room has a cathedral ceiling and considerable natural light. The large window shown is the one on the front of the house. The room has wide aisles between furniture making it easy to move about.*

ABOVE BOTTOM: *This is a small conversation area providing a place for informal visiting. It opens onto the courtyard.*

Courtesy Major General (Ret.) and Mrs. Paul Hodges

LEFT & BELOW: *The foyer has a high ceiling giving a spacious feeling. It has a hardwood floor and is lighted by a wrought iron chandelier. The dining room is seen in the background.*

Courtesy Major General (Ret.) and Mrs. Paul Hodges

ABOVE: *The kitchen arranges the white cabinets along the walls forming a U-shaped kitchen. The small office is part of these cabinets. The island counter is the focal point of the kitchen. A small breakfast area is just outside the kitchen.*

LEFT: *This custom-built island counter has a polished granite top into which a cooking unit has been placed.*

Courtesy Major General (Ret.) and Mrs. Paul Hodges

ABOVE: *The master bedroom was planned to accommodate two queen size beds. This requires a very large room. The atmosphere is enhanced by the natural light flowing through the full length curtains.*

RIGHT: *This is a small powder room off the foyer. The white cabinet stands out against the combed, walls that are painted hunter green.*

Courtesy Major General (Ret.) and Mrs. Paul Hodges

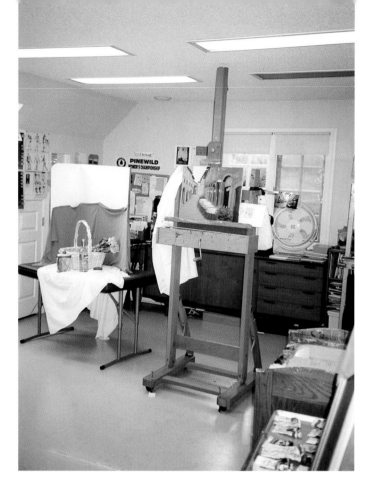

RIGHT & BELOW: *Mrs. Hodges has her studio on the second floor. The artificial light provides the same illumination as natural northern light. Skylights that can be shielded are also available.*

Courtesy Major General (Ret.) and Mrs. Paul Hodges

ABOVE: *In the den is a large home office with a computer and cabinets providing considerable storage.*

LEFT: *An office in the kitchen is used for the many daily household duties.*

Courtesy Major General (Ret.) and Mrs. Paul Hodges

An open courtyard enclosed on three sides by walls of the house has a slate floor. It is ideal for entertaining. The open end is enclosed by a high hedge with an iron gate which is typical in Europe. One wall has a lion head fountain.

Courtesy Major General (Ret.) and Mrs. Paul Hodges

CONCRETE HOMES—STRENGTH, QUIET, SAFETY

ABOVE: *This beautiful house was built with concrete walls and faced with a brick veneer. Concrete homes have airtight walls that reduce energy loss. The mass of the concrete wall is an effective sound barrier. Lower energy bills and insurance costs are other features as is the safety provided during tornadoes, hurricanes, and earthquakes. The design of the house and the arrangement of the rooms is completely flexible as with other types of construction.*

RIGHT: *The beautiful living room in this concrete house features a large conversation area focused on the fireplace. The massive structure is not only strong but forms a design element for the room and the exterior of the house.*

Courtesy Portland Cement Association, Skokie, IL

LEFT: *These concrete walls have been finished with a plaster coating. The concrete mass provides the quiet desired in a bedroom. The windows provide considerable natural light and have reed shades to provide privacy when desired.*

BELOW: *This unusual L-shaped kitchen has glass doors on the wall cabinets and a large island counter containing a surface cooking unit that also serves as a snack bar. The concrete floor is slightly colored and provides a durable, fire-resistant surface.*

Courtesy Portland Cement Association, Skokie, IL

A CONTEMPORARY HOME WITH A VIEW

ABOVE: *This contemporary home was designed to blend into the surrounding landscape. The tan stucco, weathered wood shake roof, and low profile provide the desired features.*

LEFT: *The living room opens onto a large porch with a fireplace. This fireplace adjoins the one in the living room.*

Courtesy Mr. and Mrs. Harvey Marcy

Designed by William Brown, A.I.A. and Mrs. Eleanor Macy, Architectural Designer

ABOVE: *The living room, dining room, and a conversation area all share this long glazed rear wall. This wall faces a glorious view of a lake, a short distance away.*

RIGHT: *The view from the rear rooms and deck is impressive.*

Courtesy Mr. and Mrs. Harvey Marcy

LEFT: *A large deck extends completely across the back of the house enabling those using it to relax and enjoy the view of the lake.*

BELOW: *The garage is a separate building and is connected to the main dwelling with a portico.*

Courtesy Mr. and Mrs. Harvey Marcy

RIGHT: *The living room has a cathedral ceiling. The fireplace backs up to a porch that also has a fireplace.*

BELOW: *This view of the living room shows how large it is and how easily it accommodates a grand piano. Notice the fully glazed wall.*

Courtesy Mr. and Mrs. Harvey Marcy

ABOVE: *The kitchen is formed into a square. The white cabinets blend with the walls and ceiling in the adjoining rooms. The light system provides general and task illumination. The breakfast area is convenient.*

RIGHT: *The formal dining room features an area carpet over the ceramic tile floor. It has a view of the lake at the rear of the house.*

Courtesy Mr. and Mrs. Harvey Marcy

ABOVE TOP: *Here is a busy home office. Notice the computer station and the separate writing table.*

ABOVE BOTTOM: *This is a conversation area on the rear of the house providing an informal, relaxed place to read and visit. It has a full view of the lake.*

Courtesy Mr. and Mrs. Harvey Marcy

A RUGGED LOG HOME

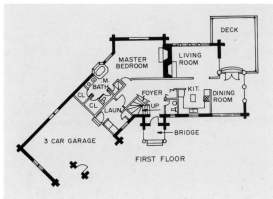

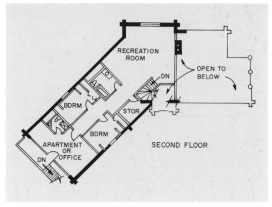

This rugged log home was built on a high elevation in northern Idaho. It is built on an angle to fit the site and maximize the view. The end wall enclosing the dining room is glazed to the roof. Notice the use of natural stone on the foundation. Overall it fits snuggly into the rugged terrain surrounding it.

Courtesy Edgewood Fine Log Structures, Coeur d'Alene, ID

The huge log truss spans the width of the home providing a wide area for the kitchen, dining, and living rooms.

Courtesy Edgewood Fine Log Structures, Coeur d'Alene, ID

The massive truss and horizontal beams support solid wood roof decking. The decking provides a warm subdued atmosphere bathed by considerable natural light from the exterior glazing. The deck is accessed from the end of the living room. Notice the railing made from locally gathered wood providing a rustic look. Notice the large glazed wall providing a great view.

Courtesy Edgewood Fine Log Structures, Coeur d'Alene, ID

The formal dining room has a breathtaking view of Silver Mountain. This design was inspired by the Japanese tradition of blurring the distinction between the interior and exterior space.

Courtesy Edgewood Fine Log Structures, Coeur d'Alene, ID

THE COTTAGE HOME

Early cottages in the United States were built by the settlers using the designs they knew in their home country. They used materials locally available and built small houses because of the time and difficulties of construction. As the years passed, people prospered, and materials were produced enabling larger houses to be built. The early Cape Cod house was one of those that developed and was copied in many parts of the country. Influences from other cultures also were reflected in the design of these early small houses.

The houses, while small and humble, were adorned with features such as brackets on the eaves, chimney caps, and hoods over the windows. The cottage became a small, affordable, and charming dwelling. Various cottage styles were built through the years from coast to coast. Local culture and materials had some influence but architects were also producing "storybook" designs.

ABOVE: *This newly built cottage reflects the charm of the early New England cottage on the exterior, yet uses the best of current thinking when planning the use of space on the interior.*

Courtesy Habitat Post & Beam, Inc., 800.992.0121

Through the past century families have become smaller and the homes being built are larger. People have begun to realize the value of a smaller home commonly referred to as a cottage. The current cottage home reflects the lifestyle of many younger people today. Many married young couples are finding the concept attractive. The number of single people is increasing and some prefer a private cottage to an apartment or duplex. The number of retired persons is increasing and some find a small, less pre-tentious, less costly cottage appealing especially if there is less maintenance. Cottages are being built today all over the country in rural and urban areas.

Currently there is still much interest in the cottage home. Architects have designed a wide array of "new cottages." One big change was away from a building with a lot of small, separate spaces toward the concept of a more open floor plan. Living areas, dining areas, and kitchens flow into each other. Also there is emphasis on a relationship to

Contemporary cottages are designed using the open floor plan popular in all types of residential planning. The living room, kitchen, and dining room meld together utilizing all of the available space rather than forming many small rooms as was typical of the early cottages.

Courtesy Habitat Post & Beam, Inc., 800.992.0121

the outdoors through the use of decks and patios. The modern-day cottage, while still quaint and charming, is quite different from those in past years and makes much better use of the space available.

The design of a cottage provides an opportunity to use the best ideas to produce an efficient, attractive living area to suit your contemporary lifestyle. As you design your cottage do not overlook the opportunity to use architectural detailing to produce character and a unique structure. Open planning can provide a feeling of spaciousness in a small area.

The cottage should have a special appeal providing a charming, cozy atmosphere, simplicity in interior and exterior design, and careful choice of materials to get the warm, intimate appeal that is part of the overall concept. The location of the building site is also an important part of the overall design. The cottage should fit into the surroundings as if it naturally grew from them. Native plantings and preservation of the site during construction are important.

Some things people like in a cottage include the use of smaller windows to fit the scale of the building, bare wood floors, exposed rafters and beams, low ceilings, use of a large deck or patio to expand the living area, an efficient kitchen, compact eating areas, modern bathroom facilities, and an adequate heating and air-conditioning system.

A fireplace is an important part of the overall plan. A rugged, rough-framed cottage may have a stone fireplace or one built from used brick. A more refined cottage may have a conventional fireplace or a manufactured unit.

The use of natural building materials on the exterior such as cedar shakes, redwood siding, natural stone walls, and chimney, and textured concrete stucco add to the ambience of the true cottage. One that will fit in its environment.

The open space and plain walls are typical of the early American cottages. Simplicity was and still is a part of the charm of this type of cottage.

Courtesy Habitat Post & Beam, Inc., 800.992.0121

A HISTORIC COTTAGE

ABOVE & BELOW: *The Longleaf Cottage, circa 1919*   **Courtesy Mr. and Mrs. Colin Bentley**

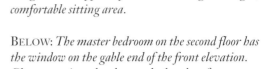

LEFT: *The living room features a wall of short double hung windows typical of this time. This gives a light, comfortable sitting area.*

BELOW: *The master bedroom on the second floor has the window on the gable end of the front elevation. Closet space is under the steeply sloped roof.*

LEFT: *This classical dining room has double hung windows typical of this era. Notice the unique wall-covering.*

ABOVE: *The foyer has been recessed into the living room forming a light, attractive entrance.*

Courtesy Mr. and Mrs. Colin Bentley

OTHER COTTAGES

ABOVE: *A real log cottage built in North Carolina in 1815. It is still maintained and used daily as a public building.*

LEFT: *A very small cottage with a quaint entry and two fireplaces. The bricks are smaller than standard and thus are in proportion to the small size of the building.*

ABOVE TOP: *This new cottage is quite large yet architecturally maintains the ambience of the cottage concept. The use of cedar shingles causes it to blend into the surroundings.*

ABOVE BOTTOM: *A symmetrical cheery cottage with wood siding and small windows that are in proportion to the size of the building. The roof over the front porch not only protects visitors in inclement weather but is a major architectural feature.*

ABOVE TOP: *A larger cottage with rooms on a second floor. The high pitch of the roof is matched by the roof over the front entry producing a balanced attractive home. Notice the hoods over the windows on the first floor.*

ABOVE BOTTOM: *A beautifully balanced cottage with a unique arched roof over the large front porch. The wood shingle roof provides a bit of character.*

This cottage uses a gambrel roof to provide considerable living space on the second floor.

This quaint cottage has cedar shingles producing a honey color when the sun strikes them. Notice the extra wide trim around the small windows. This is typical of early cottage designs.

BUILD SMALL—EXPAND LATER

Some people do not have the funds to buy a three bedroom house yet want a place of their own. One way is to find a nice site and purchase it. As the payments become manageable, you can then plan the house you wish to build. This can be done in two or more stages. First, build a minimum house in which to live—crowded, but a home. When you have accumulated enough equity, you can secure a loan to build the addition. The example on these pages illustrates how this may be accomplished. One caution when you buy the site: Check local ordinances to be certain you can build a house with a small number of square feet of living space. Some have minimum sizes which would prohibit building in this way.

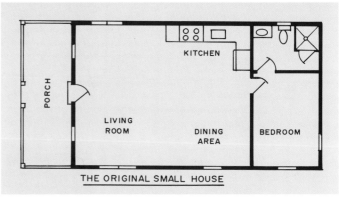

ABOVE: *This small house has a porch manufactured from a polymer providing an attractive and low-maintenance architectural feature.*

Courtesy HB and G Permaporch Systems

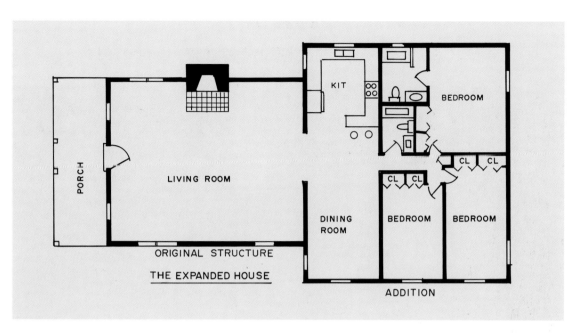

ORIGINAL STRUCTURE

THE EXPANDED HOUSE

PORCH

LIVING ROOM

DINING ROOM

KIT

BEDROOM

CL CL

BEDROOM

BEDROOM

CL CL

ADDITION

FRONT ELEVATION—EXPANDED HOUSE

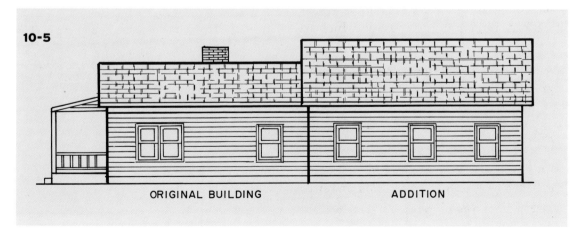

10-5

ORIGINAL BUILDING

ADDITION

A TOUCH OF FRENCH COUNTRY

ABOVE: *This home with its large steep hipped roof and solid masonry walls reflects the images of the classic French Country House. It has vinyl clad, double glazed, energy efficient windows and requires very little exterior maintenance. The high roof not only adds to the architectural mass, but also provides space for several rooms on the second level and a loft over the kitchen.*

RIGHT: *The 19-foot ceiling in the living area permits the construction of a loft over the kitchen.*

Courtesy Dr. and Mrs. William P. Spence

ABOVE LEFT: *Access to the second floor is through a series of arches.*

ABOVE RIGHT: *The massive fireplace extends two stories high. It also serves as a sound barrier for the bedrooms behind it.*

LEFT: *The sunroom provides a wide view of the countryside.*

Courtesy Dr. and Mrs. William P. Spence

ABOVE TOP: *The living room has a wall of glass opening onto a sunroom.*

ABOVE BOTTOM: *The loft provides a private area for relaxing and reading. It can serve as an extra bedroom.*

Courtesy Dr. and Mrs. William P. Spence

AN OLD NEW ENGLAND POST-AND-BEAM BARN

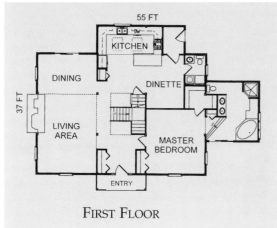

FIRST FLOOR

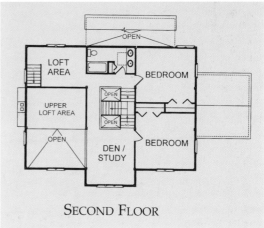

SECOND FLOOR

ABOVE: *This house features the architectural elements of the early New England post-and-beam barn. The large interior volume provides a chance to design a contemporary floor plan within the structure and have living space on three levels. The natural wood provides the charm found in the early structures.*

Courtesy Habitat Post & Beam, Inc., 800.992.0121

LEFT: *This stair and walkway lead to an inviting third level.*

BELOW: *This is a conservatory that has been added to the floor plan providing space for additional family activities.*

Courtesy Habitat Post & Beam, Inc., 800.992.0121

ABOVE: *The volume of the interior space enables the construction of a multilevel open beam framework. This room has a vast open feeling enhanced by the natural wood framing.*

LEFT: *The living room has a high ceiling enhanced by a stone fireplace.*

Courtesy Habitat Post & Beam, Inc., 800.992.0121

AN EXTRAORDINARY CONTEMPORARY HOME

ABOVE: *The walk to the main entrance is covered with a portico starting at the street.*

RIGHT: *The right wing of the house is used for entertaining large groups. It opens to a beautiful pool.*

Courtesy Mr. and Mrs. Robert Menzies

LEFT: *The tower is a dynamic structure providing a 360-degree view of the surrounding countryside.*

BELOW: *The wing to the left of the front entrance contains the family living areas and has access to the tower and gazebo.*

Courtesy Mr. and Mrs. Robert Menzies

ABOVE & RIGHT:
The house is connected by an elevated walkway to a screened gazebo.

Courtesy Mr. and Mrs. Robert Menzies

ABOVE & LEFT: *Two views of the entertainment area. Notice the beautiful, durable tile floor.*

Courtesy Mr. and Mrs. Robert Menzies

LEFT: *The living room has a vaulted ceiling with exposed trusses. Notice the beautiful pine flooring.*

BELOW: *The dining room has a wall of windows and overlooks the heavily wooded countryside.*

Courtesy Mr. and Mrs. Robert Menzies

LEFT: *The hall flows from the foyer to the entertainment area on one side of the house and to the rest of the house on the other side.*

BELOW RIGHT: *The foyer has a high ceiling and is lighted by this unusual luminaire.*

BELOW: *The glazed double entrance doors and side lights provide considerable natural light into the foyer.*

RIGHT: *This small home office has cabinets and paneling that are coordinated with the wood flooring. Notice the large window that provides natural light.*

BELOW: *A peninsula kitchen counter separates the kitchen from a small dining area. A large window provides natural light and a view.*

Courtesy Mr. and Mrs. Robert Menzies

AT HOME IN HAWAII

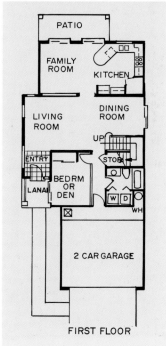

FIRST FLOOR

PATIO

FAMILY ROOM

KITCHEN

LIVING ROOM

DINING ROOM

UP

ENTRY

LANAI

BEDRM OR DEN

STOR

W D

WH

2 CAR GARAGE

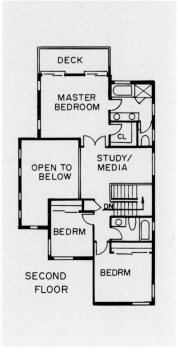

SECOND FLOOR

DECK

MASTER BEDROOM

CL

OPEN TO BELOW

STUDY/ MEDIA

DN

BEDRM

BEDRM

ABOVE & LEFT: *This award-winning house has a concrete stucco exterior finish, a clay tile roof, and vinyl windows providing a maintenance-free exterior. The living area is open to a vaulted ceiling. Notice that the area over the dining room is used as a study/media area, which is open to the living area. A covered entry lanai protects visitors from inclement weather. The exterior design consists of a series of rectangular structural elements providing emphasis for the mass of the structure.*

Courtesy Sculer Homes, Inc. Honolulu, Hawaii

ABOVE: *The living and dining areas are on the open plan and have considerable window area providing natural light and a view of the surrounding area. The two-story vaulted ceiling over the living room is dramatic. The railing that is along one wall of the study/media area on the second floor provides an interesting architectural feature. The dining and living spaces use area carpets to give them identity.*

RIGHT: *The kitchen/family room areas open into each other providing access and an informal dining space and relaxation area. Large glass doors provide a view of the beautiful countryside. Since the kitchen is near the patio outdoor entertainment is facilitated.*

Courtesy Schuler Homes, Inc., Honolulu, Hawaii

A CONTEMPORARY POST-AND-BEAM HOUSE

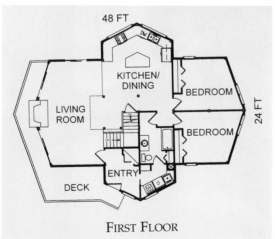

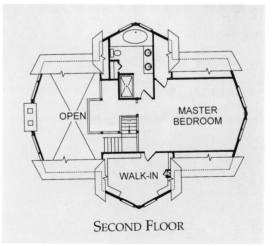

This contemporary design features a two-story wall of glass lighting a living room with a cathedral ceiling. Natural wood framing and finish materials provide a warm, pleasant atmosphere.

Courtesy Habitat Post & Beam, Inc., 800.992.0121

This two-story glass wall frames the dramatic fireplace and provides an expanded view of the lake.

Courtesy Habitat Post & Beam, Inc., 800.992.0121

ABOVE: *This spacious kitchen has a beautiful beamed ceiling that also supports the rooms on the second floor. The windows provide a generous view of the heavily wooded surrounding area.*

LEFT: *A unique bathroom on the second floor has a whirlpool tub below a glazed gable. The natural wood ceiling provides an attractive architectural feature.*

Courtesy Habitat Post & Beam, Inc., 800.992.0121

AN ECLECTIC COUNTRY HOME

ABOVE: *This home was built on a multi-acre, heavily wooded site slopping to the rear. The brick veneer is painted white. The home has a long rambling floor plan.*

RIGHT: *The front entrance is protected with an arched porch roof that was a design element found in early Roman buildings.*

Courtesy Mr. and Mrs. Robert Clark

Designed by Robert Clark, A.I.A.

ABOVE: *The back of the house has living and dining areas with an expansive view of the large, heavily wooded site.*

LEFT: *The left wing has a large garage with several rooms and a bath above. They are spacious and enjoy considerable natural light.*

Courtesy Mr. and Mrs. Robert Clark

ABOVE & LEFT: *The exterior is enhanced by a number of architectural features. Architectural detailing contributes a great deal to the overall appearance of a home.*

Courtesy Mr. and Mrs. Robert Clark

LEFT: *The massive custom-built fireplace has a five-foot-wide firebox. It is painted white to coordinate it with the brick exterior walls. The wood floor in this and most of the other rooms is also painted white.*

BELOW: *The living room has a large conversation area in front of the fireplace.*

Courtesy Mr. and Mrs. Robert Clark

LEFT: *The kitchen cabinets, walls, and ceiling are white as are all the walls, ceilings, and floors in the other rooms.*

BELOW: *The dining room has a ceramic tile floor with the table centered on an area carpet. The window faces the rear wooded area.*

Courtesy Mr. and Mrs. Robert Clark

ABOVE TOP: *This is a small conversation area located off the living room. It provides a more intimate space to visit with friends.*

LEFT & ABOVE : *The entertainment center gets the television away from the formal living room. It also is a quiet place to relax and read.*

A UNIQUE DREAM HOUSE

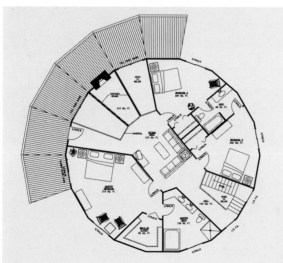 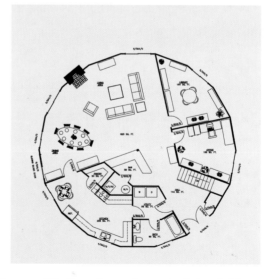

This unique round house provides a panoramic view from all the rooms. The floor plan can be custom designed. The circular roof is built with trusses meeting at the center. Therefore, the entire interior is free from load-bearing walls.

Courtesy Deltec Homes, Asheville, NC

ABOVE: *The curved, glazed exterior wall of the living room provides a panoramic view of the mountains in the distance.*

LEFT: *The dining room windows open to a deck that curves along the exterior wall. Natural light brightens the room.*

Courtesy Deltec Homes, Asheville, NC

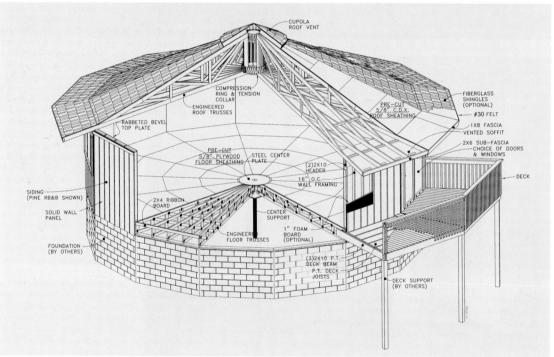

ABOVE TOP: *The kitchen cabinets line the curved exterior wall giving an interesting overall appearance. Notice the considerable glazing providing natural light and a view.*

ABOVE BOTTOM: *A cutaway illustration showing the unique structural system of this type of house.*

Courtesy Deltec Homes, Asheville, NC

This bedroom has the curved exterior wall as shown on the floor plans. This gives room for large windows providing ventilation and natural light. Notice the wood ceiling.

Courtesy Deltec Homes, Asheville, NC

AN IMPRESSIVE MEDITERRANEAN HOME

ABOVE: *This Mediterranean home has a clay tile roof and stucco exterior walls. The symmetrical design of the front elevation is especially appealing.*

RIGHT: *The front entrance is approached through a loggia sheltering the front entryway and is the focal point of the front elevation.*

Courtesy Mr. and Mrs. Conley Williams

Staggard and Choa, architects; Longstreet Construction Co.; Southern Landscape Co., Village Interior Decorators.

ABOVE: *Architectural details enhance the visual appeal and produce a very interesting structure.*

ABOVE LEFT: *The arched ceiling has been painted to reflect the sky with clouds drifting by.*

ABOVE RIGHT: *A convenient vanity.*

RIGHT: *The master bathroom has many special features.*

Courtesy Mr. and Mrs. Conley Williams

ABOVE & LEFT: *The main living area is centered around an unusual fireplace. Notice the wood paneling and cabinets, which provide a rich, warm atmosphere. The entire area has a ceramic tile floor.*

Courtesy Mr. and Mrs. Conley Williams

ABOVE: *The large area occupied by the living room and dining room has a high, heavy trussed roof structure, which adds to the open feeling of the area.*

RIGHT: *This attractive fountain adjoins the living room. Notice the extensive glazing providing natural light and a view of the grass patio area outside.*

Courtesy Mr. and Mrs. Conley Williams

ABOVE: *The dining room has French doors opening on to an exterior porch. Notice the use of an area carpet on the ceramic tile floor.*

LEFT: *This cabinet separates the dining room from the living room to create a large living area free of partitions.*

Courtesy Mr. and Mrs. Conley Williams

ABOVE TOP & LEFT: *The kitchen is organized around a large island counter. The cabinets and refrigerator have matching wood surfaces.*

ABOVE: *A pleasant dining area is part of the overall kitchen layout.*

Courtesy Mr. and Mrs. Conley Williams

ABOVE: *This balcony is off the master bedroom. It has a view of the golf course and a lake.*

LEFT: *The beauty of this waterfall and lily pond is obvious.*

ABOVE & LEFT: *Considerable attention has been given to exterior design features.*

Courtesy Mr. and Mrs. Conley Williams

ABOVE TOP & BOTTOM: *These exterior porches are very unusual. They have a masonry foundation and wood floor joists, over which narrow wood decking has been installed.* **Courtesy Mr. and Mrs. Conley Williams**

ABOVE TOP & BOTTOM: *Landscaping was a big part of the overall plan for the house. The gate with a wrought iron fence and the driveway with plantings provide a frame through which the house is viewed from the street.*

Courtesy Mr. and Mrs. Conley Williams

HOUSE 19

A SOUTHERN HOME ON A LAKE

ABOVE & RIGHT: *This home is typical of some large Southern houses built in the early days of this country and is still a popular choice.*

Courtesy Mr. and Mrs. Theodore Shebs

ABOVE: *The sunroom on the right side of the house is entered from the living room and the dining room.*

LEFT: *The Carolina room on the back of the house has large windows. Notice the circle top windows that project natural light toward the high ceiling.*

Courtesy Mr. and Mrs. Theodore Shebs

ABOVE: *The dining room and living room are open to each other providing a spacious living area.*

RIGHT: *The living room and dining room have 24-foot ceilings. They both open onto the sunroom.*

Courtesy Mr. and Mrs. Theodore Shebs

LEFT: *The kitchen has a large gas-fired cooktop and a microwave. The custom cabinets blend into the wall.*

BOTTOM: *The spacious kitchen is built around a large custom-built island counter that doubles as a breakfast area.*

Courtesy Mr. and Mrs. Theodore Shebs

ABOVE: *The sunroom is accessed from the living and dining rooms. It provides an expanded area for entertaining large groups.*

LEFT: *This is the Carolina room on the back of the house. It faces the lake and has a great view through the large windows. It has a 16-feet high ceiling.*

Courtesy Mr. and Mrs. Theodore Shebs

Above Top: *The deck faces the lake and provides a large area for entertaining as well as a great view of the lake.*

Above Bottom: *The back of the house is finished with wood siding to be more compatible than brickface with the lake and the wooded area.*

ABOVE TOP & BOTTOM: *The deck has a full view of the lake and provides a place for a cookout.*

Courtesy Mr. and Mrs. Theodore Shebs

NESTLED IN THE COUNTRYSIDE

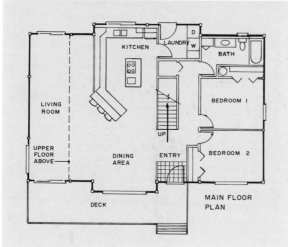

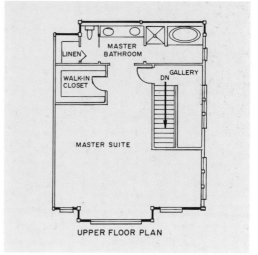

ABOVE TOP & BOTTOM: *This beautiful contemporary western red cedar home nestles quietly into its environment. The cedar siding provides a natural, pleasing color that tends to give a warm glow especially when the sun strikes it. Western red cedar is resistant to decay and attacks by insects such as termites. This house has vinyl windows contributing to a low-maintenance exterior. The cedar shakes on the roof contribute to the overall ambience of the building.*

Courtesy Pan Abode Cedar Homes, Waterford, MI, www.panabodehomes.com

ABOVE: *The massive beams supporting the western red cedar roof decking provide a large open bedroom area. The cedar walls give a warm frame to the large glazed opening. The floor is covered with a lighter brown shade of carpet, tying the room together.*

RIGHT: *This well lighted kitchen provides a large, cheerful food preparation area. The oak cabinets are stained to blend with the western red cedar walls and ceiling. The ceramic tile floor blends in and provides a durable surface.*

Courtesy Pan Abode Cedar Homes, Waterford, MI, www.panabodehomes.com

The living and dining areas are open to each other and are spanned by massive beams supporting the master bedroom above. The wood-burning stove and fire-resistant brick wall behind it blend harmoniously with the cedar wall paneling and ceiling.

Courtesy Pan Abode Cedar Homes, Waterford, MI, www.panabodehomes.com

A GALLERY OF HOMES **99**

AT HOME ON THE FAIRWAY

ABOVE: *This golf course home has a cedar shingle roof and stained vertical cedar siding. It blends into the surrounding wooded countryside. Windows on the front were held to a minimum to preserve privacy.*

RIGHT: *This chimney is an interesting bit of architectural detailing. Such details add much to the overall appearance of the house.*

Courtesy Mr. and Mrs. Don Edwards

ABOVE: *The back of the house faces the golf course and has considerable glazing, giving interesting views of the fairway from each room.*

LEFT: *The fairway as viewed from the kitchen breakfast area, dining room, living room, and the deck.*

Courtesy Mr. and Mrs. Don Edwards

RIGHT & BELOW: *The entryway into the foyer provides access to the stair to the second floor bedrooms. The second floor hall has railings instead of a solid wall providing an interesting architectural feature.*

Courtesy Mr. and Mrs. Don Edwards

ABOVE: *The large living room has a high cathedral ceiling and an entire wall glazed to the floor. This room faces the golf course.*

LEFT: *The fireplace is enclosed in a wall extending to the top of the cathedral ceiling. The second floor hall passes behind it and has railings rather than walls adding to the feeling of spaciousness of the living room.*

Courtesy Mr. and Mrs. Don Edwards

ABOVE: *The kitchen features white cabinets and appliances, light wallpaper, all set off by the hardwood floor.*

RIGHT: *A breakfast area is at the end of the kitchen facing the fairway.*

Courtesy Mr. and Mrs. Don Edwards

ABOVE: *The television/reading room has book storage, comfortable chairs, and good lighting for reading and television viewing.*

LEFT: *The foyer is spacious and has considerable natural light provided by the sidelights and transom windows.*

Courtesy Mr. and Mrs. Don Edwards

A PICTURESQUE FARM HOUSE

ABOVE & RIGHT: *The American farmhouse is a popular style home. This attractive home has a porch wrapping around three sides of the house.*

ABOVE: *The house has a metal roof and bevel siding.*

LEFT: *This detached garage with living quarters above is reminiscent of the barn on the old family farm.*

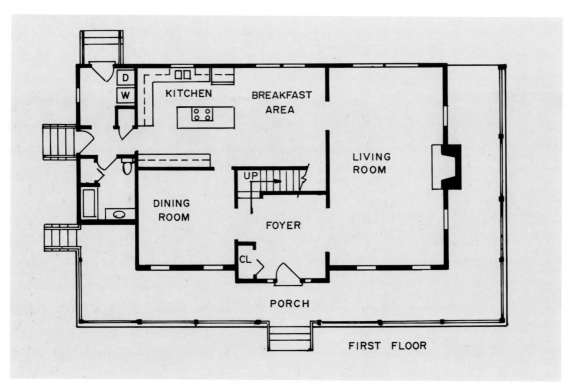

A formal entry hall provides access to a large living room, dining room, and stairs.

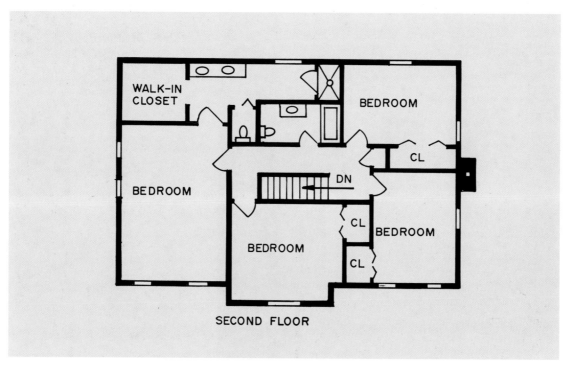

The second floor has a large master bedroom and master bath plus three additional bedrooms and a second bath.

A CUSTOM DUPLEX

ABOVE: *This custom duplex overlooks the rugged terrain in a Colorado resort area. The lower level has recreation rooms with walkout doors and full windows. The main floor houses the bedrooms, bathrooms, deluxe kitchen, and a dramatic, spacious great room.*

LEFT: *From the great room on the main level a stair leads to a loft area. The balustrade has been left natural to blend with the open beam ceiling and wood roof decking. Notice the roof windows that let in additional natural light.*

Courtesy Habitat Post & Beam, Inc., 800.992.0121

LEFT: *A corner of the great room has a totally glazed wall providing a spectacular view. The furnishings and the area carpet provide a subdued, comfortable sitting area.*

BELOW: *The large kitchen has cabinets of wood that blend with the structural framing. The view of the countryside from the kitchen is magnificent.*

Courtesy Habitat Post & Beam, Inc., 800.992.0121

LEFT: *The corner whirlpool bath in a spacious bathroom has a beautiful view of the rugged surrounding territory.*

BELOW: *The recreation room is on the lower level. Notice the heavy beamed ceiling supporting the rooms above. Recessed lights provide general illumination.*

Courtesy Habitat Post & Beam, Inc., 800.992.0121

CREATIVE DESIGN—MASS & FORM

The home can be conceived with the use of natural materials as a creative interplay of mass and form. The design and construction of these residences make use of redwood, a durable natural material, to create dynamic and elegant expressions of form. These range from a reproduction of the old Texas ranch house to the contemporary California house. The use of this durable material is reflected in the residences built in Minnesota where the weather can be severe in winter.

ABOVE: *This Texas ranch house incorporates the overall mass of the traditional house of years ago, yet makes creative use of glazing that did not exist earlier. The redwood siding provides an earth color and will withstand the climate typical of the area. The use of a wood shingle roof and a huge stone fireplace completes the overall blending of materials.*

Courtesy California Redwood Association, Novato, CA

RIGHT: *This creative California house has extensive glazing, which brings the exterior view into the house. It basically has a rectangular mass. Notice the redwood siding has been applied vertically, which gives emphasis to the height. The siding has been applied diagonally on the walls of the inset outdoor sitting area. Overall it is finished with a deck running the full length of the house.*

BELOW LEFT: *This multi-level California house takes advantage of a sloping site, setting the garage into the bank. The house itself is a series of rectangular-mass living areas on two levels, each complemented with a deck. The redwood siding has been applied horizontally, which emphasizes the length of the residence.*

Courtesy California Redwood Association, Novato, CA

ABOVE RIGHT: *This dramatic contemporary residence uses vertically applies redwood siding. The complete covering of all the exterior wall area without the intrusion of a roof fascia establishes a distinct appearance. Even the chimney is covered with redwood siding. The first impression upon viewing this house is the unusual mass. Then one begins to notice the details, such as the deck and glazing.*

Courtesy California Redwood Association, Novato, CA

ABOVE: *A house designed to fit into the wooded territory in Minnesota. The horizontal redwood siding blends naturally with the wood shingle roof. The sloping site permits the left wing to have a basement, a first floor in line with the floors of the other sections of the house, plus a second floor. The three-story glazing provides a bold architectural feature, including the windows set on both sides of the corner of the house.*

RIGHT: *Wood can be formed to produce some striking architectural features. The redwood railing along a deck high above the earth below is a creative use of wood. It combines the beauty of the redwood with the gracefulness of the design.*

Courtesy California Redwood Association, Novato, CA

A REMODELED DREAM HOUSE

Sometimes creating a dream house involves rethinking and remodeling an existing structure. This house was basically a simple rectangular seventy-year old structure that had green wood siding and was in a choice location. With the assistance of an architect, the owners reconceived the design while saving the basic structural frame. A major design feature is the new roof, which sets the architectural tone of the house. The slate roofing provides a rich look of quality. An L-shaped addition was created and the siding is stucco. The result is truly a dream house.

ABOVE TOP & RIGHT: *The garage and guest house were added on the site and connected to the main house with a breezeway. All of the elements have the same architectural characteristics as the main house.*

PLANNING THE HOME

PLANNING THE ROOMS

The homeowner usually has in mind specific features wanted in each room. As each room is planned these are considered, but it is also wise to review articles in magazines that speak to the home and life there. Often additional good features are noticed and if used will increase the usefulness and livability of the room. A visit to dealers selling products used in these rooms and the examination of the many catalogs available give many good ideas. Catalogs and magazines show rooms with various color schemes and these help visualize the finished room (**2-1**).

Decisions must be made concerning the furniture to be used and the size of the room. While it is hard to visualize the size of a room as stated on a drawing you can measure the rooms where you are living and get a good idea of how the newly planned room will turn out. Furniture sizes vary considerably. A visit to furniture, cabinet, and appliance dealer showrooms will help establish furniture sizes. Many brochures with specific sizes are available. Basically the room size will depend upon the furniture to be placed in the room. Make a list of these items and record the possible sizes. This will be used as you plan each room. Reducing the size and number of pieces of furniture is another option.

Furniture Templates

Furniture templates may be made by drawing each piece of furniture on cardboard to a scale allowing ¼ inch (6mm) to represent one foot (305mm). Label the templates and cut them out.

2-1 *Color photos found in magazines and catalogues of companies and trade organizations that supply products for the home are an excellent source of ideas. This photo shows the beauty of redwood paneling, ideas for the use of glazing, and a possible furniture arrangement.*
Courtesy California Redwood Association

Develop Room Arrangements

Decide the approximate size of each room remembering the size will influence the cost. The actual size and shape will be changing throughout the planning process until a final layout of furniture and the floor plan is achieved. It may be that you have some idea about how the floor plan will be laid out before you begin planning each room. This will place some restrictions on the freedom to try a variety of designs but is still a good process.

Draw the outline of the proposed room on a sheet of graph paper having ¼-inch (6mm) squares. Each square represents one foot (2-2). If you are working in metric units use a metric graph paper divided into 1 mm squares with light lines and 5 mm squares with heavy lines. At a 1:50 metric scale 1 mm would represent 50 mm. Therefore each 5 mm square represents 250 mm (2-3).

Try placing the furniture templates in different ways to try to find a good arrange-ment. Mark any possible window locations on the graph paper because this will certain-ly influence the layout. The door could be in several places and can even be moved as the various rooms are arranged into a floor plan. As the floor plan is arranged it may be nec-essary to rearrange some of the furniture. All of this is done observing the principles of good room planning. Carefully observe the planning recommendations and traffic flow within the room. These recommendations are presented in the following chapters.

Consider Room Sizes

The sizes of the room will depend upon the desires of the homeowner, the furniture to be housed, and the cost of the space. You can possibly get an estimated cost per square foot for a house of the type being considered from a local builder. This cost multiplied by the number of square feet in a room will give a rough estimate of the cost of the room. The larger the rooms the more expensive

Table 2-1: Suggested Room Sizes

	Small		Medium		Large	
	sq ft	m²	sq ft	m²	sq ft	m²
Living Room	12 × 18	3.7 × 5.5	14 × 20	4.3 × 6.1	20 × 25	6.1 × 7.6
Dining Room	10 × 14	3 × 4.3	12 × 15	3.7 × 4.6	14 × 18	4.3 × 5.5
Kitchen	8 × 12	2.4 × 3.7	10 × 16	3 × 4.9	12 × 18	3.7 × 5.5
Bedroom	10 × 12	3 × 3.7	12 × 14	3.7 × 4.3	14 × 16	4.3 × 4.9
Bath	6 × 8	1.8 × 2.4	7 × 9	2.1 × 2.7	9 × 12	2.7 × 3.7
Den	10 × 10	3 × 3	10 × 12	3 × 3.7	14 × 16	4.3 × 4.9

the house becomes. Large rooms increase the heating and air-conditioning costs. A room that is too small is a constant annoyance and not a good investment. Use your experience by recalling the sizes of rooms you have had in the past and use them as one source for planning the size. The size of the house will also influence room sizes. For example a house with four bedrooms is typically designed for families of four or more people. Therefore the living room, kitchen, dining areas, and recreation space should be larger than those in a two-bedroom house. Careful planning will help arrive at the best size for the circumstances.

While it is not possible to set firm standards on room sizes for houses occupied by families of various sizes, the data in **Table 2-1** can serve as a guide for possible minimum room sizes. As stated earlier observe your needs and wishes and the furnishings expected to be in the room as sizes are established.

As You Proceed

After making the preliminary decisions about the house begin working on the rooms. Planning details are covered in Chapters 3 through 10 and developing the floor plan is covered in Chapter 11.

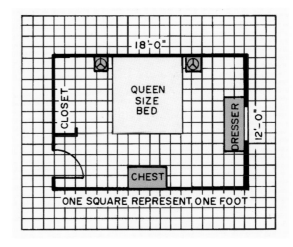

2-2 *Room layouts can be tried by using furniture templates on a scale drawing of the room. This plan uses ¼-inch squares to represent one foot.*

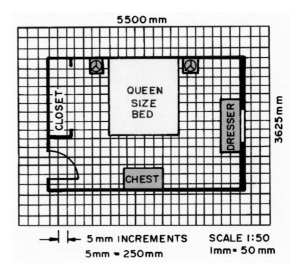

2-3 *The room layout example uses metric size templates and room grid. It is at a 1:50 scale that uses 1mm to represent 50 mm.*

PLANNING THE FOYER, LIVING ROOM, FAMILY ROOM, DEN, RECREATION ROOM, HOME OFFICE & BASEMENT

The rooms discussed in this chapter are all actively occupied and form the main daily living area of the house. They are often close together and carefully separated from the quiet areas, as the bedrooms. The den and home office are sometimes located away from the more active noisy areas.

The Foyer

The foyer is the entryway from the front door to the interior rooms of the house. It serves as the focal point from which those who enter move to the rooms within the house **(3-1)**. The size depends upon the wishes of the homeowner and how the floor plan is laid out. The example in **3-2** shows that it provides direct access to the stair, family room, and living room and a hall through which traffic flows to other rooms.

3-1 The foyer is the entryway into the house. All traffic flows from it to the other parts of the house. The large inlaid area in this foyer enhances its overall appearance. **Courtesy Kentucky Wood Floors**

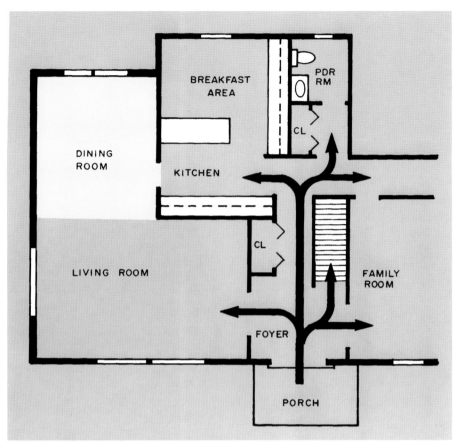

3-2 Notice how the traffic flow from the foyer moves smoothly to the various parts of the house and the stairs.

BREAKFAST AREA

PDR RM

CL

DINING ROOM

KITCHEN

CL

LIVING ROOM

FAMILY ROOM

FOYER

PORCH

It usually is a showplace because it gives the first impression when a visitor enters the house **(3-3)**. A coat closet is often placed along one wall of the foyer.

The floor must be a durable material that will withstand moisture and is easily cleaned. Ceramic tile, slate, brick, and stone are often used. Vinyl floor covering material is also used **(3-4)**.

The foyer should be well-lighted, yet have a soft light so the visitor is not blinded when entering from a dark outside. Natural lighting by sidelights or skylights is good.

3-3 The foyer gives the first impression to the visitor and deserves special consideration.
Courtesy Designed Stairs, Inc. 1-877-4Stairs

3-4 *This foyer has a durable ceramic tile floor leading from the entryway to the stairs and other parts of the house.* **Courtesy Designed Stairs, Inc. 1-877-4Stairs**

3-6 *A fireplace adds a great deal to the atmosphere and enjoyment of the living room.*

3-5 *The living room is a good place to display art and family artifacts.*

Planning the Living Room

In many houses the living room is the most heavily used room. It may serve as a sitting room, television and music room, an office or computer room. It can also serve as a library, possible dining and snack room, and an extra bedroom if there is a sofa bed. Art and sculpture displays as well as other family artifacts are prominent (3-5). It can have a fireplace or wood-burning stove for atmosphere and a little heat (3-6). In a small house it could be the children's play area. Usually it is the largest room in the house and the best furnished. Guests are ushered directly into the living room and get their first impressions of the house. In larger, more expensive houses some of these activities are housed in other rooms commonly referred

3-7 *This is a comfortable living room designed to provide a pleasant conversation area.* **Courtesy American Walnut Manufacturers Association**

to as family rooms, dens, and recreation rooms. In a large, more expensive house the living room is often rather formal and contains quality furniture and art and is used mainly for conversation **(3-7)**.

Frequently the living room and dining room are designed to flow as one large room with no division between them **(3-8)**. This makes both rooms appear larger and is an important consideration in smaller houses. Another technique is to open the kitchen to the living room and dining room again providing a large open area combining the major areas of a house.

Living Room Planning Considerations

The living room should be in a central location easily reached from the front entrance.

The front entrance should open into a foyer as shown in **3-2**, not the living room. If the foyer is omitted part of the living room must serve as a hall. This means people must walk through the living room to get to the other rooms. This breaks up the unity of the furniture arrangement and is annoying to those in the living room. A

foyer is especially important when access to a stair is required.

The living room and dining room should be located near each other as shown in **3-2**. Guests normally visit in the living room before moving to the dining area. Remember, the dining area must be very near the kitchen.

Decide if an open or closed living room is wanted. The open room flows into the

3-8 *When the dining room flows from the living room both rooms seem larger.*

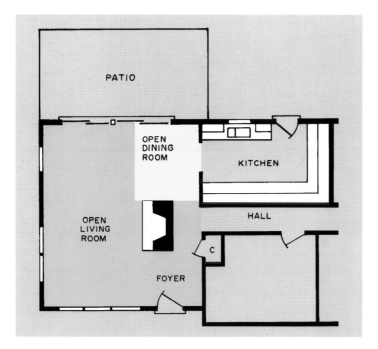

3-9 An open living room permits the area to flow into other rooms and makes all the rooms seem larger.

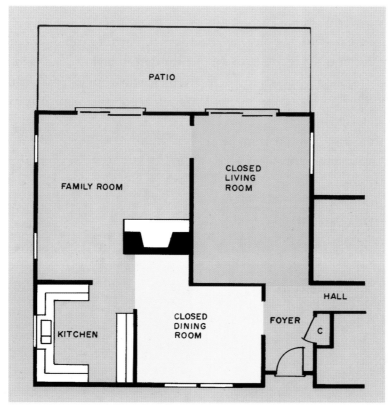

3-10 A closed living room is a private, separate room. It usually has to be a bit larger than an open room holding the same furniture. Notice the dining room is accessible from the kitchen and living room.

3-11 *The living room should face a pleasant view. The site and local conditions will control its location on the floor plan. Glass doors provide a large viewing area and access to a deck facing the view.*
Courtesy Weather Shield Manufacturing Company

3-12 *These sliding doors open up the living room on to a deck and the view beyond.*
Courtesy Kolbe and Kolbe Millwork Co., Inc.

dining room and often into other parts of the house as shown in **3-9**. A closed living room has walls and ceiling completely surrounding it and some form of arched opening providing access **(3-10)**.

The living room should face a pleasant view. This usually requires it to be on the back of the house unless a multi-acre building site is being used **(3-11)**. If the site is a typical small lot the yard can be fenced or landscaped to provide an attractive garden.

Frequently the living room will open on to a deck, patio, screened porch, or sunroom **(3-12)**. This provides additional living space and the pleasant view is still available. Usually a large glazed wall area is provided

3-13 *Sunken living rooms define the space when an open floor plan is used. It is important to clearly mark the step down so those entering do not fall. In these examples the type of flooring is different. The foyer has ceramic tile while the living room and dining room are carpeted.* **Courtesy Mr. and Mrs. Theodore Shebs**

*3-14 The fireplace in the living room was chosen to be the focal point of this living room and a conversation area was centered on it. The oak floor sets the tone for the colors in the room. **Courtesy Harris-Tarkett, Inc.***

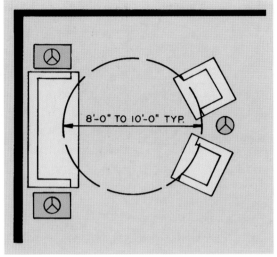

3-16 Chairs forming a conversation area generally are placed abut 8 to 10 feet apart.

on this wall. Energy efficient glazing is important to control energy loss and gain.

Some like the unusual effect of a sunken or raised living room **(3-13)**. This clearly identifies it and provides unusual interior decorating opportunities. However the steps need to be clearly marked and have handrails available on at least one side. A change in the floor covering often calls

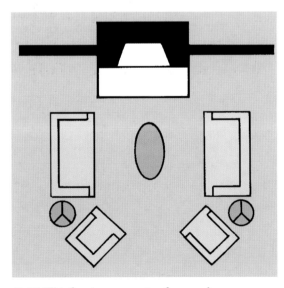

3-15 This furniture grouping forms a pleasant conversation area.

attention to this difference in floor level.

As the room is planned it should be centered about a focal point, as a fireplace, a large window, or special cabinets **(3-14)**. This can also form a pleasant conversation area **(3-15)**. Chairs are often grouped in a section of the living room forming a small conversation area **(3-16)**. They should be grouped about 8 to 10 feet (2440 to 3050mm) apart. If beyond 10 feet conversation becomes difficult.

A large living room can have other furniture groupings featuring an activity, such as a television viewing area, game table, a quiet reading area, or a piano **(3-17)**.

Built-in units, such as bookcases, televisions, planters, or log boxes by the fireplace add convenience and attractiveness to the room. The location of these is influenced by the plan for the placement of furniture and traffic within the living room.

Study the traffic patterns that flow through the living room. These influence

3-17 Small activities areas can be located in parts of a living room. This entertainment center will hold the TV, stereo, VCR, and compact disc player. **Courtesy KraftMaid Cabinetry, Inc.**

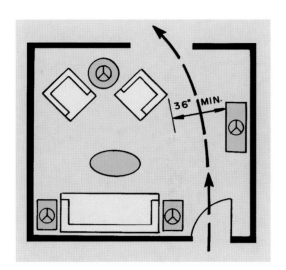

3-18 Avoid routing traffic through the living room to get to other rooms. If this must be done allow at least a 36-inch passageway. This occurs in small homes where space is tight.

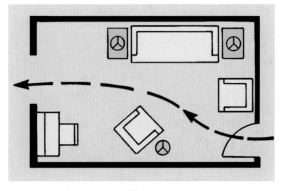

3-19 Avoid routing traffic through a conversation or activity area. This routing makes the room a major hall.

the size and shape of the room as well as furniture placement. The overall floor plan can cause troublesome traffic in the living room or be designed to reduce it to a minimum **(3-18)**. Avoid routing traffic through the room to get to other rooms **(3-19)**.

The furniture plan must allow for easy movement within the room. Aisles for most traffic should be at least 3'-6" (1067mm) or wider. A minor aisle can be as small as 2'-0" (610mm) but this is tight. The aisle that leads guests from the front entrance to the

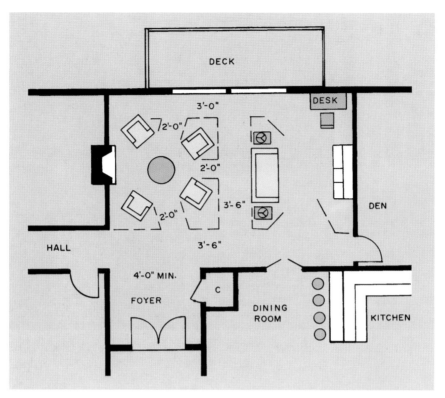

3-20 Carefully plan traffic flow within the living room. You should be able to move about the room without disrupting conversation or other activities.

seating area should be 4'-0" (1220mm) or wider **(3-20)**.

When possible orient the exterior wall of the living room south. This wall receives many hours of sunlight and produces a bright, well-illuminated room. In the winter the exposed glass windows or doors provide solar heat. In the summer the glazing needs to be protected from the direct exposure of the sun and requires energy efficient glazing **(3-21)**.

Windows and exterior doors selected for the living room should be consistent with the style of the house. Their location should fit in with the furniture plan yet be pleasingly balanced when viewing the exterior. Work the window locations and furni-

3-21 If the living room faces south the glass on that wall will provide considerable natural light and solar heat but must be protected during the hot summer days.
Courtesy Weather Shield Manufacturing, Inc.

3-22 The finish on interior walls and ceiling has a dramatic influence on the overall atmosphere of the living room. This room has a ceiling with exposed beams. The dining area has a pendant light fixture providing local illumination. **Courtesy Thomas Lighting**

3-24 As furniture and artwork are located remember to consider the location and types of lighting needed.

ture carefully to get the maximum value from each. Consider the need for privacy when locating windows and deciding upon their size.

As the living room is designed consider the possible floor covering to be used. Plush carpet is nice, wood and ceramic tile are also popular choices. The floor covering is a dominant element when viewing a living room. Refer to **3-4** for a ceramic tile floor, **3-8** for a carpeted floor, and **3-14** for a hardwood floor.

Consider the finish for the interior walls and ceiling. Gypsum drywall is the dominant material but wood paneling is also popular. This choice is very important in setting the overall scene. Exposed beams in the ceiling are popular but do not fit every style of house **(3-22)**. Cathedral ceilings provide a tall open appearance but make more space to heat and air-condition **(3-23)**.

Lighting requires careful consideration. Some form of subtle general illumination is needed. Special features like a fireplace or painting might require a spotlight fixture. Lamps for reading are also necessary and should be part of the furniture plan **(3-24)**.

3-23 This cathedral ceiling and living room walls are finished with gypsum wallboard and are painted a light color giving a bright, open feeling.

3-25 Furniture can be located out in the room away from the walls. Remember to place electric outlets for lamps to be with this furniture.

Since furniture will most likely be rearranged occasionally locate electrical outlets to provide total room coverage.

While it is easier to arrange furniture in rectangular rooms than square rooms other shapes can be considered.

The plan should provide sufficient wall

3-26 This family room has a game table and comfortable chairs and a reading area and book shelves. Notice the pool cues for a table not shown. A television is almost always in a family room. **Courtesy Haris-Tarkett, Inc.**

space to hold the furniture needed. Some furniture can be located out in the room away from walls **(3-25)**. A room with too many doors or windows is difficult to arrange.

Planning the Family Room

The family room is a comfortably furnished room serving as a second living room. It is where much of the day-to-day living takes place. Here various activities, such as sewing, working on hobbies, watching TV, and just relaxing, occur **(3-26)**. It serves as a play area for small children. It has durable furniture and floor covering. The formal living room is used for guests and is spared the wear and tear of day-to-day family activities.

When planning the room consider the activities that will occur here. A TV viewing area is almost essential. Cabinets and tables for sewing, card playing, and other family activities need to be located. A relaxing area or a small grouping of chairs for conversation is typical and is often located so that it looks out upon a pleasant scene. A fireplace is a plus.

Since the room gets heavy use durable materials that are easily maintained should be used. It should be a cheerful place and have plenty of electrical outlets and choices of lighting. Noise is a typical problem so sound-deadening insulation in the walls and possibly acoustical ceiling tile would be used.

The family room can be located on the floor plan in any convenient location. Since it may be noisy at times it should be away from the sleeping area. Often it is near the kitchen because it is a good place for snacks and in some cases is combined with the kitchen as a large open area. A snack bar may be used to separate the kitchen from the family room.

Sometimes a family room and living room are located back-to-back with a movable partition, such as a large folding door, between them. When opened, this provides an expanded area for entertaining a large number of guests.

Storage is an important consideration. Since it serves as the center for multiple activities plan for adequate storage, including cabinets and closets.

Planning a Den

The den is an area where you can study, write, or read. It is a quiet area and needs to be located away from the busy, noisy activity areas. Since it is not a room that is part of the active day-to-day flow of things, it can be located in a quiet out-of-the-way place on the floor plan.

The furnishings typically include bookshelves, a desk, a couple of comfortable chairs, and lamps for reading. The computer could be here if you do not have a home office. Other items, depending upon the activities planned, may be included. Good general illumination is helpful as well as lights and lamps for reading and study (3-27).

Planning a Recreation Room

A recreation room is used for activities of a more vigorous nature than you wish to have occur in a family room. For example, table tennis, pool, dancing, or children's parties may occur here. It could also be the center for hobbies such as ceramics or painting pictures.

3-27 *This den has extensive, high quality cabinetry and a handsome desk. Notice the subdued lighting and quiet, relaxing atmosphere.*
Courtesy KraftMaid Cabinetry, Inc.

Since it is a noisy area it should be located away from the sleeping area and the center of day-to-day activities. A basement location is good. If there is a swimming pool in the yard it may open toward it, providing access to the house and possibly also include a half bath.

Obviously durable materials on the walls and floor are necessary and an acoustical ceiling is a big help.

Storage cabinets and large closets are needed to store the items used in the various activities. Good general illumination is also important.

Planning the Home Office

More people are now working full-time at home or have to bring work home from their job away from home. Some have part-time employment with duties that can be performed at home. The need for a well-planned, efficient home office is becoming one more factor to consider as a new house

3-28 This is a well-planned efficient home office suitable for someone who has many duties to handle. The efficiency is enhanced by using cabinetry and furniture designed especially for this purpose.
Courtesy Yorktowne, Inc.

3-29 The tower is conveniently stored in the side of the cabinet on a sliding shelf. This provides easy access and it can be stored and covered. **Courtesy Yorktowne, Inc.**

3-30 This desk has the keyboard mounted on a sliding shelf. It can be put under the top out of the way and protected from dust and damage. **Courtesy Yorktowne, Inc.**

is planned **(3-28)**. A little planning will produce a workspace that is efficient and comfortable.

The use of cabinetry planned for use with the computer will save space and improve efficiency. Notice the cabinet features in **3-29** and **3-30**.

A small home office may be planned in part of a den or family room. This small unit can serve the family needs for paying bills and handling correspondence **(3-31, 3-32, 3-33)**. Those using the home office for employment purposes would be wise to dedicate an entire room to this purpose. It enables the operation to be expanded as needed and most important provides privacy from interruption by family members. Cabinet manufacturers have many units designed to provide efficient home offices.

3-31 This small, efficient home office provides space for a computer, an open countertop, and protected storage. **Courtesy KraftMaid Cabinetry, Inc.**

The cabinetry is as attractive and of the same quality as kitchen and bathroom cabinets.

The home office is usually placed in a quiet location on the floor plan. However, if it will have visitors regularly it needs to be located so it can have an outside door and be accessible from the front of the house. This avoids tracking business contacts through the family living quarters, which can be annoying to the family and the visitor. One frequently used location is to develop the space over the garage. It can have an outside

3-32 This small home office is placed along one wall and provides considerable file space and a computer desk. **Courtesy Decora Cabinetry**

3-33 This interesting home office utilizes the space under a stairway. This is very effective use of floor area. **Courtesy Aristokraft Cabinets**

stair and an inside stair connecting to the living quarters.

Begin planning by listing the equipment and furniture required. This will no doubt include a computer that is more effective if placed on a furniture unit designed for this purpose. File cabinets, bookshelves, open table space, storage cabinets, and a number of chairs are typically required. Consider the location of the copy machine, telephone, fax machine, electrical outlets, and lighting. Good general illumination is very important (3-34).

There are many ways to arrange the furniture depending upon what is needed and the relationship between the units. One arrangement places the equipment on

3-34 A large home office will contain most of the frequently used office machines, such as a fax, computer, copier, and computer. Storage is very important.

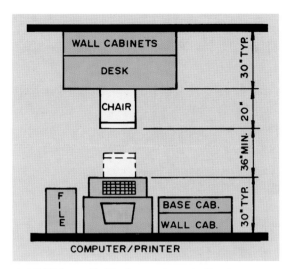

3-35 This small office layout places the furniture on opposite walls making it necessary to turn around to use the equipment on the opposite wall. It does use a minimum of space.

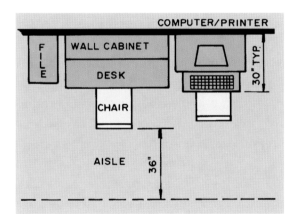

3-36 This small office places the equipment along one wall. This is effective for a minimum installation.

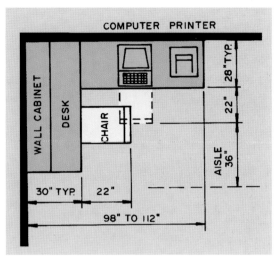

3-37 An L-shaped office layout is efficient because both work areas can be reached with a minimum of movement.

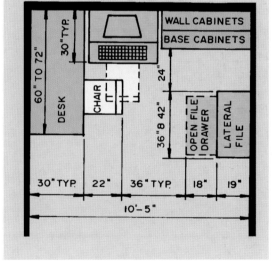

3-38 A U-shaped office is effective for a larger installation. It can contain the equipment in an efficient arrangement, provide good storage and considerable open countertop area.

opposite walls **(3-35)**. This requires the person to spin the chair around to use the computer. This is not a big problem if the flooring is a hard material so the chair moves easily.

Another way to arrange a small office is to place the furniture along one wall **(3-36)**. Storage space is limited to wall-hung cabinets but would be adequate for family use.

A more efficient arrangement is the L-shaped layout in **3-37**. It uses little floor area and is easy to move from the desk to the computer. On this small plan storage is limited to wall hung cabinets.

The U-shaped office in **3-38** retains the efficiency of the L-shaped plan but has considerably more storage. It is important to provide adequate space between the desk and the cabinets or files on the opposite wall. A crowded situation will become intolerable quite soon.

A plan for a home office containing most of the equipment needed by someone operating a business full-time from it is in **3-39**. This is only one possible arrangement. A great many changes and variations are possible. Actually after using the office awhile it is likely the furniture will be rearranged based on experience. Provide plenty of electrical outlets and several telephone jacks in various parts of the room. Remember, you may want a separate telephone line for the computer. If you plan to do a lot of mechanical drafting the installation in **3-40** is very efficient.

Planning Basements

In areas with a high water table or layers of rock near the surface of the ground it is usually not advisable to build a basement. While it can be done it is very expensive and usually the above grade floor area is expanded much easier. In warm climates basements are also not commonly built. The footings here sit near the top of the soil so a basement would require considerable excavation. In northern areas the footings have to go below the frost line, which could be four to six feet into the soil. In this case a basement becomes economical space because deep excavations are needed anyway.

Some view a basement as a dark, damp place. When properly designed and constructed this is not the case. There are excellent waterproofing systems that provide leak-free walls. A dehumidifier can easily remove any humidity in the air. It is a distinct advantage if the house is on a sloped lot because in many cases one or more basement walls are completely out of the ground (**3-41**). This permits the use of standard doors and windows providing natural light,

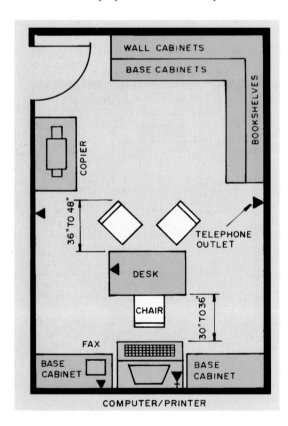

3-39 A large office like this will serve someone who works here all day and has an occasional visitor to discuss business matters. There are many other possible arrangements for the furniture and equipment.

3-40 *This is an efficient mechanical drafting workstation. It does not require much floor space.*
Courtesy California Redwood Association

3-41 (TOP RIGHT, BOTTOM LEFT, AND BOTTOM RIGHT) *When the lot slopes enough one or more walls of the basement can be above grade allowing the use of standard windows and access doors.*

3-42 *This polyethylene window well is assembled and mounted to the basement wall over a window opening in the wall.* **Courtesy The Bilco Company**

3-44 *The large window area provided by a window well makes it possible to have a light, airy bedroom in the basement.* **Courtesy The Bilco Company**

3-43 *The window well has a terraced step design and serves as a means of egress in an emergency.*
Courtesy The Bilco Company

3-45 *A basement sitting room is enhanced by the use of large window wells.*
Courtesy The Bilco Company

3-46 *A window well in the basement brightens up an area where you can relax and read.*
Courtesy The Bilco Company

3-48 *The finished installation of an exterior basement access door system.*
Courtesy The Bilco Company

3-47 *This is a prestressed concrete basement entry stairway. It has a steel door installed protecting the area from the weather.* **Courtesy The Bilco Company**

ventilation, and access to the outside. If the basement is pretty much fully in the ground window wells can be used to provide ventilation and natural light. One such product is shown in **3-42**. This window well is made from high-density polyethylene and is impervious to soil and moisture damage. It is assembled on the site and mounted to the foundation. A view looking down into the finished installation **(3-43)** shows the terraced step design meeting building codes for emergency egress.

As you plan the use of a basement it can serve many purposes. If properly designed and constructed it can serve as a bedroom area **(3-44)**, a sitting area **(3-45)** or just a nice place to read using the natural light from the window well **(3-46)**.

3-49 *The doors open providing easy access to the base-ment.* **Courtesy The Bilco Company**

If the basement is fully in the ground, easy access to the outdoors can be had by installing a basement entry. These can be cast-in-place concrete walls and steps or you can install a prefabricated entry system. The one shown in **3-47** is a prestressed concrete unit bonded to the basement wall over the door opening left in the wall as the foundation was built. The unit then has a steel door that fits on top of the stair unit **(3-48)**. It is opened providing wide access to the basement **(3-49)**. It also provides emergency egress.

The basement is also used for a recreation area, play area, workshop, hobby area, laundry, and a place to put the furnace and water heater. If the lot is sloped enough it could serve as a garage **(3-50)**. Plan the use of basement space as carefully as you do the rest of the house. The results will be rewarding **(3-51)**.

3-50 *A basement can serve as a garage if the lot slopes enough. Be certain to observe fire codes that apply when you have an automobile in the basement.*

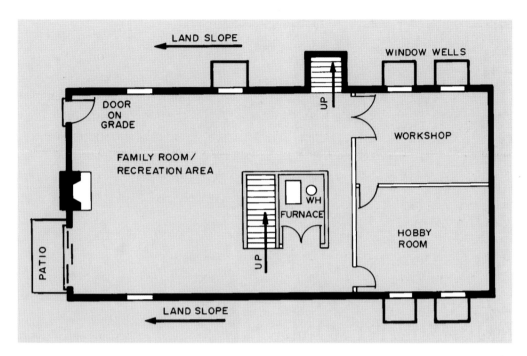

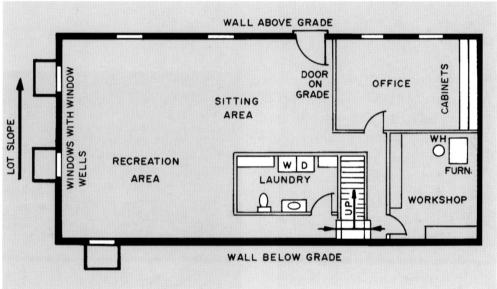

3-51 Typical basement plans indicating the division of space into areas for activities desired by the family. Notice the outside exits and use of window wells.

PLANNING KITCHENS
& DINING ROOMS

Planning the Kitchen

The planning of the kitchen deserves considerable attention. It is possibly the most heavily used room and the most expensive because of the wide range of appliances available. Kitchens can be the center of more activities than food preparation and cleanup. Many have an eating area and often a small office setup **(4-1)**. Some will have a recreation area or sitting area with a TV or stereo tied in with the kitchen **(4-2)**. Sofas, comfortable chairs, and space for a hobby area are often included. The kitchen may have a snack counter and freezer. It serves as an informal gathering place during parties and must provide storage for food, linens, utensils, china, and silver. It can be seen that the kitchen is often a multipurpose room in which several people are

4-1 A small desk for recordkeeping and correspondence is a nice addition to a kitchen. Notice the durable finished floor. **Courtesy Congoleum Corporation**

4-2 Kitchens frequently include provision for other activities such as dining and relaxing.
Courtesy Congoleum Corporation

cal and plumbing needs and be certain to meet local codes. Also consideration of ventilation and lighting become part of a final plan.

Work Areas

Kitchen planning for the food preparation activities involves providing a pattern of work flow for storing, processing, and cooking food as well as serving the prepared items and cleaning up after the preparation and after the meal has been finished. The basic kitchen is planned around three major appliances that comprise the cooking/baking unit, a refrigerator/freezer and the sink/dishwasher **(4-3)**. A fourth area, the preparation area, requires a large open section of counter space.

The activities involved with these three work areas overlap as shown in **4-4**. For example, the cleanup center countertop allocation can also be used during food preparation. As you plan consider using the location of other appliances as a microwave, compactor, full freestanding freezer, or garbage disposal.

active in their individual pursuits. This demands that efficiency in planning the location of facilities, ingress and egress, and traffic patterns within the room is essential.

Consider the shape of the room. It does not have to be a standard rectangle but can branch off providing a better traffic pattern and widen the use of the space. Get information on the many appliances available including cost, size, and features. You need this as you plan space for them. Plan for the electri-

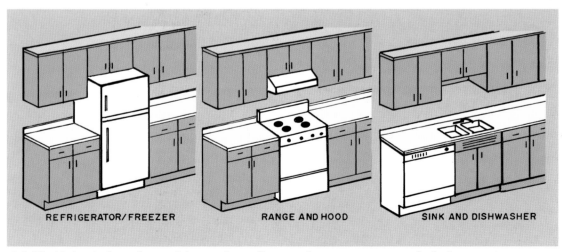

REFRIGERATOR/FREEZER   **RANGE AND HOOD**   **SINK AND DISHWASHER**

4-3 The kitchen is planned around three major appliances and some open countertop for food preparation.

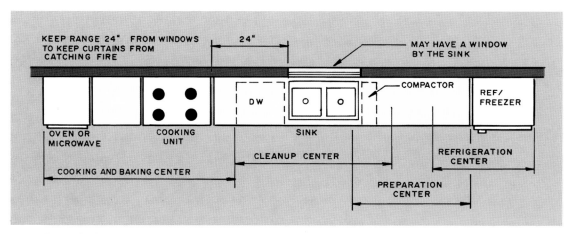

4-4 *The areas allotted to work activities in the kitchen are closely related and overlap. Consideration of these relationships is important when planning a kitchen.*

The Cooking/Baking Center

Food is heated, broiled, baked, boiled, or fried in the cooking center **(4-5)**. Since food generally leaves the cooking area and goes into the dining area, it helps if it is near it in

4-5 *The cooking center is where food is boiled, baked, fried, or broiled. Notice the microwave located above the range. While this is convenient, the microwave can be located in other areas of the kitchen.*
Courtesy Whirlpool Corporation

order to make serving easier. While the cooking appliance and oven are the major units a microwave may also be located here. Typical cooking appliances include cooktops and ranges with one or two ovens and separate wall-hung ovens. The cooking area should be near the food preparation area. Separate wall-mounted ovens do not need to be in the cooking area because they are not heavily used and once food is in the oven it does not require constant attention. The microwave should be in or very near the cooking area because food items go in and come out rapidly.

Ventilation in a kitchen cooking area is important. Cooking appliances should have a hood over them to remove fumes and water vapor developed during cooking **(4-6)**. Utensils used for cooking should be stored in or near the cooking area. Counter space for small cooking appliances, as a toaster, broiler, or coffeemaker, is important. Remember to have electrical outlets above the countertop for these appliances.

Counter space is also needed for the

4-6 *This island counter serves as a cooking center and has a small snack counter so the large hood above is essential for removing fumes. The durable floor covering serves well in a kitchen.*
Courtesy Congoleum Corporation

placement of cooking utensils and food to be cooked. Typical minimum spacing requirements are in **4-7**.

Locating the Microwave

The microwave is possibly used more than the range or oven. It heats food fast and with the pressures of time and the use of frozen food it has become a major appliance. Give careful consideration as to where it is located. Since there is little relationship between the microwave and the range or oven it need not be in the cooking area. Consider locating it near the refrigerator/freezer because it is there the items to be heated are located. The microwave is frequently located above the range but this is not always the best location **(4-5)**.

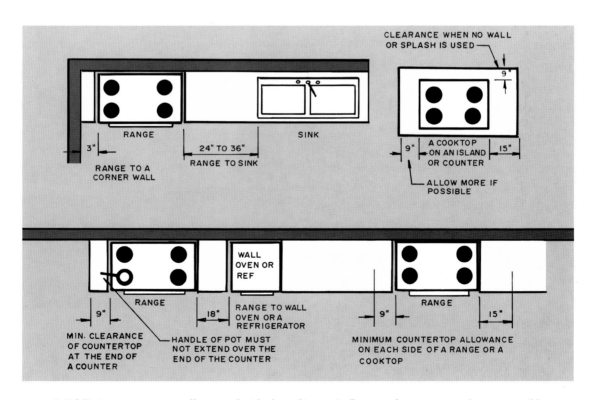

4-7 *Minimum countertop allowances beside the cooking unit. Increase these amounts whenever possible.*

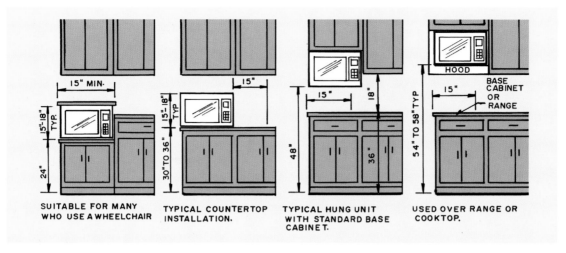

| SUITABLE FOR MANY WHO USE A WHEELCHAIR | TYPICAL COUNTERTOP INSTALLATION. | TYPICAL HUNG UNIT WITH STANDARD BASE CABINET. | USED OVER RANGE OR COOKTOP. |

4-8 Recommended positions for a microwave indicate the bottom should be at least 24 inches above the floor but not over 48 to 58 inches above the floor.

The bottom of the microwave should be 24 to 48 inches (610 to 1220mm) above the floor. It needs to be in a position where it is easy to reach—not too high or too low **(4-8)**.

The Refrigerator/ Freezer Center

Here fresh foods are kept refrigerated until used and frozen foods are stored **(4-9)**. These can be very large appliances so provision must be made for their width and height as the cabinets are chosen. Provide at least 15 inches (406mm) clear countertop on the latch side of a single door refrigerator unit. If it is a two-door unit with a freezer on one side put 15 inches (406mm) of countertop on each side. This area is needed for placing food items being removed from or being put into the unit.

The Preparation Area

The preparation area is where foods are mixed, vegetables cleaned, and other steps are taken for preparing food. The size of the work area will vary depending upon whether

the family does a lot of food preparation from "scratch" or uses mostly packaged prepared food items. Minimum recommendations are

4-9 The refrigerator/freezer is the major appliance in the refrigeration center. Notice the preparation counter between it and the sink. Notice that the resilient floor covering blends in with the wall color.
Courtesy Congoleum Corporation

in **4-10**. The area should be near a sink and a refrigerator.

The Sink/Dishwasher Center

The area is where the pots and pans are cleaned and dishes, silverware, and food storage containers are rinsed and washed. The sink is the major item and usually has a double bowl **(4-11)**.

The dishwasher is located next to the sink making it easy to place dishes in it.

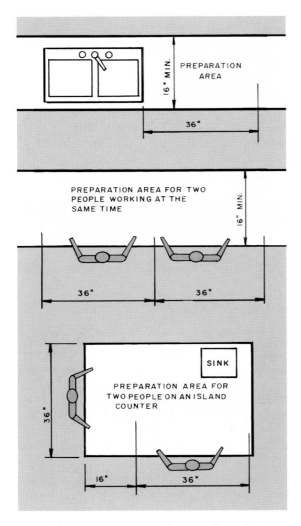

4-10 Minimum countertop allowances for various size food preparation areas.

4-11 The most commonly used kitchen sink has two bowls; however, single- and triple-bowl sinks are available. **Courtesy Elkay Manufacturing Company**

Usually it is located on the left of the sink for right-handed persons **(4-12)**. The trash compactor is placed on the side of the sink opposite the dishwasher.

A disposal is installed on one of the sinks to grind up and dispose of soft items through the house waste disposal system. The switch to operate it should be far enough away from it so that a person could not have fingers in the unit and turn it on at the same time. Some building codes prohibit the use of disposals.

Some prefer to place a window by the sink. While this is pleasant it is not necessary (**4-2** and **4-9**). Sinks are commonly placed in cabinets along a wall. However large kitchens may have two sinks, one that is often placed in an island cabinet. Generally the sink is placed in a central location because it is used when working in all areas of the kitchen.

Remember to plan for some way to store disposable dry trash and collect recyclable materials. These are typically in plastic bins located below base cabinets.

Recommendations for locating the sink and dishwasher and minimum clear coun-

4-12 The dishwasher is located beside the sink.
Courtesy GE Appliances

tertop for cleanup and food preparation near a sink are in **4-13**. If a sink is to be located near the corner of an L-shaped counter its relationship with other activities and the refrigerator are in **4-14**. Notice the corner base cabinet has a lazy Susan. This means you need at least 12 inches (305mm) between the

Table 4-1 Recommended Minimum Storage Capacity

	Kitchen 150 sq ft or less	Kitchen larger than 150 sq ft
Base Cabinet Frontage	156 inches	192 inches
Wall Cabinet Frontage	144 inches	186 inches
Drawers		
(Individual Total Frontage)	120 inches	165 inches

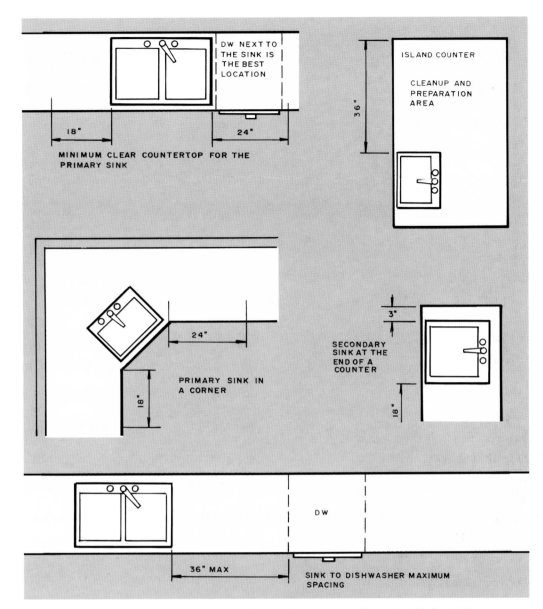

4-13 Minimum spacing recommendations for primary and secondary kitchen sinks.

edge of the sink and the corner of the base cabinet with the lazy Susan. A sink to lazy Susan installation is shown in **4-15**. A sink installed in the corner is shown in **4-11**.

Kitchen Storage

Storage is required for packaged and fresh foods, frozen foods, kitchen accessories, utensils, dishes, silverware, small electrical appliances, cleaning supplies, mops, brooms, and other such items. A large house will require a larger kitchen and more storage than a smaller house. Typical minimum storage recommendations made by The National Kitchen and Bath Association are in **Table 4-1**.

In **4-16** is a typical layout for a kitchen having less than 150 square feet. A layout for a larger kitchen is in **4-17**.

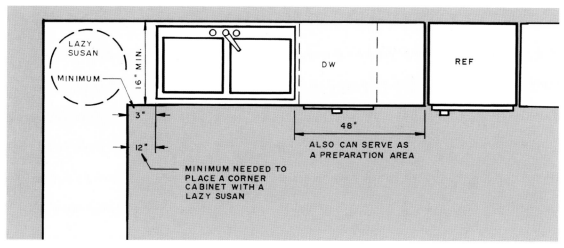

4-14 *When a sink is near a corner of the cabinets locate it at least 3 inches (76mm) away. Have at least 48 inches (1220mm) clear countertop between the sink and the refrigerator for cleanup and food preparation. Move the sink 12 inches (305mm) from the corner if a lazy Susan is to be in the corner base cabinet.*

4-15 *This installation has a corner base cabinet with a lazy Susan installed next to the sink.*

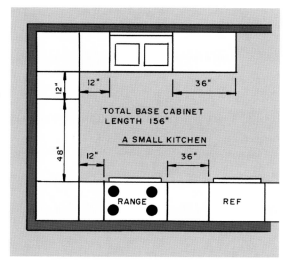

4-16 *A typical base cabinet layout for a kitchen with less than 150 square feet of floor space. It has the minimum lineal inches of base cabinet storage space. The base cabinets must be at least 21 inches deep.*

As you plan the storage space, locate items, such as utensils and food products, as near as possible to the work center where they will be used. Cabinet manufacturers have many very efficient storage accessories built into the cabinets (**4-18**). Take advantage of these and order them when you order the cabinets.

If there is room on the plan consider adding a pantry. A pantry is a small closet lined with shelves including small wire racks mounted on the door.

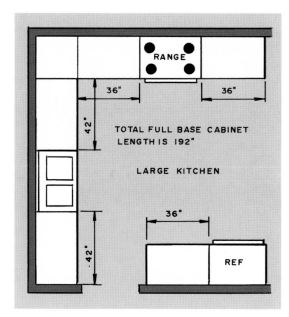

4-17 A typical base cabinet layout for a kitchen with more than 150 square feet of floor space. This plan provides the minimum lineal inches of storage.

A freestanding freezer is a major storage appliance for large quantities of frozen foods. They are usually quite large and are placed in a garage or basements. Small quantities of food are moved occasionally to the refrigerator/freezer for daily use.

4-18 Take advantage of the many special storage features cabinet manufacturers can provide.
Courtesy CraftMaid Cabinetry.

A Planning Area

Some enjoy having a small desk or low cabinet to use as a place for planning meals, handling household finances, and taking care of general correspondence. This can be built in the kitchen area outside of the food preparation, cooking and cleanup activities. If a cabinet is built for this the top should be 30 inches (762mm) above the floor **(4-19)**.

Planning a Small Dining Area

It is very convenient to have a small dining area within the kitchen plan for breakfast and snacks. This could be a small area with a table and chairs **(4-20)** or a counter that may be a peninsula or island unit **(4-21)** or a booth. If a counter is used it is designed for use by tall stools or standard chairs. Design recommendations are in **4-22** and **4-23**. Booths vary in size but the one in **4-24** is typical. See the section in this chapter on planning dining rooms for more detailed information.

4-20 A small dining area in a section of the kitchen is a popular feature. The light color of the resilient flooring enhances the dark cabinets and dining furniture.
Courtesy Congoleum Corporation

4-19 A planning area is a very useful part of a kitchen. Since it is not directly involved in food preparation or cleanup it can be placed in a less accessible area.
Courtesy GE Appliances

4-21 This island counter serves as a dining area and provides a work surface for food preparation. The resilient tile floor is durable and will withstand the use of the chairs. **Courtesy Congoleum Corporation**

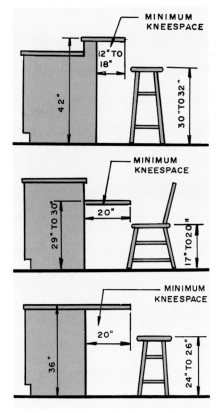

4-22 The height of eating counters depends upon the height of the chair or stool to be used.

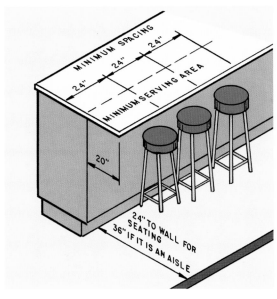

4-23 An eating counter should provide at least 24 inches of clear countertop for each person and adequate kneespace below the top.

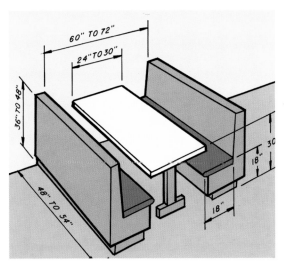

4-24 Booths are popular in the kitchen eating area. These are typical sizes for a booth to seat four people.

The Work Triangle

The concept of the work triangle has been used for many years as a means for checking the efficiency of a kitchen. This is the total straight-line distance from the refrigerator to the stove to the sink. This is the distance you would walk as you move between these three appliances. Typically each side of the triangle should fall between 5 to 10 feet.

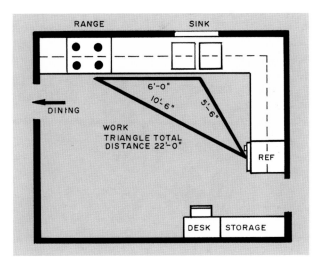

4-25 This L-shaped plan shows a typical small kitchen with an adequate work triangle. The work triangle is used to check the efficiency of the plan.

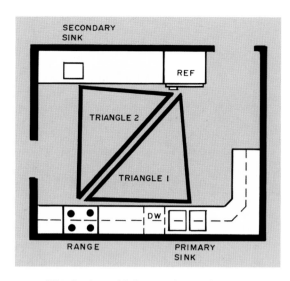

4-26 This kitchen added a secondary sink and was arranged with two work triangles, enabling two people to work at the same time.

The total of all three sides will average out around 22 to 26 feet **(4-25)**. This total can be somewhat larger or smaller than this, but it is best if it is in this range. Likewise if one side is very short, less than 5 feet, the

4-27 An island counter can be used to reduce the size of the work triangle, thus reducing the number of steps between the work areas. **Courtesy Aristocraft, Inc.**

4-28 The peninsula counter can have a sink or range, thus shortening the distance between work centers. It can also serve as an eating area. **Courtesy Aristokraft, Inc.**

appliances are too close together and may be difficult to use, especially if two people are working in the kitchen.

When you add a second sink or plan a large kitchen for two cooks working at the same time, you will have to vary the distances somewhat and possibly plan two work triangles **(4-26)**.

If the kitchen is very large, you can use an island counter or a peninsula to shorten the distances between work centers. The island counter or peninsula may allow you to have two triangular paths or a set of paths with more than three sides. However, the goal is to access the work centers with the minimum number of steps **(4-27** and **4-28)**.

Basic Kitchen Shapes

The rooms in a typical home are generally either rectangular or nearly square. When designing a new house you might consider planning how you would like a kitchen and dining area and arrange the walls to accommodate the plan. In any case, kitchens tend to fall into a number of rather standard shapes. These shapes include an L-shaped kitchen,

4-29 This L-shaped kitchen has an oven in the corner cabinet and a cooktop and microwave around the corner. Notice the doors on the refrigerator match those on the cabinets. **Courtesy GE Appliances**

U-shaped kitchen, a double L-shaped kitchen, a G-shaped kitchen, an I-shaped kitchen, and a corridor kitchen. These shapes can be altered and enhanced a little by adding an island counter or a peninsula.

L-Shaped Kitchen

The L-shaped kitchen has cabinets and appliances along two butting walls forming a corner **(4-29)**. The efficiency is reduced if

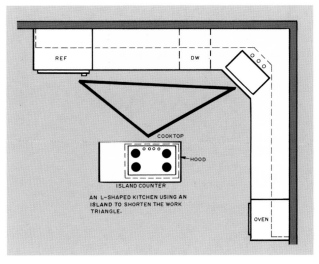

4-31 The island counter cuts down on the distance between work centers producing a very efficient layout. However, it would be crowded for two people to work at the same time.

the cabinets on one wall are very long and the other short. This kitchen leaves a large open floor area that could be used for dining or other activities. The layouts shown in **4-30** have the work triangle below 22 feet.

The efficiency can be improved by adding an island counter as shown in **4-31**

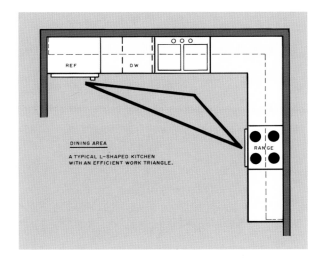

4-30 This L-shaped kitchen layout for a small kitchen has an efficient work triangle.

4-32 This L-shaped kitchen places a cooktop on an island counter, reducing the distance between work centers. Notice the placement of the other appliances. **Courtesy Whirlpool Corporation**

4-33 A U-shaped kitchen is very efficient.
Courtesy Wellborn Cabinet, Inc.

and seen in **4-32**. The island can be used for a range, cooktop, or sink. It can also provide a surface for a small dining or snack area.

U-Shaped Kitchen

A U-shaped kitchen has cabinets on three sides of the room. Arranging cabinets in this way reduces the walking distance between

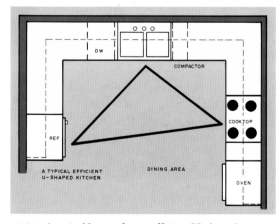

4-34 A typical layout for an efficient U-shaped kitchen.

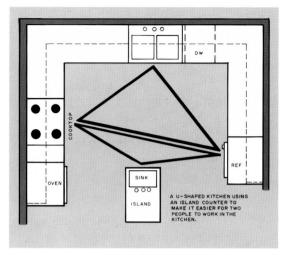

4-35 This large U-shaped kitchen has a second sink making it easy for two people to use at the same time. The use of two work triangles is an effective technique in developing an efficient large kitchen.

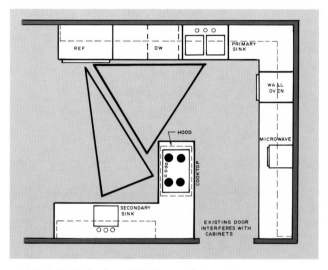

4-36 A double L-shaped kitchen can help make a useful layout when a window, door, or other obstruction interferes with the cabinets along the wall.

the work centers, producing an efficient kitchen. A small dining area can be located on the open side. The U-shape can be formed using a peninsula counter on one side instead of a wall (**4-33**). Some typical plans are shown in **4-34** and **4-35**. If two people are to work in the kitchen, be certain the aisles are wide enough to allow easy access to the appliances.

Double L-Shaped Kitchen

A double L-shaped kitchen is a useful design if you want a U-shaped kitchen but a door or window interferes with the layout. It will involve developing two work triangles that can be effective if you add a secondary sink in a convenient location. A typical example is shown in **4-36**.

G-Shaped Kitchen

The G-shaped kitchen is efficient but requires that the cabinets be spaced far enough apart so two people may work at the same time. It can be formed using the fourth

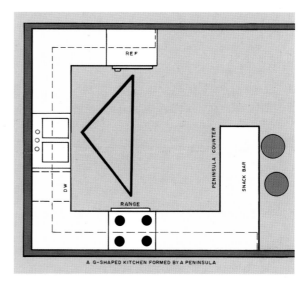

4-38 A G-shaped kitchen can add additional cabinet space and sometimes shorten the work triangle.

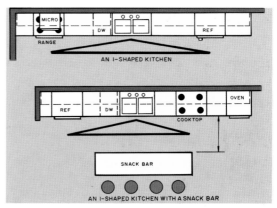

4-39 The I-shaped kitchen stretches along one wall and is suitable for use by only one person.

4-37 This G-shaped kitchen has a peninsula counter with a second sink off the stone wall on one side of the kitchen. **Courtesy Merillat Industries, Inc.**

wall of a kitchen or installing a peninsula across the end of the open side of the U-shaped kitchen as shown in **4-37**. One typical layout is shown in **4-38**.

I-Shaped Kitchen

The I-shaped kitchen has the appliances and cabinets along one wall. It is used in small apartments and small houses. All of the utilities are in one wall. The problem is trying to get everything you need along the wall without its getting too long. Typically it will only let one person work in the area **(4-39)**.

A shortage of clear countertop makes it difficult to have a place to put everything. Basically it is useful for those who do very little food preparation but is of little use for the person who likes to cook.

The Corridor

The corridor kitchen has appliances and cabinets on two opposite walls. It can be used when space for a kitchen is limited to a long narrow area. It can be designed to have a short work triangle and is an efficient design. However, it is difficult for two people to work in it at the same time **(4-40)**.

You have to be especially careful that you do not place appliances with doors

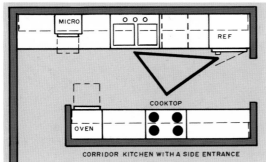

4-40 The corridor kitchen can be built in a long narrow space. While it is efficient to use, generally only one person can work in it.

4-41 This kitchen occupies a large area and uses an island to carry the cooktop to make the work triangle efficient. A small dining area is connected to the island. Notice how the finishes on the appliances are coordinated providing an attractive kitchen.
Courtesy Whirlpool Corporation

directly across from each other. With the minimum width between walls, open appliance doors will cause some difficulty.

Island Counters

Island counters are freestanding units allowing a means for adjusting the work triangle, providing additional storage, or serving as a small dining area. They can contain a sink or appliances. In a large kitchen a second sink is often located here. An island counter with a cooktop and dining area is shown in **4-41**.

A peninsula is a section of counter connected on one end to the cabinets along the wall. It goes across the open end of the kitchen forming a divider to the next room.

4-42 This kitchen has a peninsular counter extending out from the wall, providing additional storage and serving as a room divider. The walls have been painted to blend with the resilient floor covering.
Courtesy Congoleum Corporation

It can be used to hold a sink, range, cooktop, storage space, or provide an extra surface for work or dining **(4-42)**.

Special Kitchens

Creative architects often produce floor designs for kitchens other than the typical square or rectangular room. The room may

4-44 This kitchen is pie shaped and the island counter containing cooking and dining facilities slopes parallel with the sides of the room. **Courtesy GE Appliances**

have a curved wall, a wall of glass, or walls that meet at angles other than 90°. The flexibility permits the kitchen designer to be creative in producing a plan that will meet or exceed the minimum spacing requirements.

In **4-43** the kitchen has a very irregular shape with cabinets flowing back into an area with large windows. This requires a number of corner cabinet units. The effect

4-43 This cabinet installation has to turn a number of corners to flow into the small area in the back with the windows. The warm wood produces a pleasant atmosphere. **Courtesy Aristokraft, Inc.**

4-45 This kitchen is very unusual and because of the sloping walls and gleaming appliances gives a bright, interesting appearance.
Courtesy GE Appliances

4-46 *This custom-made cabinet provides considerable storage and holds a refrigerator at a height that makes it easy to use. The antique finish on the cabinet helps diminish the appearance that it is part of the kitchen.* **Courtesy Sub-Zero Freezer Company, Inc.**

The kitchen in **4-44** is wider at one end, so the island counter has been tapered to match the slope of the walls.

The kitchen seen in **4-45** I consider to be a great kitchen. The side walls are on angles and the end wall makes an acute angle. Notice how the appliances have been worked in with the cabinets to produce an exciting kitchen.

Custom-built cabinets can provide considerable storage as shown in **4-46**. This configuration also holds a refrigerator unit up off the floor so that it is easy to access. The refrigeration unit can be installed in cabinets such as these or set back in walls, allowing access to it wherever refrigerated storage is needed.

4-47 *Creative planning was used to hide an island counter with this bright sofa and to coordinate the wall colors with it. The refrigerator and cabinets blend together forming a unified whole.* **Courtesy Whirlpool Corporation**

4-48 *This kitchen does not have the "kitchen" look but a more formal appearance. The dark hardwood cabinets contribute to this impression. Notice the paneled island counter and small dining table with classic Queen Anne legs.* **Courtesy Merillat Industries, Inc.**

of this nook is to produce a visually pleasing kitchen area. Actually, rather than a kitchen, the room has the look of a pleasant family room.

In **4-47** the "kitchen look" is diminished by placing a colorful sofa up against an island counter that contains a sink. The white wood framing and cabinets flow easily into the white refrigerator-freezer. The bright wall colors also diminish the look of a typical kitchen.

In **4-48** a special effort was made to give the kitchen the appearance of a more formal room. The dark cabinets with considerable detailing including paneling, the use of cabinets with glass doors, and the use of wallpaper all contribute to the pleasant appearance.

Traffic Patterns

When you locate the kitchen on the floor plan you must consider certain traffic patterns to reach it and possibly through it. For example, it is typical to place the kitchen next to the garage. This makes it easier to move food into the kitchen and to carry out the

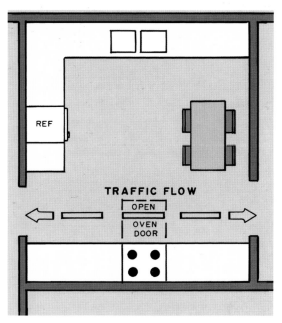

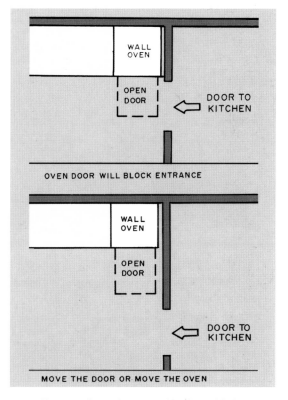

4-50 Be certain that the door from an appliance does not interfere with the flow of a primary traffic aisle.

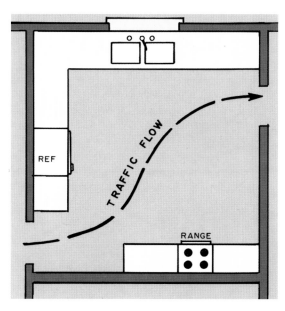

4-49 When the primary traffic flow is through the center of the kitchen it can disrupt food preparation activities.

4-51 Position the appliances so they do not block the entrance into the kitchen.

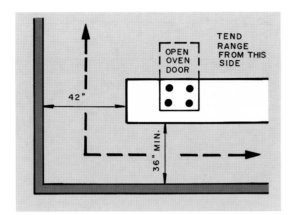

4-52 A 36-inch wide aisle is recommended for traffic flow past a counter where no appliance is to be used. If aisles intersect one should be at least 42 inches wide.

4-53 Range hoods remove cooking fumes and disperse them to the outdoors They are available to match the range or cooktop. **Courtesy Aristokraft, Inc.**

waste. However, you may have caused a traffic flow pattern through the work triangle to reach the rest of the house from the garage **(4-49)**. Also be careful you do not block the flow into the kitchen by opening appliance doors **(4-50)**. Traffic flow should not interfere with someone working in the kitchen.

You need to consider the impact of major traffic flow through the kitchen as you locate the appliances. A major flow of traffic should not go past major appliances, as shown in **4-51**. A traffic aisle along the side of a counter where no appliance will be used should be 36 inches wide. When aisles meet at 90°, one should be at least 42 inches wide. This will also allow a person in a wheelchair to make the turn **(4-52)**.

Ventilation

Mechanical ventilation is an important part of kitchen design. Cooking activities generate moisture, fumes, grease in the air, and odors that eventually cling to cabinets, walls, curtains, flooring, and other exposed

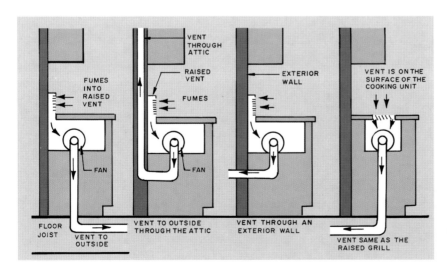

4-54 Some surface cooking units have a downdraft venting system that pulls the fumes off the cooking surface and exhausts them to the outside.

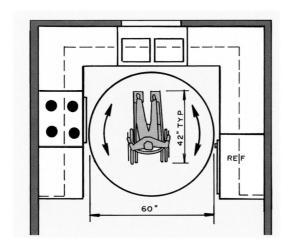

4-55 *A wheelchair has a turning diameter of 60 inches.*

4-57 *Base cabinets are available where the height of a sink or cooktop can be adjusted to a height suitable for someone in a wheelchair. Notice the area below the sink is open permitting the legs of the person in the wheelchair to move below the sink.* **Courtesy GE Appliances**

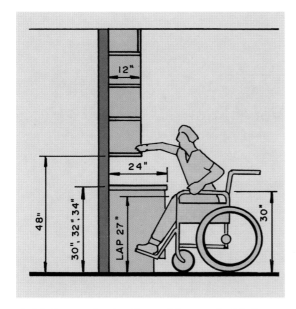

4-56 *A person leaning forward from a wheelchair can reach about 48 inches above the floor. This requires open space below the countertop for the persons legs.*

items. Range hoods and exhaust fans are commonly used to disperse these pollutants.

A range hood is placed over each range or cooktop (4-53). They vent the fumes through a pipe to the exterior of the house. One type cycles the fumes through a system of filters and returns the air to the room.

A downdraft venting system pulls the fumes from the cooking surface and exhausts it outdoors (4-54).

Accessible Work Centers

There are many things that can be done to increase the accessibility of various work centers in a kitchen. One consideration is providing adequate floor space so someone who is wheelchair bound can easily move around. Doors into the kitchen should be 36 inches (914mn) wide. A wheelchair has a 60 inch (1524mm) turning radius so spaces between cabinets, furniture, and appliances should be at least this wide but making the space larger is a tremendous help (4-55).

Another consideration is providing shelving that can be reached and open

4-58 This kitchen has ceiling mounted fluorescent fixtures for general illumination, hanging pendant lights for task lighting over the island counter and recessed spotlights over the sink and countertop.
Courtesy Thomas Lighting

spaces below the countertop at areas where food preparation will occur **(4-56)**. The highest shelf that can be reached from a wheelchair is 48 inches above the floor and the lowest shelf is 9 inches above the floor.

Access to sinks and cooktops requires that the space below be open so the wheelchair can fit under them. Cabinets are available that have tops that can be lowered to a 30 inch (762 mm) height **(4-57)**. Wall cabinets are also available that can be raised and lowered on wall-mounted tracks.

Lighting

As the kitchen is planned remember you will need general lighting to provide overall illumination of the room. This can be diffuse illuminaries **(4-58)** on the ceiling. You will need task lighting, which puts light on a specific area, as a sink **(4-59)**. You can also use special lighting to enhance a feature or provide dramatic illumination of some aspect of the kitchen.

Planning the Dining Room

As the design of the house proceeds, considerations of the habits of the family should be considered. If the family entertains guests for dinner as part of their active lifestyle a full formal dining room is necessary. This

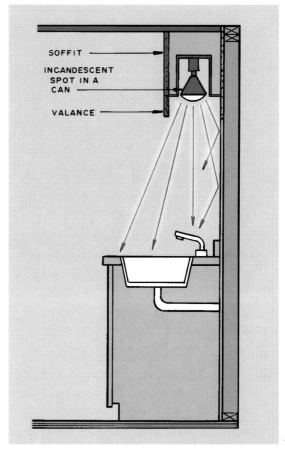

4-59 Incandescent spots recessed into the soffit above the sink provide excellent task lighting.

room will also make the house more valuable, cost more, and easier to sell. List the other eating areas that are wanted such as a space in the kitchen for family meals and quick snacks or provisions to entertain on a deck, terrace, porch, or patio and provide for them as the plan is developed. The dining room should not be a part of the living room but can have an open wall leading into it from the living room.

Dining Room Planning Considerations

Locate the dining room near the kitchen. This reduces the number of steps needed to

4-61 *This hutch provides storage for china, silver, and linens used in the dining room.* **Courtesy KraftMaid Cabinetry**

4-60 *This walnut dining room table has the chandelier positioned over its center providing general illumination. The dimmer switch controls the intensity. The hutch stores the china and silver used for formal dinners.* **Courtesy Thomas Lighting**

move items from the kitchen to the table and makes removing dishes easier. Refer to the following drawings in Chapter 3, **3-8, 3-9**, **3-10**, **3-20**.

Locate the dining room so guests can reach it without going through the kitchen. Typically guests wait in the living room so unhindered access between the living room and dining room is important. Refer to drawings in Chapter 3.

Plan so you can reach the kitchen without going through the dining room.

It is desirable if the dining room can have windows or doors overlooking a pleasant view.

Provide for variable intensity of general illumination. The lighting should be able to

4-62 *This table and cabinet are convenient for glassware and art objects.*

Courtesy KraftMaid Cabinetry

4-63 *Small tables are a nice way to display silver and art objects.*

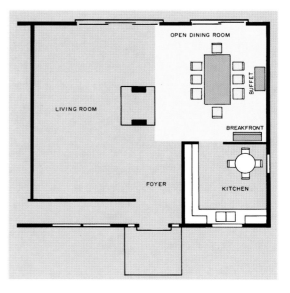

4-64 *An open dining room has one or more walls omitted permitting it to flow into the next room.*

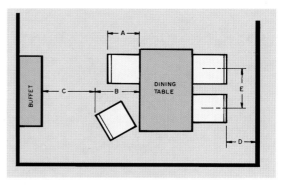

Dining Room Space Requirements

A. A seated person requires 18 to 22 inches.

B. To rise from the table requires 32 to 38 inches.

C. An aisle to allow someone to easily pass behind a seated person should be 40- to 44-inches wide (a major aisle).

D. An aisle to allow someone to slip by a seated person should be 18- to 24-inches wide (a minor aisle).

E. Minimum center-to-center spacing between chairs is 24 inches.

4-65 *Recommended minimum spacing for dining room tables and chairs.*

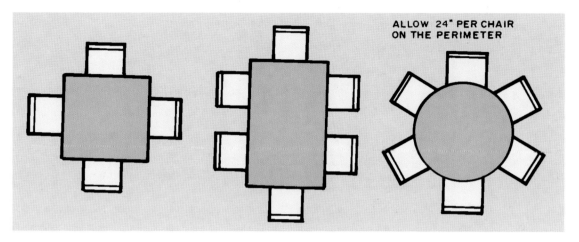

ALLOW 24" PER CHAIR
ON THE PERIMETER

Square Tables		Rectangular Tables		Round Tables	
40" × 40"	4 persons	30" × 48"	4 persons	36" dia.	4 persons
48" × 48"	6 persons	36" × 60"	6 persons	48" dia.	6 persons
54" × 54"	8 persons	36" × 78"	8 persons	68" dia.	8 persons

4-66. *Typical table sizes and seatng recommendations.*

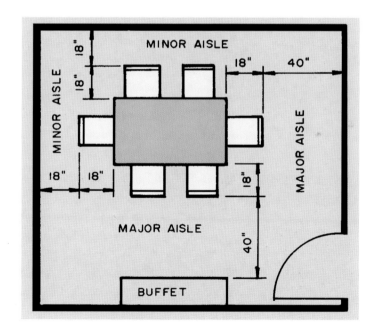

4-67 *This is basically a minimum dining room that will seat six people. If the minor aisles are eliminated everyone could still be seated but one person could not get out until the person beside him leaves the table. If the meal is to be served it would be difficult to serve those seated along a wall.*

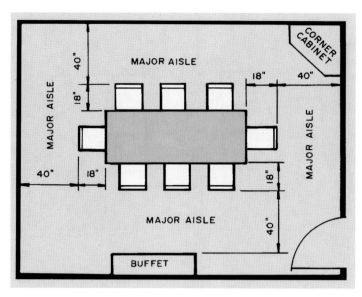

4-68 This is a more spacious layout seating eight people and permitting guests to be served on all sides of the table. It can also have room for a corner cabinet or other furniture.

be dimmed so the atmosphere is subdued and luxurious. A chandelier is commonly used and can be controlled with a dimmer switch (**4-60**). It is usually placed over the center of the dining table.

Provide for storage of china, silver, and linens in or very near the dining room. Notice the breakfront in **4-60** and the hutch in **4-61**. Also consider tables and cabinets in which glassware, silver, and decorative art objects can be displayed (**4-62** and **4-63**).

A dining room can be open or closed. A closed dining room has walls on all four sides as shown in **4-67**. An open dining room flows into another room, usually a living room (**4-64**).

The dining room can be any shape desired. However, a rectangular room is easier to arrange. Consider if the table is to be round, square, or rectangular.

Consider the furniture to be placed in the dining room. Obviously a table and chairs will be the central items. However, buffets, breakfronts, corner cabinets, and serving carts are often used.

Allow sufficient space so a person can be comfortably seated with room to rise and leave the table. Allow aisle space so people can move around the table to be seated and serviced. Recommended minimum spacing is in **4-65**. Notice that a chair requires at least 32 inches (813mm) for someone to slide it back and rise from the table. A narrow aisle behind seated persons must be 18 to 24 inches (457 to 610mm) while a wider aisle permitting easy passage should be 40 to 44 inches (1016 to 1176mm) wide. The table should be long enough to permit the chairs to be spaced 24 inches (610mm) apart center-to-center.

Decide on how many people will be seated. This will directly influence the amount of floor space needed. Remember if the table can be expanded to seat additional

4-69 *The choice of floor covering in the dining room should be made considering the color scheme for the room and the durability of the flooring covering material. This hardwood floor provides a durable, warm floor.*
Courtesy Harris-Taikett, Inc.

people for a large dinner extra space must be allowed in the room.

Recommendations for table sizes for seating several people are shown in **4-66**.

A plan for a minimum dining room for six people is in **4-67**. The dining room in **4-68** seats eight people and a major aisle has been provided on all sides of the table. This is more convenient but still is at minimum recommendations.

Consider the floor covering. It should be easy to clean, withstand abrasive action of the chairs, blend with the colors of the walls and furniture, and enhance the style of furniture to be used (**4-69** and **4-70**).

Consider the finish wall and ceiling material. While gypsum wallboard is most often used, consider a wood wainscoting or

4-70 This dining room has adequate seating for eight and can easily accommodate ten persons. Notice the displays of china and crystal. The durable sculptured carpet adds an additional feature.
Courtesy Mr. and Mrs. Theodore Shebs

paneling one entire wall. There are many types of wall covering materials (commonly called wallpaper but are not paper) available that can set the tone for the room **(4-71)**.

4-71 The color and wall finish material must be coordinated with the floor, furniture, and the overall color scheme for the house. **Courtesy American Walnut Manufacturers Association**

CHAPTER
5

PLANNING THE BEDROOMS, LAUNDRY ROOMS, STORAGE FACILITIES & UTILITY ROOMS

The bedroom area occupies a large part of the total square feet in a house (**5-1**). A first decision is how many are needed. When houses are advertised for sale the number of bedrooms and bathrooms is almost always a part of the description. A three bedroom house will usually be easier to sell than one with two bedrooms. Even if you may not need three bedrooms they can be used for other purposes such as a sewing room or hobby room. Young couples will generally start a family and the extra bedrooms become an essential part of the house. It is desirable if each child can have a private room.

As you begin the planning process consider the possible uses for the room. First make preliminary decisions on the furniture to be used. A king or queen size bed requires

5-1 Bedrooms occupy a large part of the total square feet in a house. A spacious bedroom makes living pleasant. A pendant light fixture provides general illumination. **Courtesy Thomas Lighting**

5-2 *It is wise to have bedrooms large enough to hold a king size bed. This walnut bedroom set is enhanced by the carpet and bedspread colors.* **Courtesy American Walnut Manufacturers Association**

a larger room than a single twin bed. While it is more expensive it might be wise in the long run to plan bedrooms that can accommodate a king-size bed even though there are no immediate plans to use one **(5-2)**.

Locating the Bedrooms

While it is typical to locate the bedrooms together in one end of the house **(5-3)** split plans are popular. A split plan will group several bedrooms together and locate the large master bedroom some distance away **(5-4)**. This provides privacy; however, small children sleeping away from parents greatly limits parental supervision, especially when a child is ill. There are communication systems that can be installed in the children's bedrooms with a monitor in the master bedroom. These provide a means for the child to contact the parents and the parents can hear if the child is having a problem.

As you locate bedrooms on the floor plan place them in quiet areas away from the noisy living area.

Noise

As you plan the bedrooms consider the need to control noise. Not only their location on the floor plan, but wall construction must be designed to block the passage of noise into the rooms. One way to do this is to place closets along a wall next to another room. Wall construction using staggered studs and acoustic insulation may be used.

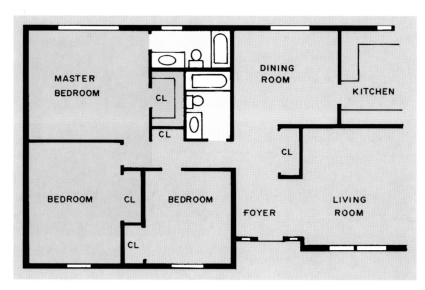

5-3 *A typical floor plan groups the bedrooms and bathrooms together in a quiet area of the house.*

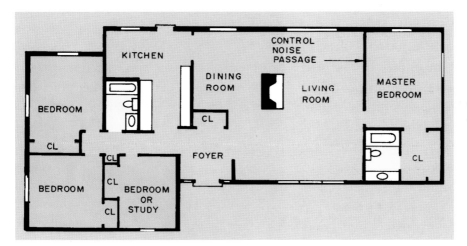

5-4 *A split bed-room plan places the master bedroom away from the other bedrooms providing privacy for the occupants. If small children are in the family this can cause some concern because of lack of supervision.*

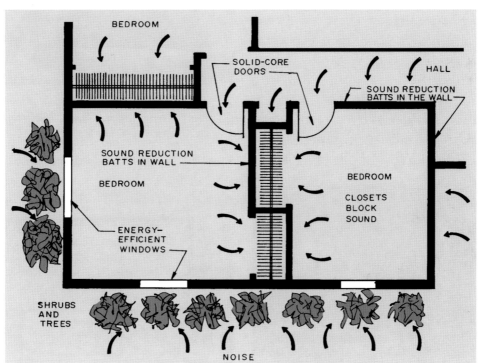

5-5 There are many things that can be done to control noise penetration into the bedroom.

Consider the location of the bedroom door and the use of solid core doors that reduce sound transmission. Exterior noise is always a difficult thing to control. When possible locate the bedrooms away from the street. Use energy efficient multiple glazed windows that are properly installed. Use storm windows over standard glazed windows. A huge fence and large shrubbery can help dampen exterior noise. Use heavy draperies inside and acoustic tile on the ceiling to dampen noise vibrations. If possible locate the windows away from the street (5-5).

Establish the Room Size

The two major factors influencing the size of the bedroom are the furniture to be used and spaces between the furniture providing aisles for easy movement within the room. Other things that may be considered include leaving space for things you feel are important, such as a dressing area related to the closets, a place for a comfortable chair for reading, or a small desk **(5-6)**. There are many possibilities for use of bedroom space in addition to just the bed. Adequate storage in the form of a dresser, chest of drawers, vanity, closets, or an armoire is important **(5-7)**.

The sizes of bedroom furniture vary from one manufacturer to another. Typical bed sizes are in **Table 5-1**.

It is recommended that you make templates of the furniture to be used. Use a

5-7 This bedroom is furnished with a beautiful bed head and foot board and matching storage units. **Courtesy KraftMaid Carpentry, Inc.**

5-6 Consider using the bedroom for quiet activities such as reading or handling family correspondence at a small desk. Notice the ceramic tile floor with a decorative border. **Courtesy Crossville Ceramics Company**

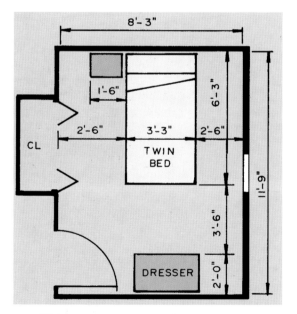

5-8 This is a minimum single occupancy room with only a twin bed, bedside table, and a dresser. It would be nice to enlarge it to permit a comfortable chair to be included.

Table 5-1 Typical Bed Sizes (in inches)	
Twin	39 × 75
Large Twin	39 × 80
Super Twin	48 × 84
Full	54 × 75
Large Full	54 × 80
Queen	60 × 80
Large Queen	60 × 84
Super Queen	64 × 96
King	78 × 80
Large King	78 × 84
Super King	90 × 96

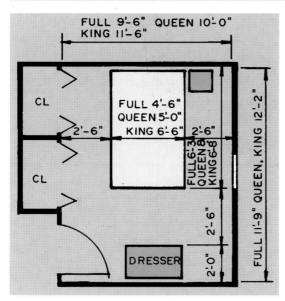

5-9 This is a minimum double occupancy bedroom with only a bedside table and dresser. A chair would be a good addition and is used frequently when dressing.

scale allowing ¼ inch to represent one foot. Arrange these on a sheet of graph paper with ¼-inch squares. Move, adjust and rearrange until the plan is acceptable. Carefully measure the space between furniture and watch what you put by windows.

Recommended minimum spacing be–tween bedroom furniture is shown in **5-8**, **5-9**, and **5-10**. A 2'-6" aisle between the bed and a wall or furniture on the side is minimum. This includes the area in front of a closet. A 3'-6" aisle in front of a closet is recommended. A major aisle usually occurs at the foot of the bed. Three feet is the minimum recommended space while 3'-6" or 4'-0" is better.

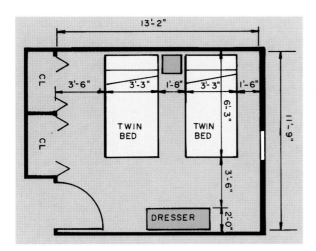

5-10 Twin beds require a larger room. This shows a minimum bedroom with only a bedside table and a dresser. A chair or other furniture would enhance the use of the room.

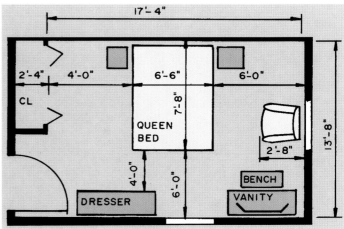

5-11 This bedroom has two bedside tables, a vanity, and a chair and extra wide aisles providing a more comfortable plan.

In **5-11** a bedroom with additional furniture is shown. This makes the room more useful and pleasant to occupy. As you work with these sizes measure the distances existing in your present bedroom to get a better feel for the sizes mentioned. Also watch for the swing of the door into the room. A 2'-8" door is minimum. Remember, some of the furniture is large so that a wide door is needed.

Notice in **5-8**, a single occupancy room must be at least 8'-3" wide and 11'-3" long if all it has is a bed and dresser. This requires 97 square feet of floor area. In **5-9** a room with a twin, queen or king size bed with one dresser requires 116, 122, and 140 square feet. A room with twin beds **(5-10)** and only a bedside table dresser requires a minimum of 149 square feet.

Closets

Design recommendations generally indicate a bedroom for a single occupant should have at least 3 lineal feet (914mm) of closet space. Actually 4 lineal feet (1220mm) is more realistic. Double-occupancy rooms should have 6 feet (1830mm) but 8 feet (2440mm) is better. These are bare minimums and more space should be provided if possible. Closet design sizes are given later in this chapter.

Some Planning Suggestions

Each bedroom should have two windows. Place them so the room will have cross ventilation. Try to avoid having the draft flowing over the bed **(5-12)**. The door, if left open, can also provide for natural ventilation.

Bedrooms should be located so that they are entered from a hall. This provides privacy and helps control noise.

If a bedroom is located near a street or sidewalk where privacy may be a problem consider using small windows high on the wall **(5-13)**. Place the sill about 5 feet (1525mm) above the floor. Remember,

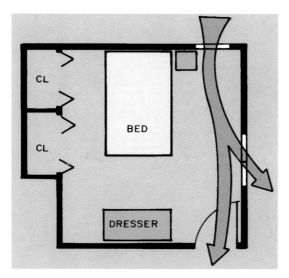

5-12 *If two windows are in a bedroom, natural ventilation is available. Try to avoid directing the airflow over the bed. The door to the hall can provide an air flow if you leave it open.*

5-13 *The use of small high windows provides privacy, allows some natural light and ventilation, and provides wall space against which a large piece of furniture may be placed.*

5-14 *A deck or patio off a bedroom provides another place to relax and enjoy the view.*
Courtesy Weather Shield Manufacturing, Inc.

codes require you also have a regular window to provide a method of escape in an emergency.

A small deck or patio off the bedroom is a nice feature. Consider using French or sliding glass doors to provide access (**5-14**). This also makes a small room seem larger.

When locating the bedrooms coordinate their placement with the bathrooms. Easy access to a bathroom from each bedroom is important. Consider a bathroom as part of a master bedroom (**5-15**). Do not place a bathroom between two bedrooms and enter it directly from each bedroom.

As you arrange the bedroom furniture consider placing mirrors and the vanity to take advantage of the natural light.

5-15 *A large master bathroom entered from the master bedroom is a very desirable feature.*
Courtesy Crane Plumbing, Fiat Products/Universal Rundle

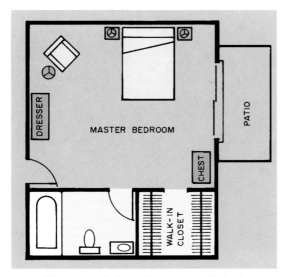

5-16 This master bedroom has a nice walk-in closet and a minimum bathroom.

5-18 This oak bedroom floor is durable, beautiful, easily maintained, and sets the color tone for the room.
Courtesy Harris-Tarkett, Inc.

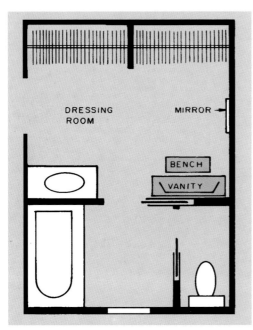

5-17 Combining a large closet, spacious dressing area, and the bath make a convenient arrangement.

While it takes some extra floor space consider adding a walk-in closet **(5-16)** and even a related dressing room that is often coordinated with the master bedroom **(5-17)**.

Give consideration to the type of wall covering and the color scheme for the room as you choose the floor covering.

The bedroom floor sets the tone for the room. Carpet and wood flooring are popular **(5-18)**. They are durable, withstand wear, and are easily cleaned.

A comfortable chair for relaxation and reading is a nice feature as shown in **5-18**.

When planning a bedroom for children consider allowing open floor area for a play area for small children **(5-19)** that may become a study area with a computer as the children grow older.

Planning the Laundry

Laundry facilities typically contain a washer, dryer, sink, countertop space for preparing and sorting clothes, ironing facilities, and in some cases a sewing cabinet **(5-20)**.

Consider the location as you plan the layout and decide what activities will occur.

A popular and convenient location is in the wing or area where the bedrooms and bathrooms are located. This is where the clothes are collected that need to be laundered. After they have been dried, folded, and ironed they will go into storage in the bedrooms so close proximity is convenient. Some prefer to place the laundry in the basement. This is inexpensive space. However, moving the clothing to and from the room is a bit of a problem. Try to locate the laundry room below a closet so a chute can be run from the floor of the closet for dropping the clothes into the basement laundry room.

Some locate the washer and dryer in the kitchen or family room and in warm climates in the garage or a room on the end of a carport. Consider the inconvenience of these locations as they relate to the area

5-20 A laundry can be designed to perform several activities related to the care and preparation of clothing and linens. KitchenAid is a registered Trademark of KitchenAid, USA. Photo used with permission.

where clothes needing washing are assembled, in the bathrooms and bedrooms.

In a small house it can be located near the kitchen and bedroom area as shown in **5-21**. Here it is between a kitchen and bathroom enabling the plumbing to be concentrated reducing the cost some. Typically the washer and dryer are located side by side in a small room designed for the laundry operations **(5-22)**.

If only a minimum facility is wanted the washer and dryer can be located in a closet in the hall to the bedroom. They can be stacked one on top of the other **(5-23)** or placed side by side. Folding doors can be used to conceal them. Sorting, preparing for washing, folding, and ironing will have to occur somewhere else.

5-19 A children's bedroom should have an open play area. This room has an Adirondack ash honey-colored wood floor that is durable and easily maintained. Courtesy Harris-Tarkett, Inc.

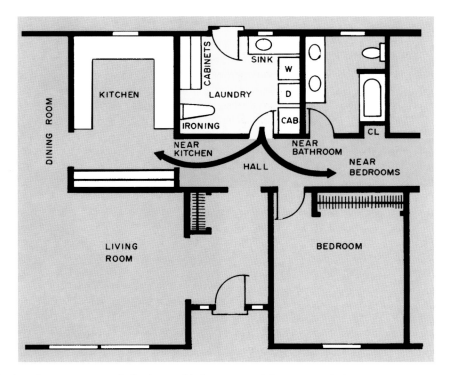

5-21 *This laundry room is near the kitchen and bedroom area. It has an outside door so it can serve as a place for children to clean up a bit before they enter the house.*

5-22 *The washer and dryer are generally placed side by side in a small room devoted to the care of clothing and other fabric articles.*
Courtesy Whirlpool Home Appliances

Some Laundry Planning Pointers

Typical washers and dryers are 26 to 30 inches (660 to 762mm) square and when installed will extend about 32 to 36 inches (812 to 915mm) into the room. Allow about 5'-6" (1677mm) of wall space for positioning these **(5-24)**.

An aisle of at least 3'-0" (915mm) is required in front of the washer and dryer **(5-24)**.

A sink is required. It is needed for the preparation of clothing before it is washed.

Plan for a cabinet with several feet of countertop and wall cabinets. This is used when preparing the clothes for washing and folding them after they have been dried **(5-25)**.

5-23 *When space is at a premium the washer and dryer can be stacked and placed in a closet. Notice the shelving provided for laundry supplies.*
Courtesy Whirlpool Home Appliances

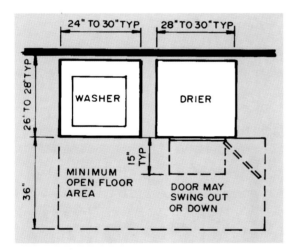

5-24 *Recommended minimum spacing requirements for a washer and dryer.*

5-25 *A counter work surface is an important part of a laundry room. It is used when preparing the clothes for washing and when folding and ironing cleaned clothes and linens. The cabinets are the major storage facility.*

Wire shelving units provide a variety of units that help hold the clothing being ironed in the laundry room. They are freestanding and can be moved as needed **(5-26)**.

Shallow closets can provide a lot of storage for laundry supplies and cleaning materials **(5-27)**.

Arrange the facilities in a sequence so that the clothes move toward the dryer.

5-26 *This freestanding moveable wire shelf unit is a big help when doing the ironing.* **Courtesy ClosetMaid**

5-27 *Shallow closets with wire shelving can store cleaning materials and require very little floor area.*
Courtesy ClosetMaid

Begin with the sorting and preparation counter and move toward the sink where bleach and special soaps may be applied. From there move to the washer. The dryer is next to the washer so clothes do not have to be moved very far. If there is an ironing area it should follow the dryer **(5-28)**.

Remember the dryer must be vented to the outside air so consider how this will be done as you locate it.

Allow at least 6 inches (152mm) of space between the back of the washer and dryer for the plumbing and venting pipes and electrical outlets.

Plan electric outlets in the wall behind the washer and dryer. The washer requires 120V current and the dryer 220 volts.

Consider placing the laundry room so it can have an outside door **(5-21)**. This serves as a rear entrance to the house and a place

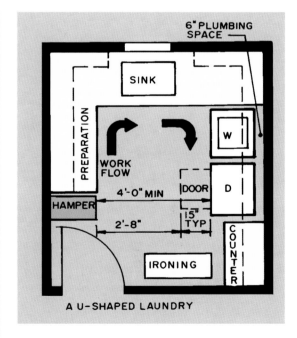

5-28 *Two typical laundry rooms with the work flow following a logical sequence.*

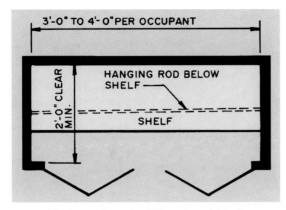

5-29 *A bedroom closet should be at least 24 inches (610mm) deep. Provision can be made for hanging long and short items, increasing the usefulness of the closet.*

5-30 *Metal shelving is available in a range of sizes and designs providing both rods to hang clothing and metal shelving.*

5-31 *Special fixtures such as shoe racks increase the usefulness of the closet space.* **Courtesy ClosetMaid**

where children at play can enter the house and clean up a bit before going into the other rooms.

Planning Storage Facilities

The location of storage facilities is as important as any part of planning the house. However it is often given little consideration. Think about the type of storage needed and where it should be located. As you plan the kitchen, bathroom, and laundry room storage considerations usually are a big part of the plan. However, for the rest of the house planning for storage is often neglected. Possibly the major storage planning revolves around closets.

Planning Closets

Closets are an important part of bedroom planning. They are also used for linen storage, in the kitchen for storing packaged foods and at the front door for guest coats.

A bedroom closet should be at least 2'-0" (610mm) deep (5-29). A bedroom closet should contain 3 to 4 lineal feet (915 to 1220mm) per person expected to occupy the bedroom. The use of wire shelving (5-30) and special fixtures as shoe racks (5-31) can greatly increase the storage capacity of the closet. It is helpful to use part of the closet for hanging long items and the rest for short items. On the short side you can hang two rows of hanging garments and shelving or a drawer unit below (5-32). Wire shelving is very versatile and permits a wide choice in arranging the closet interior (5-33). Storage for hanging items, shelves for boxes and other items and special racks are available (5-34).

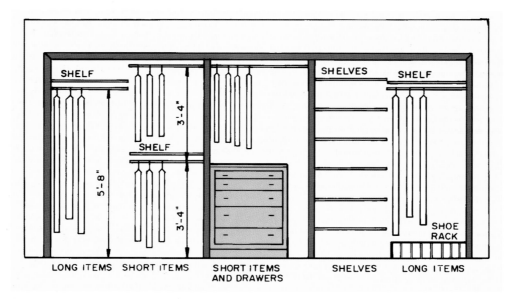

SHELF

3'-4"

SHELF

5'-8"

3'-4"

SHELVES   SHELF

SHOE
RACK

LONG ITEMS   SHORT ITEMS   SHORT ITEMS
AND DRAWERS   SHELVES   LONG ITEMS

5-32 One side of a closet can have two rows of hanging short clothing or shelves and the other can hang long items.

5-33 Manufactured wire shelves provide great versatility in designing closet storage and permit air to circulate, which is very important in hot, humid climates where closet interiors tend to develop mold.
Courtesy ClosetMaid

5-34 This arrangement allows for hanging long garments and a series of pockets for shoes and other small items. **Courtesy ClosetMaid**

5-35 Bifold doors open up the entire closet making it easy to reach everything.

As you plan the closets consider using folding doors because they open the entire width of the closet **(5-35)**. Remember to put a light in the closet.

Walk-in closets are popular in larger homes **(5-36)**. A walk-in closet is an area with shelving and hanging rods on all sides. Allow at least 2 feet (310mm) for hanging the clothing and an aisle of 2'-6" (762mm). A wider aisle is a big help **(5-37)**. A larger closet with a dressing area including a small vanity is in

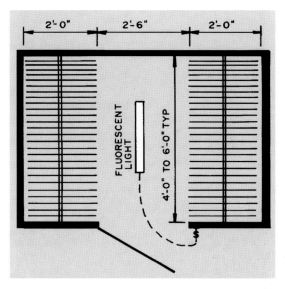

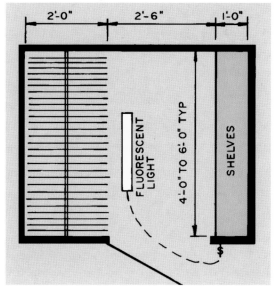

5-36 This walk-in closet has metal shelving on three sides providing several kinds of storage capabilities.
Courtesy ClosetMaid

5-37 Typical minimum walk-in closets. Good lighting is important.

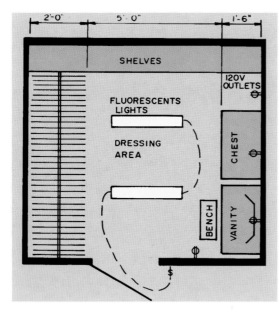

5-38 Larger walk-in closets can have a dressing area, vanity, and storage facilities.

5-38. Good general lighting and some wall-mounted duplex electrical outlets are helpful.

It is a good technique to place closets between rooms. This helps reduce noise transfer through the wall.

Closets should be planned so they do not extend into the room. It is best to extend the closet the full length of the room or use half the length for a closet in the next room (**5-39**).

Other Types of Storage

The more commonly used types of storage include built-in furniture containing shelves and closed cabinets, storage in carports, garages, and basements, and cabinets of various types. If you have a workshop considerable planning is necessary for tool and material storage. A den will need storage for books and papers to be filed. Some provision must be made for lawn mowers, garden tools, bicycles, ladders, and other home maintenance items. If you have a trailer or recreation vehicle it has to be stored somewhere. Some communities require these to be out of sight or prohibit them entirely. How will you handle garbage and trash disposal?

Planning Utility Rooms

Many homes do not have basements so the water heater and furnace have to be located elsewhere. If a house has a crawl space there are a number of furnaces that can be placed in it below the floor. The water heater can also be located here. Carefully work out these details as you plan the house. If you have a house with a concrete slab floor it is usually best to plan to have a small utility

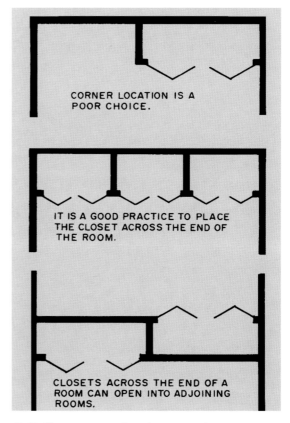

5-39 Proper ways to place closets.

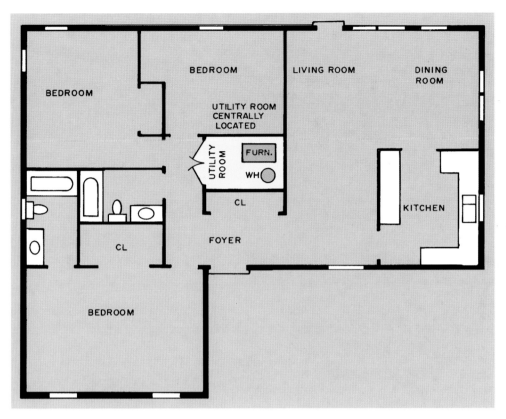

5-40 *A utility room typically holds the furnace and water heater and is centrally located.*

room to hold the furnace and water heater **(5-40)**. Sometimes the washer and dryer are also placed in this room as are a toilet and small lavatory. Some furnaces can be placed in a small closet. Observe building codes when doing this installation.

When planning a utility room consider the following suggestions:

An outside door, while not required, is helpful for servicing the unit.

Consider the need for a chimney or vent pipe. Plan how it will run and how it looks from the outside.

Mechanical ventilation or a window is needed.

Locate it so that the noise generated does not infringe on the living and sleeping areas.

Locate it to provide the shortest possible duct runs to the various rooms. This tends to be a compromise between noise, venting, and an efficient heat and cooling distribution system. A central location on the floor plan is desired.

Observe codes for furnace installation.

Leave enough room so the furnace can be easily serviced.

PLANNING THE BATHROOM

When planning a new house you have the freedom to select the shape and size of the areas to form the bathrooms. Do not limit the plan to a simple rectangle but consider other options **(6-1)**. The choice of fixtures is wide and varied. Basically you have to decide what you want in a bathroom and how many you feel are needed. In many homes the bath off the master bedroom is the family pride and joy. It can contain a whirlpool, dual lavatories, a toilet in a compartment and luxurious lighting **(6-2)**.

In addition to the master bathroom a second full bathroom is needed for other bedrooms. In a three-bedroom house this second bathroom will serve two bedrooms. A four-bedroom house can easily use two bathrooms in addition to the master bathroom. If the house is two stories typically the second floor will have three or four bedrooms. In this case locate a half bath on the first floor. A half bath consists of a toilet and lavatory **(6-3)**. This is often called a powder room and is located in a place where it is convenient for guests, yet provides privacy. It is frequently located near the living room, family room, or other entertainment area. If a full basement exists consider placing a half bath there.

As you plan the bathroom, consider other uses that may occur there such as laundry facilities, a dressing area with mirrors, a sauna, a whirlpool, or exercise and sunbathing equipment.

In addition, an extensive array of fixture cabinets form an important part of the bathroom. They are available in a range of designs and species of wood **(6-4)**. Custom-built cab-

6-1 *A bathroom can be a spacious, interesting room that is warm and inviting. The use of quality fixtures, natural woods, carefully selected colors, and natural light all contribute to the restful atmosphere.* **Courtesy American Standard, Inc.**

6-2 *This bathroom features a large whirlpool bath, a pedestal lavatory, and a toilet in a compartment. Notice the lighting sconces for special light and a large glazed yet private wall using natural light to enhance the area.* **Courtesy Jacuzzi Whirlpool Bath**

6-4 *These cherry wood cabinets provide considerable storage for items needed in the bathroom and a rich warm atmosphere is created. It does not look like a bathroom. Notice the cherry wood boxing around the tub.* **Courtesy Aristokraft, Inc.**

6-3 *These fixtures fit nicely into a small powder room for guests and occasional use by the family. The pedestal lavatory requires a minimum of space, which helps when planning the layout.* **Courtesy Kohler Company**

6-5 *This series of curved custom-made bathroom cabinets produces a very interesting scene. Notice the glass countertop and spotlights over the lavatory.* **Courtesy Merillat Industries**

inets having special countertops and shapes greatly enhance a bathroom **(6-5)**.

The plan must meet local building codes for plumbing and electrical systems. In addition ventilation is important. Bathrooms without windows must have mechanical ventilation. It is very helpful if mechanical ventilation be provided in all bathrooms regardless of the existence of windows.

Locating the Bathroom

If a house has only one bathroom it should be centrally located. If several bathrooms are planned consider where they are most needed. Typically the bedroom area is the high use location. However, one should be near and easily accessible from the living room, dining room, and the kitchen area. Bathrooms to be used by those in several bedrooms should be entered from the hall. Do not have several bedrooms directly entering the bathroom. This causes privacy problems and locked door problems.

Consider grouping several bathrooms together. They might share a common wall. This can reduce the cost of plumbing. Second floor bathrooms can be located over first floor bathrooms to save plumbing costs. If a more efficient location requires separating them

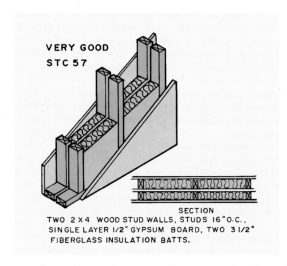

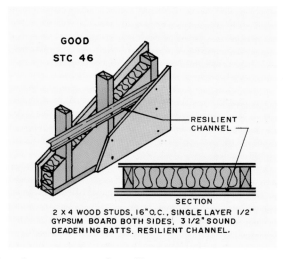

6-6 *Several types of interior wall construction used to reduce the transmission of sound between rooms.*

the efficiency is more important than the reduction in plumbing costs.

Sound Transmission

While reduction of sound between rooms in a house is important for all rooms it is especially important for bathrooms. Sound transmission characteristics are specified in terms of the walls Sound Transmission Class (STC). The higher the STC rating, the greater the ability to limit the transmission of sound. STC ratings for bathroom walls should be 52 or greater. While there are several ways to build interior walls with high STC rating those in **6-6** are typical. Special sound deadening batts used on interior wall greatly reduce sound transmission **(6-7)**.

Consider Floor Loads

The floor needs to be reinforced to carry the weight of a bathtub or whirlpool. Since these hold large quantities of water they are very heavy when full. Water weighs 8.3 pounds per gallon or 0.95 kilograms per liter so the weight when full can be calculated.

Typical Types of Bathroom

A house will usually contain at least two of the following types of bathrooms:

- **Master bedroom bath suite**
- **General family bathroom serving several bedrooms**
- **A powder room (half bath)**
- **The universally accessible bathroom**

The master bedroom bath suite is designed to fit into the overall plan for the master bedroom and any special storage

6-7 These Noise Reducer™ *sound-deadening batts will greatly reduce sound transmission through interior walls.* **Courtesy Certainteed Corporation**

such as walk-in closets, dressing rooms, and storage cabinets. The master bedroom bath suite is usually large, has multiple fixtures, and is rather extravagant. It exists for the comfort and pleasure of the occupant **(6-8)**.

The general family bathroom tends to have fixtures spaced so that it may under certain circumstances be used by two people. For example, the tub or shower and

6-8 This master bathroom is spacious and has high-quality fixtures. Notice the unique design of the fixtures and the use of wood paneling on the wall and around the whirlpool. **Courtesy Kohler Company**

toilet could be located in one space and one or more lavatories be in a separate space within the room **(6-9)**. This provides two private compartments allowing two people to use the bath at the same time. Some place the toilet by itself in a private compartment.

Family bathrooms require you to give consideration to the needs of children. A small platform in front of one lavatory will help and can be removed as the children grow up. A shower instead of a tub or in addition to a tub will help them. Fixtures that can be adjusted for height are available.

One helpful idea to reduce congestion in the family bathroom is to locate a small lavatory and mirror in each bedroom.

Rather than one large family bathroom, some prefer to build two smaller rooms each complete but using minimum spacing requirements.

A powder room is also referred to as a half-bath. It will have a lavatory and toilet and be allowed only minimum clear floor

6-10 This bathroom has a shower with a seat and grab bars and a tub with a seat and grab bars making it accessible to those with physical limitations. Considerable floor area is needed for wheelchair users. **Courtesy HEWI, Inc.**

area, although some extra space is recommended. It is typically located near the area where you entertain, and so falls near the living room, family room, or other large-size room. The entrance should somehow be sceened or located off a hall so when guests use it they can do so with some degree of privacy. When used for the family to supplement the other bathrooms rather than for guests, it can be placed in a utility room, under a stair, or in some other less valuable but still accessible space. Some like to make it accessible from outside so children playing in the yard can access it without running through the house.

The universally accessible bathroom is designed for use by almost anyone regardless of physical condition. It meets all the requirements of the U.S. Disabilities Act. It will accommodate children because the height of fixtures is varied and large enough for wheelchair users to maneuver. A typical example of a universally accessible bathroom is in **6-10**.

6-9 This family bathroom has two pedestal lavatories separated by a cabinet enabling two people to use the bathroom at the same time. **Courtesy Kohler Company**

Planning Guidelines

After you have decided on the fixtures you want in each bathroom make scale drawings on ¼-inch graph paper and try several arrangements of the fixtures. Some may require considerable space, being the focal point of the room (**6-11**). Following are planning guidelines to help locate and space the fixtures. These are minimum recommendations for designing a satisfactory bathroom.

Lavatory Clearances

The minimum clear floor space in front of a lavatory is shown in **6-12**. This can run parallel with or perpendicular to the fixture. When you have two lavatories in a single cabinet you will want to allow at least 60 inches of clear floor space parallel to the

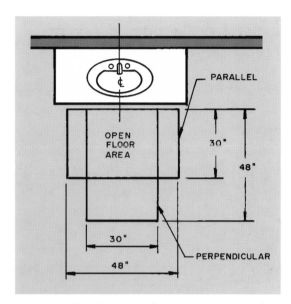

6-12 *A 30 by 48 inch open floor area is recommended in front of a lavatory.*

6-11 *Plan for luxury items you want in the bathroom, such as this custom shower or a whirlpool.*
Courtesy Alumax Bath Enclosures

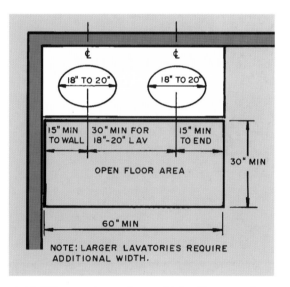

6-13 *When two lavatories are side by side you need at least 60 inches of open floor area to comfortably use both at the same time.*

cabinet with the lavatories 30 inches apart (**6-13**). Typically this distance is made larger for a more private and luxurious installation. A lavatory should be at least 15 inches from a side wall as shown in **6-13**.

Lavatory Cabinet & Mirror Heights

The height of the lavatory cabinet can be varied to suit the needs of the user. For some a 30-inch height is comfortable and for others up to 40 inches is best. Usually family members vary in height so some make one lower than the other **(6-14)**. A height of 32 inches is commonly used. Pedestal lavatories are typically 32 to 36 inches high **(6-15)**.

When installing mirrors, the bottom edge of a mirror mounted flat against the wall should not be more than 40 inches (1016mm) above the floor. If you tilt the mirror some, you can raise it to 48 inches (1219mm) **(6-16)**. Tilting the mirror makes it easier for those wheelchair bound to use it.

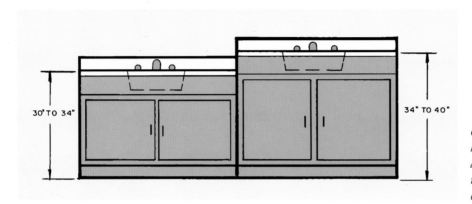

6-14 You can have lavatories at different heights to make them easier to use.

6-15 Pedestal lavatories are available in several heights. They provide open floor space on all sides.

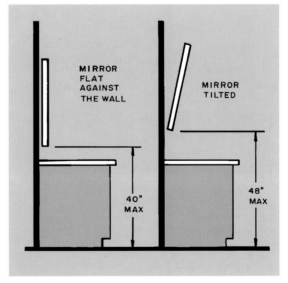

6-16 When mounting a mirror over the lavatory try several heights until you find one that is best for you.

Shower Recommendations

The minimum dimensions needed for an enclosed shower are shown in **6-17**. The grab bars or a folding seat, if present, may project into this minimum size. Typical larger sizes **(6-18)**, which are as much as 34 x 50 inches or 34 x 62 inches, provide much needed space for bathing and seats.

Larger showers will have a built-in seat. Permanent built-in seats should not encroach on the minimum 34 x 34 inches clear shower floor area. Shower doors should open into a clear floor space in the bathroom.

Bathtub Recommendations

The size and shape of the clear floor space required beside a bathtub depends upon the direction from which you have to approach it. If it is located so you walk along the side (parallel) a clear space of 30 x 60 inches is minimum **(6-19)**. Should you have to walk perpendicular to it, the minimum floor area

*6-18 Larger showers are more convenient to use and can provide easy access. **Courtesy Alumax Bath Enclosures***

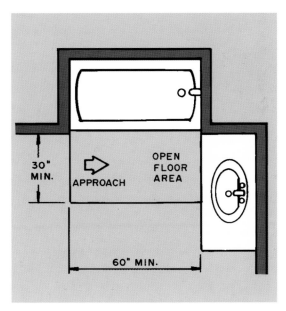

6-19 A bathtub with a parallel approach requires at least a 30 by 60 inch open floor area. Increase this if possible.

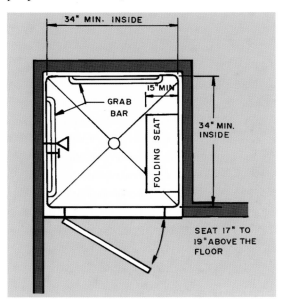

6-17 This minimum shower provides tight quarters.

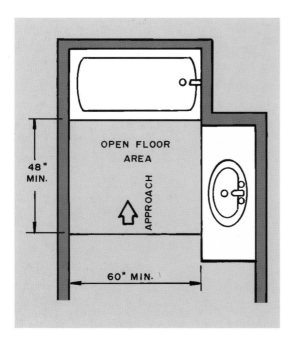

6-20 If you approach perpendicular to the bathtub you need a minimum of 48 by 60 inches of open floor area.

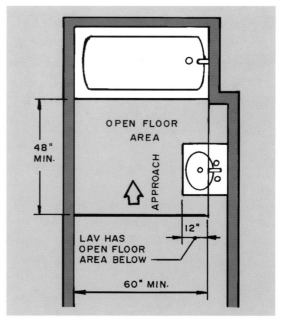

is as shown in **6-20**. If a cabinet has a recessed area providing an unobstructed floor area, at least 12 inches of this can be counted as part of the overall minimum clear floor area **(6-21)**. Remember, these are minimums. If you can allow larger clear floor areas the bathroom will be greatly improved.

Toilet & Bidet Recommendations

The minimum clear floor space in front of the toilet is 48 x 48 inches as shown in **6-22** and **6-23**.

If it is not possible to get the full 48 inches in front, this can be reduced some but do not go below 30 inches.

The clear floor area can have a door swing over it because the door is closed after you enter the bathroom (refer to **6-23**). Up

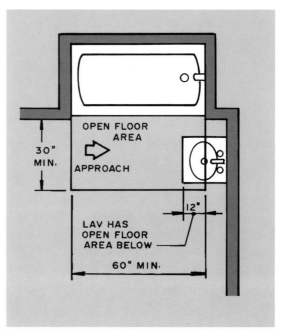

6-21 (TOP AND ABOVE) You can use 12 inches of open floor area below a cabinet by the bathtub as part of the minimum floor area.

to 12 inches of the clear floor space can extend under a nearby lavatory or cabinet.

The principles applying to a toilet all apply to a bidet. The ideal situation is

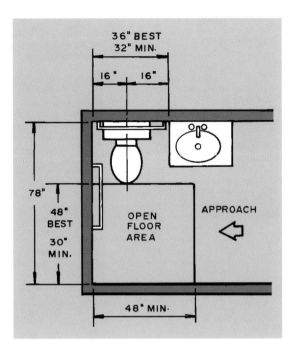

6-22 *It is best to allow 48 inches of open floor space in front of the toilet when you have to approach it from the front.*

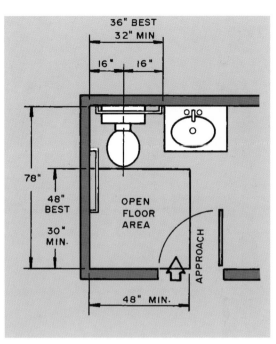

6-23 *When you approach a toilet from the side you need 48 inches open floor area in front of it.*

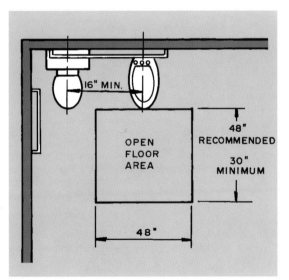

6-24 *A bidet requires a 48 by 48 inch open floor area. This area can overlap the toilet open floor area.*

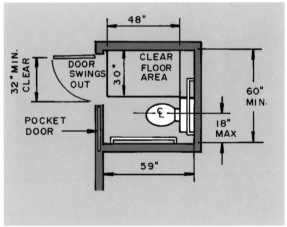

6-25 *This privacy toilet compartment provides adequate room for comfortable use.*

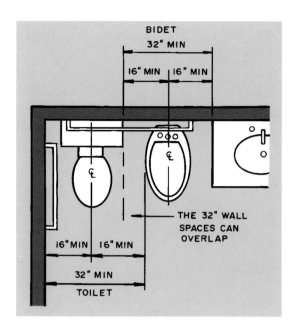

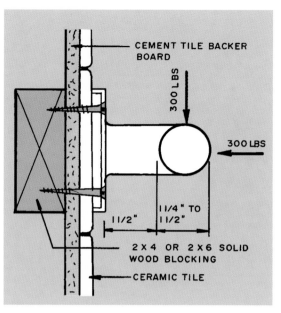

6-26 The recommended spacing of the toilet and bidet when they are placed side by side is 32 inches (813mm). However, 16 inches of this can overlap.

6-27 Grab bars must be securely fastened to solid wood or thick plywood underlayment.

6-28 Grab bars can extend on each side of the toilet if it is not next to a wall.
Courtesy HEWI, Inc.

6-29 Grab bars around the bathtub provide a great safety feature and allow access in and out with minimum danger of falling. **Courtesy HEWI, Inc.**

shown in **6-24** with the 30-inch clearance as an absolute minimum. The open floor area for the toilet and bidet can overlap as long as the centerline of the bidet is 16 inches (406mm) from the centerline of the toilet.

In **6-22** and **6-23** it shows a toilet requires at least 32 inches (813mm) of clear wall space. This is very tight and 36 inches (914mm) or more is recommended. When a toilet is built into a privacy compartment make the compartment at least 36 inches (914mm) wide. However this is very tight and 60 inches (1524mm) is recommended (**6-25**).

Generally the toilet and the bidet are placed side by side. This requires less total clear floor area and simplifies the plumbing. The recommended spacing of these fixtures is shown in **6-26**. The 32-inch minimum wall space can overlap provided the minimum clear floor area is available for each.

Locating & Installing Grab Bars

Grab bars are an essential part of bathroom planning. They are needed by everyone using the facilities. They must be installed by screwing to a solid backing material such as 2-inch (51mm) lumber or ¾-inch (19mm) plywood (**6-27**). A grab bar should be 1¼ or 1½ inches (32 or 38mm) in diameter and have 1½ inches (38mm) space between the bar and the wall.

Grab bars beside a toilet are in **6-28**, a bathtub in **6-29**, and a shower in **6-30**.

Bathroom Storage

You will need to incorporate in your plan some storage cabinets for towels, toiletries, soap, and other supplies. If the room is large, base cabinets and wall cabinets add a great deal (**6-31**). For most bathrooms, the lavatory vanity cabinets will be the major storage center, especially if the cabinet is longer than the minimum needed for the lavatory bowl (**6-32**). There are many variations of small

6-30 This shower has colored nylon grab bars and seat providing safety and comfort. It is open permitting entrance by a wheelchair bound person. **Courtesy HEWI, Inc.**

6-31 These beautiful bathroom cabinets provide considerable storage as well as accommodate the lavatory. They are finished in a maple color. The total installation produces a refined look not seen in many bathrooms. **Courtesy Wellborn Cabinet, Inc.**

6-32 This small lavatory cabinet provides considerable storage.

6-34 This lavatory and countertop are made as a single piece from a synthetic composite material. **Courtesy Avonite, Inc.**

6-33 This wall-hung cabinet is typical of many such storage units available for use in the bathroom.

6-35 This striking lavatory has a glass bowl, top, and pedestal. **Courtesy American Standard, Inc.**

6-38 *This one-piece toilet is often called a low-profile toilet. It only uses 1.6 gallons per flush. It is made from vitreous china.* **Courtesy Eljer Plumbingware, Inc.**

6-36 *This is a kiln-fired solid glass lavatory bowl mounted in a glass top.* **Courtesy Jacuzzi Whirlpool Bath**

6-37 *This vitreous china self-rimming countertop lavatory is set into a tile-surfaced countertop providing a durable and beautiful installation.* **Courtesy American Standard, Inc.**

6-39 *This two-piece toilet has the tank made separately and has it bolted to the back of the bowl.* **Courtesy Crane Plumbing/Fiat Products/Universal Rundle**

6-40 *This bathtub has been set on a platform. The sides and step are finished with ceramic tile.* **Courtesy American Standard, Inc.**

6-42 *This whirlpool has been set into a raised platform. Notice how the colors are coordinated with the lavatory. The oval shape is very popular.* **Courtesy Aqua Glass Corporation**

6-41 *The free-form sculptured bathtub has been enclosed providing a smooth finished appearance. Notice the freshness added by the natural light.* **Courtesy American Standard, Inc.**

wall-hung cabinets that are good for medicines and other small articles (**6-33**).

Bathroom Fixtures & Accessories

Bathroom lavatories available include a striking array of products and materials. A widely used lavatory is made from synthetic materials and the bowl and countertop are cast as a single unit (**6-34**). A striking European design with a glass bowl, top, and base is in **6-35**. A kiln-fired glass bowl set in a glass countertop provides a striking appearance (**6-36**). A charming vitreous lavatory set in a ceramic tile finish countertop is decorative and durable (**6-37**).

Toilets are typically one-piece (**6-38**) or two-piece (**6-39**).

Bathtubs are available in enameled

6-43 *This unique whirlpool is shaped to fit into a corner. Notice it has been set into a recess in the floor so the tub and pump are below the floor.* **Courtesy Jacuzzi Whirlpool Bath**

6-45 *A metal-framed glass shower enclosure makes a bathtub serve as a shower.* **Courtesy Alumax Bath Enclosures**

6-44 *This is a shower made as a complete unit. It has no seams to leak. All that is needed is to install a door.*

6-46 *This corner shower uses a fiberglass pan on the floor enclosed by a metal-framed glass enclosure assuring a watertight installation.* **Courtesy Alumax Bath Enclosures**

steel, enameled cast iron, acrylic, fiberglass with a gel coat or an acrylic coating, and ABS plastic. The shapes vary considerably ranging from rectangular to square **(6-40)** to freeform **(6-41)**.

Whirlpool tubs are made from the same materials as bathtubs. They have a series of jets operated by pumps that produce a stream of water under pressure across your body, helping you to relax **(6-42)**. Some are set on platforms while others are recessed into the floor **(6-43)**.

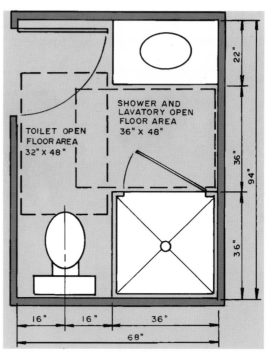

6-47 This striking shower shows how you can use manufactured glass enclosures and water-resistant materials on the floors and walls to create an unusual installation. **Courtesy Alumax Bath Enclosures**

6-49 When space on the floor plan is tight consider using a shower in second and third bathrooms. This is sometimes referred to as a three-quarters bathroom.

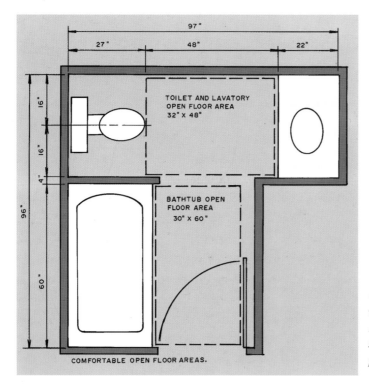

Showers may be prefabricated units of acrylic or fiberglass having the floor and walls made as a single unit **(6-44)**. Some have a seat built into them. An inexpensive way to get a shower is to plumb in a shower head on the wall at the end of a bathtub. Then add a metal-framed glass shower enclosure **(6-45)**.

Shower enclosures of various shapes are available. In **6-46**

6-48 A layout for a full bathroom, with comfortable open floor allowances. However, these are considered minimum so allow more open area, whenever possible.

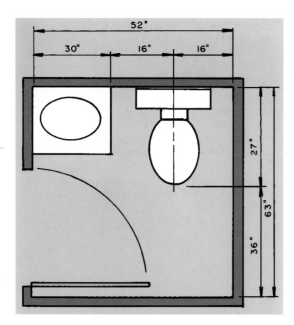

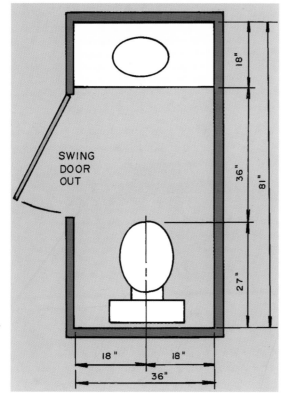

6-50 These are usable but tight layouts for half baths. If space is very tight use a pocket door.

is a corner enclosure. The metal-frame glass walls fit into a cast fiberglass pan forming the floor. The walls are covered with ceramic tile. Another striking installation is in **6-47**. The glass enclosures are set against glass block walls and on a ceramic tile floor.

Some Bathroom Layouts

After you have listed the fixtures to be in the bathroom and made some brand selections you have the basic sizes of each. Using this information and the possible amount of space you want to allocate to each bathroom make some trial layouts. Use templates of the fixtures and ¼-inch square graph paper upon which you draw the size and shape of the room. Start arranging the fixtures observing the planning principles.

In **6-48** is a full bathroom that meets the minimum space requirements. This provides a full bathtub, which could also serve as a shower. Notice the door swings against a wall and there is enough open floor area to permit you to enter the room and close the door. If space on the floor plan for a second or third bathroom is limited consider installing a shower instead of a bathtub. One such plan is in **6-49**.

A minimum layout for a half bath, often called a powder room, is in **6-50**. A key to a successful half bath is the placement of the door. If a swinging door is used it must clear the fixtures and there must be enough open floor area for you to stand in so you can open and close the door. In really tight situations use a pocket door or swing the door out. Also select small fixtures, including a wall hung or pedestal lavatory.

Another full bathroom layout with the

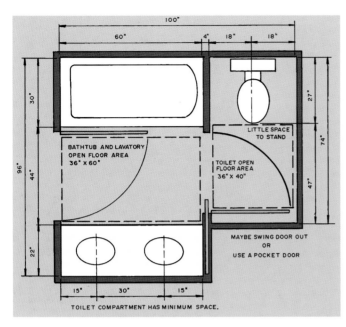

6-51 *This full bathroom layout has the toilet in a compartment. Since the compartment allows minimum space for you to stand as the door is opened a pocket door is recommended.*

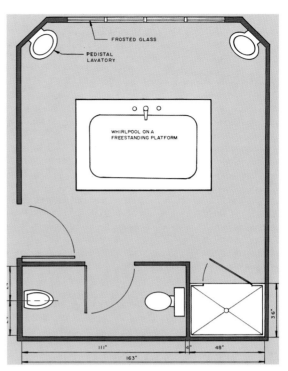

6-52 *This large luxurious bathroom has a freestanding whirlpool as the focal point of the room. A large shower is provided as well as a compartment for the toilet and bidet.*

6-53 *A freestanding whirlpool beautifully enclosed with wood paneling is the major feature of this spacious bathroom.* **Courtesy Crane Plumbing/Fiat Products/Universal Rundle**

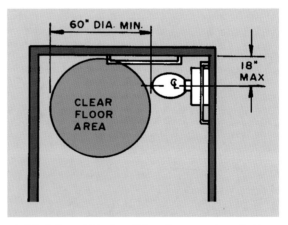

6-54 *At least 60 inches of clear floor area is needed in front of the toilet for easy access by those who are wheelchair bound.*

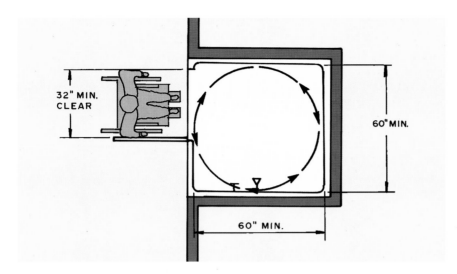

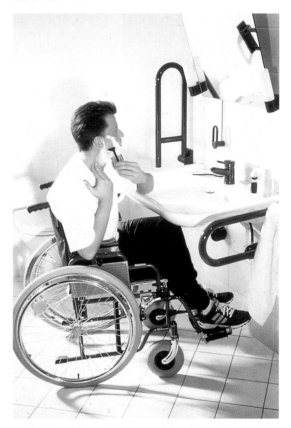

6-55 *A shower should allow a wheelchair to enter and rotate. At the floor it must retain water inside yet permit the wheelchair to roll over this into the shower.*

toilet in a privacy compartment is in **6-51**. Notice the privacy compartment must have a pocket door because the swinging door leaves no place to stand. There are many other possible room layouts. Those just shown give good examples of some that meet the minimum space recommendations.

Opposite are examples of luxurious layouts with large open areas and multiple fixtures. The layout in **6-52** has the toilet and bidet in a spacious compartment and two pedestal lavatories. The focal point of the room is the large whirlpool in the center, which is raised and enclosed similar to the one in **6-53**. The number of possible luxurious layouts is great.

Planning Bathrooms for the Wheelchair Bound

Since a wheelchair requires an area 60 inches (1524mm) in diameter to turn this is the key factor in bathroom planning. The area in front of the toilet **(6-54)** and in a shower **(6-55)** must be this large. Also needed is an unobstructed area below the lavatory so a person's legs can fit under it permitting

them to get close to it **(6-56)**. Grab bars are also essential.

6-56 *A wall-hung lavatory with nylon gripping rails provides barrier-free access to the fixture.*
Courtesy HEWI, Inc.

PLANNING PORCHES, DECKS, PATIOS & SUNROOMS

Porches, decks, patios, and sunrooms provide a pleasant extension of the house to the outdoors. While each serves a slightly difference function each should be considered as a house is planned. They can add a special feature that will be appreciated for years to come.

Porches

Porches have been a part of residential architecture for a long time. Some of the classic styles must have a porch to accurately reflect the architectural style (**7-1** and **7-2**). They do have a major influence on the exterior appearance of the house so they should be carefully designed to be compatible with the overall style.

Porches are located wherever needed. They are typically used to provide shelter over an exterior door and a sitting area (**7-3**). They are often placed off a bedroom, dining room, or living room and are often situated to provide a sheltered dining and sitting area (**7-4**). Some are screened to keep out insects.

Porches are exposed to the elements so the materials used must be durable and easily maintained (**7-5**). Decay-resistant woods such as redwood and cypress are often used as is a concrete floor.

When planning a porch that is to shelter the front entrance and protect those waiting at the door, at least a 4-feet-wide roof would be required (**7-6**). If it is to also be used for relaxing in a comfortable chair it should be at least 8 feet wide. This allows room for the furniture and space for someone to walk past those seated (**7-7**).

7-1 *This is a concrete framed country farmhouse. Even with the latest construction techniques the porch is the dominant feature of this style house. It provides shelter and a place to sit and rock.*
Courtesy Portland Cement Association

7-2 *The portico on this Southern Colonial style home forms the major identifying element of the structure. It provides shelter for the entrance and is the dominant architectural feature.*

7-3 *This porch fully shelters the front entrance and provides a private sitting area.*

7-4 *This large porch off the living area provides a place to dine, , and enjoy the countryside. The columns are made from a polymer.*
Courtesy HB and G Permaporch Systems

7-5 *This front entrance shelter is of masonry construction and has no maintenance to worry about.*

7-6 *This front porch has the roof extending out at least four feet providing adequate protection from the weather.*

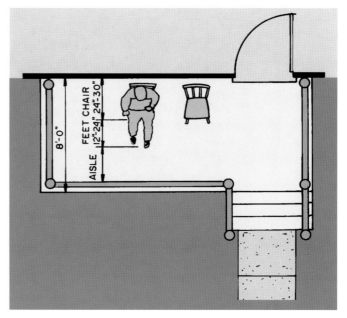

7-7 *A porch to be used for comfortable sitting should be wide enough for an aisle to permit a person to pass by those seated.*

7-8 *This porch is over 30 inches above the ground so a railing is required. Many codes specify a 36-inch high railing.*

7-9 *This front porch was finished with stucco. The material and color blend harmoniously with the light tan brick walls.*

Building codes typically require that a porch over 30 inches above the ground have a protective railing often specified as 36 inches high. When a railing is required remember it influences the overall appearance of the house. The design of the railing should be carefully considered. A railing can also interfere with the view for those on the porch **(7-8)**.

Porches take many forms and often use materials that are different from the walls of the house **(7-9)**. Whatever material is chosen it must be visually compatible with the wall material. The house in **7-10** used the same finish material on the porch and exterior wall. This creates a different visual reaction from the one shown in **7-9**.

A long striking front porch is shown in **7-11**. The house is constructed from logs and rugged structures and great lighting creates an inviting front entrance.

7-11 This log framed front porch with pleasant lighting creates a visually prominent and inviting front entrance.
Courtesy Edgewood Fine Log Structures, Coeur d'Alene, ID

Decks

Decks form an additional living area that is different from ordinary rooms. They can serve as a place to have an early breakfast or a quick lunch, a place for sunbathing and exercise equipment, and a place to relax and enjoy the view **(7-12)**. Decks let you enjoy the natural breezes and the warmth of the

7-10 Stucco was used to finish the exterior walls and the porch. The porch blends into the overall appearance of the house.

7-12 A deck is a place to relax and enjoy the view.
Courtesy Brock Deck Systems, Royal Crown Limited

7-13 *This multilevel deck was made using decking and railings manufactured from a composite material. It cuts and drills and is fastened like wood. It has a wood grain and is resistant to termites, rot, and decay.*
Courtesy WeatherBest Composite Decking and Railing, Louisiana-Pacific Corporation

7-14 *A properly designed stair providing access from a deck to the ground is an important feature. Use standard stair tread and riser sizes so it does not become steep and difficult to use.*

7-15 *This redwood deck and railing present a warm, beautiful appearance. Redwood is dimensionally stable, resists warping, cupping and checking. It has resistance to decay and insects.*
Courtesy California Redwood Association

7-16 *This beautiful, spacious deck and railing is made from a Hi-Polymer material manufactured from special high-impact weather-resistant polyvinyl chloride compound. It will not rot, split, or require painting or other maintenance.*
Courtesy Brock Deck' Systems, Royal Crown Limited

7-17 *This deck and railing system is manufactured from polyvinyl materials producing a product that requires no maintenance and is easy to install.* **Courtesy Thermal Industries, Inc.**

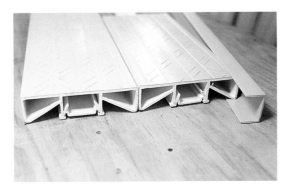

7-18 *This is a sample of polyvinyl decking. The heavy gauge members formed in a truss-like structure provide a sturdy, solid deck.* **Courtesy Thermal Industries, Inc.**

7-19 *This pool is surrounded by a deck and railing made from composite decking. Another example is shown in 7-13.* **Courtesy WeatherBest Composite Decking and Railing, Louisiana-Pacific Corporation**

7-20 *This is a sample of the composite deck used on the installations in 7-13 and 7-19. It is strong, can have a wood grain, and is resistant to termites, rot, and decay.* **Courtesy WeatherBest Composite Decking and Railing, Louisiana-Pacific Corporation**

7-21 *This deck is another manufactured composite product. It is made by mixing wood-like cellulose fibers with reclaimed plastic from products such as milk containers. The decking is a hollow cellular plank that is light in weight yet will span joists spaced 24-inch on-center. It resists termites, bacteria, and moisture.* **Courtesy Nexwood Industries, Limited**

sun. It is pleasant to relax at night and watch the moon rise and the stars come out.

Decks are wood platforms frequently added off a bedroom, living room, or dining room. They can be built on several levels and in almost any shape **(7-13)**. Typically they will have steps providing access to the ground **(7-14)**. They are made using decay resistant woods such as redwood **(7-15)** and from a number of vinyl **(7-16, 7-17,** and **7-18)** and composite wood products **(7-19, 7-20** and **7-21)**.

7-22 This polyvinyl railing has sturdy posts, a smooth (no splinters) handrail, and balusters sized to form a pleasant, balanced railing.
Courtesy Thermal Industries, Inc.

7-24 While in many areas this deck would not be required to have a railing it is still a good safety feature. Some put potted plants along the edge to mark it.
Courtesy Thermal Industries, Inc.

7-23 This poolside redwood deck has quite a drop off. The redwood railing will have to meet local codes and be carefully installed for maximum safety.
Courtesy California Redwood Association

Railings must be sturdy and meet building codes. In **7-22** is a close look at a polyvinyl railing. The parts are designed to quickly be assembled. The redwood railing along the edge of the deck in **7-23** is maintenance-free and is a strong installation. Local building codes will detail minimum railing requirements. Typically this requires a deck that is over 30 inches above the ground to have a railing. The railing will have to be 30 to 36 inches high depending on the local code. The deck in **7-24** would not be required to have a railing but it is decorative and a good idea for safety reasons.

It is important that floor framing be sturdy enough to carry the weight of the decking, railing, furniture, and people who occupy the deck. Good bracing to prevent rocking is necessary.

A very attractive variation is shown in **7-25**. The redwood deck has a partial sunscreen formed by a room built with spaced

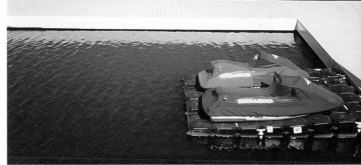

7-25 *This redwood deck has a sunscreen over it providing partial shade most of the day and almost full shade in the early morning and late evening. The effectiveness depends upon the orientation of the house to the path of the sun during the day.*
Courtesy California Redwood Association

7-27 *This water-level dock is made from polyvinyl materials.* **Courtesy Thermal Industries, Inc.**

redwood 2 x 4 inch members. It provides partial shade part of the day and total shade as the sun rises and sets.

Should you have a house on the water deck materials are used to build piers and docks (**7-26** and **7-27**).

Patios

Patios are ground-level paved areas. They are a place to relax, do some outdoor cooking and dining, and growing some flowering plants. They are often paved with bricks set

7-26 *This deck is built over the water and has steps leading to a lower level to which a boat is docked. Preservation and low maintenance are important in these conditions.* **Courtesy Thermal Industries, Inc.**

7-28 *This patio was paved with bricks set in a bed of sand. After the area has settled a mortar grout was placed between the bricks. They could have been laid touching each other and no mortar is needed between the bricks.*

7-29 *This beautiful patio furniture is the focal point of the patio. It provides a comfortable area to read, dine, and relax.* **Courtesy Tidewater Workshop, Egg Harbor City, NJ**

7-30 *This patio is surrounded by plantings and has a terrific view. The furniture is made using mortise and tenon joints and waterproof epoxy and finished with a weather-resistant high-gloss finish.*
Courtesy Weatherend Estate Furniture.

7-31 *A sunroom provides a bright, pleasant place to relax and read.*
Courtesy Four Seasons Solar Products Corporation

7-32 *It is very pleasant to dine in the sunroom. It provides a wide view of the surrounding countryside.*
Courtesy Four Seasons Solar Products Corporation

7-33 A sunroom provides space for exercise equipment and a hot tub. The area is cheerful and sliding windows admit outside air if wanted. **Courtesy Four Seasons Solar Products Corporation**

7-34 The sliding glass doors on the living room will open the area into the sunroom providing an expanded living area.

7-35 These energy efficient shades slide back to the wall when the summer sun passes on. In the winter they provide insulation against heat loss.

in sand **(7-28)**. However other masonry paving units are available. Comfortable chairs and perhaps an umbrella and decorative plantings make a pleasant area **(7-29)**. A patio area is often under an extended roof providing some shelter. This is especially nice if you plan to have informal dinners on the patio. Those fortunate to have a location with a view can make especially good use of a patio **(7-30)**.

Sunrooms

Sunrooms are glass-enclosed areas providing a sheltered area for daily activities. They are used as a place to relax and read **(7-31)**, have informal dining **(7-32)**, grow plants, or have a hot tub and exercise equipment **(7-33)**. They may be placed on a concrete slab on grade or on a floor like a deck, raised above the ground level. They are especially useful in enlarging the living area. When the living area has a glass wall between it and the sunroom the entire area appears larger

7-36 *This sunroom is joined to the wall of the house. This wall can have large glass sliding doors to provide access to the sunroom or a conventional door and windows.* **Courtesy Four Seasons Solar Products Corporation**

(7-34). Sunrooms can be heated and air-conditioned. Energy efficient glazing and the use of insulated shades **(7-35)** help control heat loss and gain.

The sunroom typically has a structural frame of heavy aluminum members. The glazing is double- or triple-glazed sections filled with krypton gas. The structure can be in the form of an all glass unit with a glazed sloping roof **(7-36).** The side panels slide open permitting natural ventilation. The unit can be heated and air-conditioned if desired. Sunrooms are available in other forms. One is shown in **7-37**. A view of the roof from the inside is in **7-38**.

7-38 *From the inside the roof gives a dramatic appearance.* **Courtesy Four Seasons Solar Products Corporation**

7-37 *Another style of sunroom gives a large floor area and an attractive roof.* **Courtesy Four Seasons Solar Products Corporation**

PLANNING STAIRS, HALLS & ELEVATORS

Stairs, halls, and elevators form the system used to move people around the house and between floors. They are not considered living space. Other than facilitating movement about a house, halls are wasted space and should be kept to a minimum **(8-1)**.

Halls

Codes typically require a hall to be 36 inches (915mm) wide from finished wall to finished wall. A wider hall provides a more pleasant passage and makes moving large furniture much easier. Often closets or other built-in storage units are located along a hall. In these cases consider how far into the hall the doors will swing. The hall should be wide enough to provide easy access to the open closet or storage unit.

8-1 Stairs and halls form the routes used to move about a house and between floors.
Courtesy Designed Stairs, Inc. 1-877-4Stairs

8-2 *Skylights can be used to provide natural light to long, dark halls.* **Courtesy Velux-America, Inc.**

8-3 *The foyer directs traffic to two stairways. One opens off the foyer and a hall leads to the other. Notice the durable floor covering.*
Courtesy Designed Stairs, Inc. 1-877-4Stairs

8-4 *This curved stairway opens off the foyer and makes an impressive architectural feature.*
Courtesy Designed Stairs, Inc. 1-877-4Stairs

8-5 *This straight stair has an open balustrade that is attractive and makes the hall or foyer seem larger.*
Courtesy Designed Stairs, Inc. 1-877-4Stairs

Bifold and sliding doors protrude less into the hall than swinging doors.

Often a long hall becomes a dark tunnel-like area. Plan adequate lighting and when possible consider using skylights to provide natural illumination. As you work on developing the floor plan try to avoid long halls **(8-2)**.

The foyer, entrance hall, and stairs connect with the halls to form a complete traffic flow system. As you develop the floor plan observe the relationship between these. Consider the use of color and various wall-covering materials to enhance and lighten halls. The floor should be a durable easily cleaned material **(8-3)**.

Stairs

There are many types of stairs available. The choice depends upon the interior style

8-7 *An L-shaped stair uses a landing to turn the stair 90 degrees.* **Courtesy Designed Stairs, Inc. 1-877-4Stairs**

of the house, the space available, and the desires of the homeowner. A large, expensive house will have a spacious foyer opening upon a grand curved stairway **(8-4)**. Possibly the most frequently used stair is the straight stair **(8-5)**. When space may be a problem the stair can be built with two flights meeting at a landing. The U-shaped stair in **8-6** makes a 180° turn. Notice that closets have been built below the top flight, making the floor area below useful. Another

8-6 *A U-shaped stairs uses a landing to turn the stair 180 degrees.* **Courtesy Designed Stairs, Inc. 1-877-4Stairs**

8-8 *This stair turns a corner of about 135 degrees. Instead of using a landing winder treads are used on the section that turns the angle.*
Courtesy Designed Stairs, Inc. 1-877-4Stairs

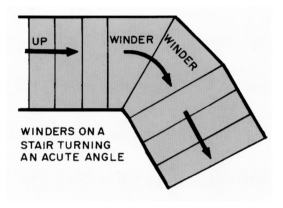

WINDERS ON A
STAIR TURNING
AN ACUTE ANGLE

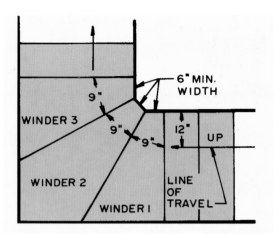

6" MIN.
WIDTH

WINDER 3

WINDER 2

WINDER 1

UP

LINE
OF
TRAVEL

8-10 Many codes require that the narrow end of a winder tread be at least 6 inches and the tread be at least 9 inches wide, 12 inches in from the narrow end.

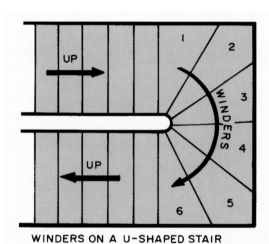

WINDERS ON A U-SHAPED STAIR

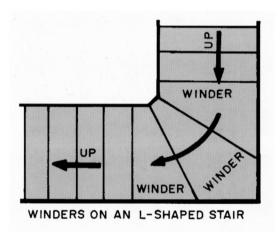

WINDERS ON AN L-SHAPED STAIR

8-9 Winders can be used to turn a stair around a corner.

8-11 Open riser stairs permit light to pass through and are an interesting structure.
Courtesy Design Stairs, Inc. 1-877-4Stairs

8-12 *Spiral stairs occupy less floor area than other types and are very attractive. They are a bit difficult to use.* **Courtesy Designed Stairs, Inc. 1-877-4Stairs**

8-13 *An attractive installation uses a curved starting step upon which the balustrade newel is secured.*

8-14 *The skirtboard protects the wall along the side of a closed stair.*

approach is to use an L-shaped stair **(8-7)**. It makes a 90° turn and provides usable space below the top flight. In **8-8** is a stair that turns a corner greater than 90 degrees. The walls of the foyer do not meet at right angles. The stair follows the walls and instead of a landing uses winders to turn the corner. Winders are triangular-shaped treads as shown in **8-9**. Winders must be designed as specified by building codes. Since they are narrow on one end they tend to be more difficult to use and likely to cause a fall **(8-10)**.

All of the stairs shown to this point had closed risers. An attractive stair with open risers is in **8-11**. This permits natural light to pass through the stair and makes the area seem open and unobstructed. A spiral stair will occupy the least floor area **(8-12)**. Spiral stairs are available in different diameters and degrees of turn. Those with larger diameters are easier to use. In all cases it is difficult to move furniture up spiral stairs.

8-15 A mitered return on the edge of the exposed tread covers the rough end grain and provides a pleasing appearance.

8-17 This wrought iron balustrade utilizes straight and curved members to produce a light, attractive installation. **Courtesy Designed Stairs, Inc. 1-877-4Stairs**

8-16 The end grain of exposed, square-end risers is concealed by installing 1/4-inch-thick decorative stair brackets.

Also check the building codes because they may require a second standard stair as a means of escape from the area served by the spiral stair.

Stairs are typically built using standard parts supplied by stair manufacturers. The choice is large so careful consideration is recommended. For example the starting

8-18 These square metal balusters have a spiral formed in the center section. They are strong yet appear light and delicate.
Courtesy Designed Stairs, Inc. 1-877-4Stairs

8-19 These balusters have a unique expanded and twisted center section which draws attention. The scrolled bands on the top crown the baluster.
Courtesy Designed Stairs, Inc. 1-877-4Stairs

8-21 A sliding disappearing stair has the ladder as a single unit. It uses special hardware to slide into the attic and fold down against the joists.
Courtesy Werner Ladder Company 1-724-588-2000

8-20 This folding disappearing stair provides an economical way to access storage in the attic and yet not permanently occupy floor space.
Courtesy Werner Ladder Company, 1-724-588-2000

step that extends beyond the width of the stair and holds the balustrade newel is a nice feature (**8-13**). A skirtboard is used to protect the wall on the side of the stair (**8-14**). The end grain of exposed treads is covered by a mitered return (**8-15**). Various types of stair brackets are available to conceal any joints on the exposed side of the stair (**8-16**).

Stock balustrades available offer a wide choice of designs. Some are shown in **8-17**, **8-18**, and **8-19**.

Disappearing stairs are used to provide access to storage areas, typically in the attic. The two types of disappearing stairs are

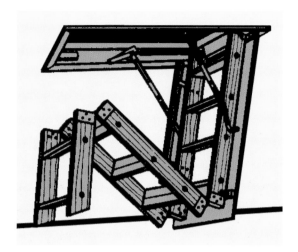

8-22 The folding disappearing stair has three sections that fold up on top of the ceiling panel.
Courtesy Werner Ladder Company 1-724-588-2000

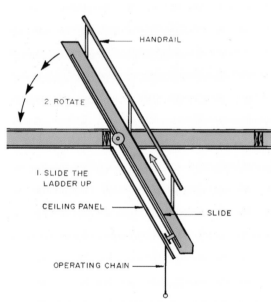

HANDRAIL

2. ROTATE

I. SLIDE THE
LADDER UP

CEILING PANEL

SLIDE

OPERATING CHAIN

I. TO OPEN PULL DOWN ON THE OPERATING CHAIN. TO CLOSE
SLIDE UP AND ROTATE.

8-23 The sliding disappearing stair slides up into the attic and folds down against the top of the ceiling joists.
Courtesy Werner Ladder Company, 1-724-588-2000

folding **(8-20)** and sliding **(8-21)**. The folding stair has three sections that fold on to the top of the ceiling panel that conceals the door when it is closed **(8-22)**. Sliding stairs are a single ladder-like unit that slide up into the area over the ceiling and fold flat against the floor in the attic **(8-23)**. These stairs do not meet codes for access to living areas.

Stair Design

The design of stairs is regulated by the building codes. Some typical requirements follow:

Stair width 36 inches (914mm)
Handrail project no more than 4.5 inches (114mm) on either side
Maximum riser height 7.75 inches (194mm)
Minimum tread width 10 inches (254mm)
Minimum headroom 6 feet 8 inches (2032mm)
Winders special requirements
Spiral stairs special requirements
Circular stairs special requirements
Handrails 34 to 38 inches (864 to 965mm) above tread, diameter 1¼ to 2⅝ inches (32 to 67mm), 1½ inches (38mm) between wall and handrail

Residential Elevators

Residential elevators provide an excellent way to move people between floors whether they are wheelchair-bound or have difficulty climbing a stair **(8-24** through **8-27)**. They are available in several sizes typically 3 x 4 feet and 3 x 5 feet. However larger sizes are available. They are operated by a hydraulic system or a cable on a drum powered by an electric motor.

8-24 This residential elevator is finished with rich woods and has a handsome decorative door.
Courtesy Inclinator Company of America

8-25 The decorative arched open cage on this residential elevation does not block the view and provides an interesting architectural feature.
Courtesy Inclinator Company of America

8-26 This residential elevator runs parallel with the stair integrating it into the traffic pattern of the house.
Courtesy Inclinator Company of America

Residential elevator cabs can have doors on one, two, or three sides enabling the passenger to enter and leave from several locations. Typical patterns are in **8-28**.

Travel distances of 50 feet are common and the cab typically moves at a rate of 30 ft/min (0.15m/s) to 36 ft/min (0.18m/s). The load carrying capabilities typically range from 500 to 750 pounds. The elevator should have an emergency light and alarm. Be sure to check your local building code to verify requirements such as electrical specifications, venting, and fire-resistance enclosing walls. The elevator should have automatic safety devices as needed in case of a broken cable or to prevent the elevation from running past the desired landing. Should there be a power failure an emergency battery system should be available to move the car to a landing.

8-27 This glass-enclosed residential elevator is freestanding inside the room providing access to the rooms above. **Courtesy Inclinator Company of America.**

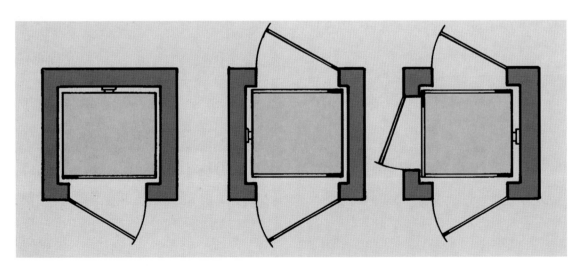

8-28 These are some of the many ways the doors opening from the elevator cab can be arranged.

GARAGES, CARPORTS & DRIVEWAYS

Climate and geographic location may influence the type and size of auto storage facility planned. In warm, dry climates many prefer a carport. A carport is a shelter with a roof and no enclosing walls **(9-1)**. It usually is attached to the house. In other localities a garage is desirable and even expected. A garage is a totally enclosed structure generally attached to the house **(9-2)**. While detached garages are built they are often prohibited by local building codes.

The location of the garage in relation to the rooms of the house is an important consideration. Since it is usually the place from which the family enters the house provision should be made to enter and pass through the house to the other rooms without causing considerable disturbance. Since the

9-1 The design of this attractive carport makes it blend into the overall design of the house.

food usually enters from the garage and trash is taken out through it a location near the kitchen is commonly used. Review the

9-2 This attached garage has the driveway passing by the front door of the house.

9-4 This two-car garage door faces on the end of the house. It is not seen from the front so does not dominate the front elevation.

9-3 This two-car garage faces the street allowing the car to be driven straight into it. This is the easier arrangement for entering a garage. Notice the area provided for guest parking.

kitchen planning suggestions in Chapter 4.

Another consideration is the location of the garage doors. The easiest solution is to have them face the street **(9-3)**. The car can drive straight into the garage. However, the large mass of the doors dominates the front elevation and is not the most aesthetic feature. Some higher-end communities ban garage doors facing the street. This means they must be on the side of the house **(9-4)**. The garage wall facing the street should have the same style and size windows typically used on the rest of the house. The house looks larger and more impressive.

If the house is on a lot that has considerable slope the garage is sometimes placed in the basement **(9-5)**. This eliminates the cost of building an above ground garage but does require you to walk up a stair every time you

Table 9-1 Typical Garage Door Sizes	
Door Heights	6'-6", 6'-9", 7'-0", 8'-0"
Door Widths	4'-0", 6'-0", 8'-0", 9'-0", 10'-0", 12'-0", 16'-0", 18'-0", 20'-0"

9-5 *A garage can be in a basement if the house is built on a lot that has considerable slope.*

put the car in the garage. It also makes bringing in groceries and other items more difficult. Be certain to check the building code for requirements for fire protection of this garage area.

Garage Sizes

The first decision is how many cars are to be sheltered. A one car garage is bare minimum and most families will want at least a two car garage. Also remember to provide an area for storage. In many cases this is where the lawn tools are stored as well as the many boxes of things a family accumulates. Three car garages are not unusual as part of a large house.

Next consider the vehicles to be stored. Today there are many different size vehicles from small compacts to large vans and sport utility vehicles. Housing recreation vehicles is a difficult problem. Many communities will not permit them to remain on the property in view of all who pass by. They are so tall extra large garage doors are required to get them into a garage. If you plan to house one in a garage it will take special design considerations and possibly a check with codes and architectural review boards.

Then get information on the sizes of garage doors available. Typical sizes are in **Table 9-1**. A choice

9-6 *A two-car garage can use two one-car doors or one two-car door.*

9-7 A third smaller overhead door is used to provide access for a lawnmower, golf cart, or other large items.

9-8 A standard door exit from a garage is a big help. This door opens toward the backyard making access to garden tools easy.

must be made on two-car garages whether to use two single doors or one double door (**9-6**). A third smaller overhead door can be added to provide access for a golf cart, or riding lawnmower, boat, or other items (**9-7**). It also helps if you provide a standard three-foot door as an exit from the garage. It provides easy access without having to open up the large overhead door (**9-8**).

A plan for a typical one and two car garage leaving minimum room on each side and no room for storage is in **9-9**. The depth and width will vary depending upon the vehicles to be housed.

A suggestion for allowing for storage is in **9-10**. In warmer climates the washer and dryer and heating and air-conditioning units are often placed in the garage (**9-11**).

Table 9-2 Typical Sizes for the Larger Automobiles Available
(Consult Dealer for Actual Sizes)

	Length	Width	Height
Luxury Sedan	210"	80"	57"
Standard Sedan	200"	73"	57"
Minivan	204"	75"	70"
Sport Utility Vehicle	183" to 219"	68"	65" to 74"

(Typical Car Door Width 42" to 48")

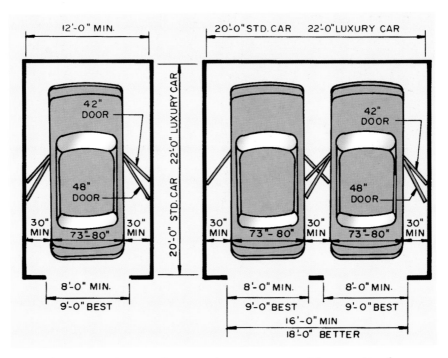

9-9 *Typical spacing requirements for one- and two-car garages without provision for storage.*

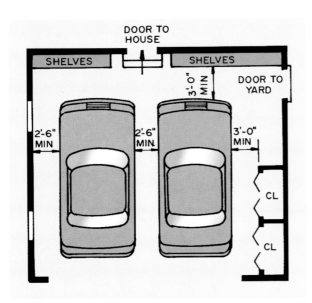

9-10 *This garage provides some closet and shelving storage in an open area for moveable items.*

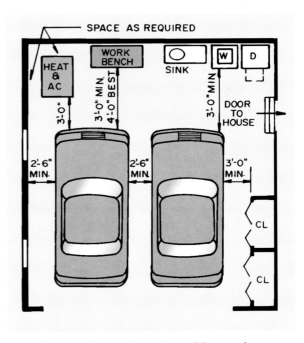

9-11 *In warm climates the washer and dryer and heating/air-conditioning unit may be in the garage. A small workbench is also helpful.*

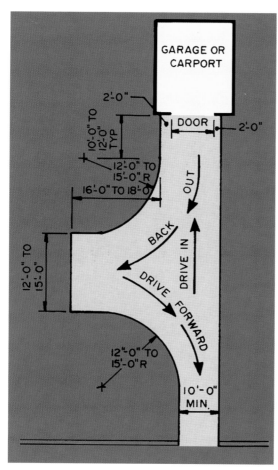

9-12 This driveway design provides a turnaround into which the car is backed and then driven forward to the street.

When selecting garage doors a range of designs are available from a solid panel door to one with a series of glazed openings. The overhead door made of several hinged panels that rolls up along the ceiling on tracks is almost universally used. It is operated by an electric motor operating some type of drive mechanism. It can be opened from the outside by a remote control.

The size of the garage can be planned for the vehicles to be stored or plan for a large luxury car. This will enable the garage to accommodate almost any car available. Some typical car sizes are in **Table 9-2.**

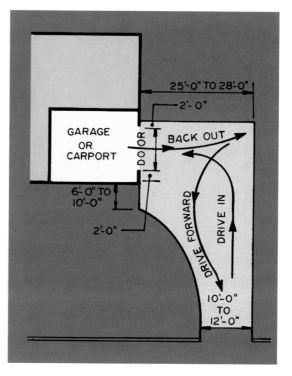

9-13 An adequate turning area is needed on the end of a house to move a car into and out of a garage.

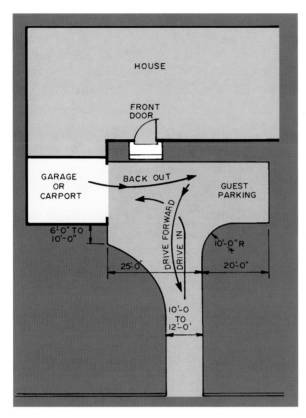

9-14 *The garage can open by the front door. When this occurs the driveway passes by the front door. Notice the guest parking area. Without it guests would have to back down the drive to the street.*

Other Garage Planning Features

The garage must meet local codes, which usually require the wall between the garage and house to have ½-inch (13mm) Fire-Shield gypsum wallboard on both sides of the studs. This gives a 45-minute fire rating. A ⅝-inch (16mm) Fire-Shield gypsum wallboard will give a one-hour fire rating.

The door opening into the residence from the garage should have a solid wood door at least 1⅜ inches (35mm) thick or a solid or honeycomb core steel door at least

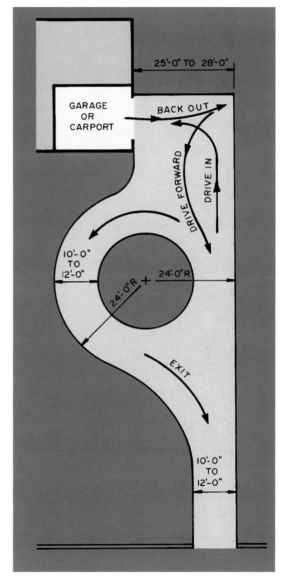

9-15 *One variation of a circle drive. The larger the radius of the curve the easier it is to make the turn.*

1⅜ inches (35mm) thick or any door with a 20 minute fire-rating.

Doors from the garage should not open into sleeping rooms.

Garage floors should be made of a non-combustible material.

Carports should be open on at least two sides.

Planning the Driveway

A suggested layout for backing out from a garage into which you drive straight in from the street is in **9-12**. This requires a back-out turn enabling you to enter the street facing it. Should you have the garage on the side of the house a layout similar to that in **9-13** could be useable. Another approach

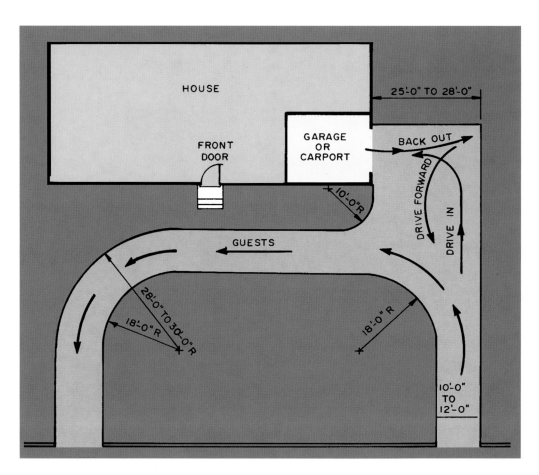

9-16 A U-shaped driveway will carry guests directly to the front door and make it easy to leave.

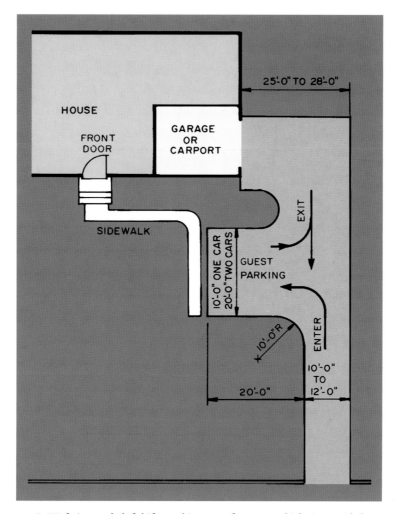

9-17 It is very helpful if a parking area for guest vehicles is provided.

that influences the exterior design of the house is to run the car in across the front entrance as shown in **9-2** and **9-14**. This will require a backup area.

Another consideration when a large lot is available is to put in a circular drive **(9-15)** or a U-shaped drive that has two entrances to the street **(9-16)**. This takes a lot of room but is very convenient and nice for holding guests' cars.

It is helpful to make provision for parking one or two guest cars without blocking the driveway. One way to do this is shown in **9-17**.

HOME AUTOMATION & OTHER SYSTEMS

Home automation is a rapidly developing concept that requires major changes in the planning of the systems within a house and provides extensive control. It enhances the lifestyle of those installing an automated system.

Home automation is a collection of controls and related devices, a total system and subsystems that interact with one another or can function separately. The key to the concept is control. The homeowner has control over all the systems such as lighting, security, and video, with in-house controls. In some cases homeowners can activate controls when they are many miles away. It helps reduce energy costs, improves security, and makes day-to-day living pleasant with the various audio and video systems available. The following pages offer a brief review of this major technical development in home design and control. Consultation with companies specializing in home automation and other systems will reveal even more information. Since this is a growing area new products and controls will be developed regularly.

The Electronic House

Whether you are planning a new house or remodeling the services provided by electronic devices, the job is complex and you have a large choice of possibilities. Begin by making a careful analysis of exactly what you want and how it will enhance your day-to-day life. Some features do routine tasks, such as controlling the air temperature, while others provide an expanded measure of pleasure, as an entertainment center. As you plan get information on the systems available so that you can compare performance. It is a good idea to get approximate cost estimates.

One other important factor is the reputation of the company installing and maintaining the equipment. Search out customers and ascertain the merits and deficiencies of the operation. Finally when decisions have been made and installers have been chosen get a detailed written list of what is to be provided including the brand and specifications and the installation charges. Establish a firm time frame for the installation. Get copies of all the warranties. The installer should carry a liability insurance policy. Finally, when all is set ask again if there are any charges you might get that have not been revealed.

Home Automation

Home automation is a collection of devices, systems, and subsystems which can interact with each other and also function independently. This enables the occupant of the house to control appliances and systems that are part of the automation system by personally inputting commands through an interface, as a push button control pad, or by automatically scheduling commands such as turning on lights as it gets dark **(10-1)**.

Home automation can help cut energy costs, increase security, control house functions when away from the house, and provide many other commands offering great convenience. For example, lights may be controlled in various rooms from a central location and security lighting can be a part of the overall security system. Radio remote controls are available allowing the occupant

10-1 Commands can be input into the automation system using a button control pad.
Courtesy Elan Home Systems

to operate appliances and lights from the yard, an auto, or other rooms of the house. The radio waves are transmitted through walls and ceilings to a transceiver. The transceiver receives the signal and transmits it over the alternating current wiring system to the desired receiving device.

Home automation may enable the occupant to control the functions included in the system by telephone. This is done by entering the proper numeric code through the number buttons on the phone. This provides access to the control program. The various systems within the house can be designed to interact with one another in many cases.

There are a range of home automation systems and components available. As a choice is made careful study of the merits and cost is warranted. A very comprehensive system can cost thousands of dollars. Decide

10-2 Automation controls can be used to light various rooms or various parts of a room on a predetermined schedule. **Courtesy CentraLite**

what you need and consider the possibility of expansion to meet future needs.

A basic system will turn on or off a number of subsystems (as lights) or individual appliances. It usually operates on a computer programmed time schedule. The central control interacts with each subsystem independently and there is no relationship between any of the systems.

Another type of system has the several subsystems integrated into one central controller. The central controller activates each subsystems so they function as designed by the manufacturer. They are not able to interact with each other. However, this is quite adequate for many home applications.

Control systems can be custom designed to meet the requirements of a specific installation. The system is designed to

not only control the subsystems but manage them so desired interrelationships can be programmed. These systems are sometimes referred to as intelligent systems because they do more than simply turn subsystems and appliances on and off but control interactions between them.

SOME CONTROL FEATURES

The type and range of features of a home automation system are many. When planning a new house an electronics architect would be useful in designing a system to meet the current needs yet provide the capability for expansion in the future. This could include installing wiring for future use as the house is being built. It is a lot cheaper to do it this way than adding it a few years after a house has been built.

Consider remote and timed control of the heating and air-conditioning system, appliances, such as an electric water heater, and lighting. Careful planning as to when these operate can reduce energy costs.

Providing zoning for heat and air-conditioning will permit conditioning the air at times when the rooms will be in use yet cut back on the temperatures at other times, as at night or during the day when no one is in the house.

Some electric companies charge less for electricity during certain hours of the day. For example, the central controller can shut off power to the water heater during high-cost hours and activate it in low-cost hours.

The convenience of being able to control lighting for the entire house, interior and exterior, from a single location is great. Automatic control of lighting is also a convenience and saves energy. It can turn on certain lights when needed, as exterior lights for security, but automatically turn them off when not needed.

A major feature of any automated control system is security. Closed-circuit television can monitor interior and exterior locations. The security mode can be set to control lights providing extra security. Also it can be used to turn on inside lights or turn on the television even though there is no one at home. This makes the house look occupied (**10-2**).

Voice- and switch-activated multimedia computers can be used to activate systems to help those physically handicapped. They can control lights and televisions. Consider a system that uses a language voice-user interface to integrate faxes, e-mail, and voice mail.

Automated Home Control Systems

An automation system controls all the subsystems within a house. Commonly used subsystems include security, lighting, heating and cooling, audio and video, and many other things such as your sprinkler system. With the press of a button on a wall-mounted keypad you can open or close casement windows, raise or lower the blinds, light the gas fireplace, and start and stop ceiling fans. These and many other control features are available.

An automated system may use one centrally located control system capable of complete control of all systems within the house or the central control may communicate with the various subsystems such as security, lighting, and audio and video components. With this automated system all of the subsystems can be controlled and managed by one consistent system using keypads, remotes, and other interfaces.

THE AUTOMATION EQUIPMENT CLOSET

The area to contain the control system is sized to hold the components to be installed. A medium-size closet centrally located is often used. If it is centrally located this reduces possible long wire runs but the actual location on the floor plan will depend somewhat upon where you can find the space. The control panels are mounted on the walls and sometimes one can be mounted above the other. They should not interfere with the installation of conduit and wires from other control boxes (**10-3** and **10-4**). Some system manufacturers provide

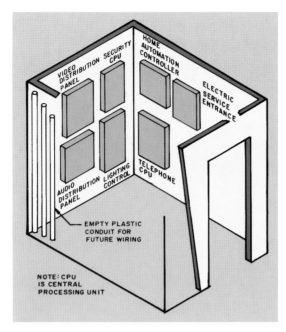

10-3 *A large automation equipment closet. The size and location of the actual components will depend upon the manufacturer and the system designer. This illustrates typical components available to build a system.*

10-5 *These components for a home automation system are mounted in a wall hung rack.*
Courtesy Elan Home Systems

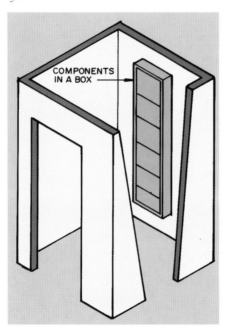

10-4 *A simple installation of automation components in a small closet. Some companies manufacture cabinets to hold the components in their system.*

equipment installation boxes to hold the components in their system **(10-5)**.

The electronic equipment needs a controlled environment where air temperature and humidity are kept at normal levels. It must be ventilated to allow air circulation. Attic locations are too hot and too cold. Basement locations are often damp and not adequate. The best location is within the living area of the house.

As you plan the automation closet allow room for future expansion, including wall space to hang additional central processing units and run some empty conduit in which wires can be pulled at some future time.

INTERFACES

While the equipment located in the automation equipment closet manages the various systems, as security and lighting, it receives electronic signals from sensors, timers, keypads, remote controls and other interfacing devices. The keypad is the most frequently used device. A keypad **(10-1)** has a variety of buttons providing signals for the control. As you plan your system it is important to decide where each is to be located. While they are not large sufficient wall space must be allowed. Sometimes they are lined up with the light wall switches providing a uniform appearance.

WIRING

Each subsystem will have its own wiring runs to the automation equipment closet. Plastic conduit is used to form wiring chases from the equipment closet to the other floors of the house. These protect the wire and allow the electrician to run additional wires through them as needed. The low-voltage wiring and 120-volt wiring systems must be kept separate. Extra conduit can be installed in walls and floors to areas where you may want future service.

Fiber Optic Connections

Fiber-optic-to-the-home systems are under development. Over the next few years there will be extensive technical developments that will make this a frequently available service. As you design your house consider if the service is available from your local electric supply company.

Fiber optics is the transmission of images and audio by bundles of fine transparent hair-like fibers.

A fiber-optic cable contains plastic or glass (silicon dioxide) fibers about the diam-

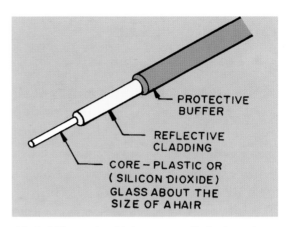

10-6 *A fiber-optic cable has very small plastic or glass (silicon dioxide) fiber core shielded by a cladding layer providing internal reflection. The outer layer protects the inner layers from physical damage.*

eter of a human hair **(10-6)**. It transmits information using infrared or visible light as the carrier. It carries audio, visual, and data information. Typical visual transmissions can be photos, drawings, television images, and video transmission between computers. Audio transmissions can include computer-generated sounds, music, and voice. It can transmit live video images enabling video conferences in separated geographic areas to be held.

The speed of transmission over fiber-optic cable is extremely fast and millions of transmissions can occur over a single fiber simultaneously.

The installation of the system means that all data, voice, and video will be digital.

Today's analog system will gradually fade from the scene. For instance, the Federal Communications Commission has mandated that all analog television will be replaced by digital by 2007. Digital audio compact disks are replacing analog. Digital video disks (DVD) are replacing VHS video.

Networks

A network is a system connecting computers, related equipment, and various communications units that allows them to file, program, and share equipment. In the home these are frequently used to operate the computers and equipment needed in a home business. When confined to a single room or a building it is referred to as a local-area network (LAN). It transfers data faster than phone line modems. It will tie several personal computers, allowing them to use a single printer, fax machine, or copier. It permits sending e-mail between computers in the system.

PC Networking

Networking is a term used to describe connecting computers, associated peripheral equipment, and any required communications equipment to allow file, program, and equipment sharing. It is very helpful for those who have home operated businesses where several people are working and several computers are in use.

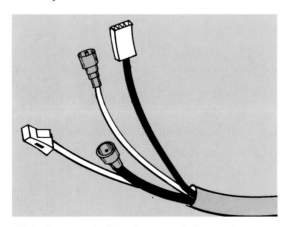

10-7 Structured cabling has several wires serving different purposes combined into a bundle. This provides for faster installation of the total wiring system.
Courtesy M&S Systems

The computers can be connected to a shared internet source using a cable modem or DSL line. The cable modem, Internet, fax, and printer can be operated from any room. Just move a laptop computer into the room and use these features. Using a high-speed LAN eliminates multiple Internet connections. The design and wiring of such a system and the installation of interfaces is the work of technicians well prepared to handle the technology.

Home Cabling Systems

The home cabling system provides integrated wiring for currently available home services and automation technology such as lighting, heat/air conditioning control, entertainment, and an interface between the home security system and the central control. It uses a unified wiring bundle instead of the typical wiring system where individual wires are run separately to each location. This bundle is referred to as structured wiring **(10-7)**.

Structured wiring is a term used to describe a wiring bundle containing several wires for systems in the house. For example, wires for lighting, heating/air-conditioning control, the security system, telephone, and video/audio might be bound in a single cable. This simplifies installation because one electrician can handle the wiring for all of these systems rather than have many different trades each installing one line, as the telephone line. There are a number of different cable groups available each carrying wires for several services.

Also structured wiring reduces the number of individual wall plates such as one

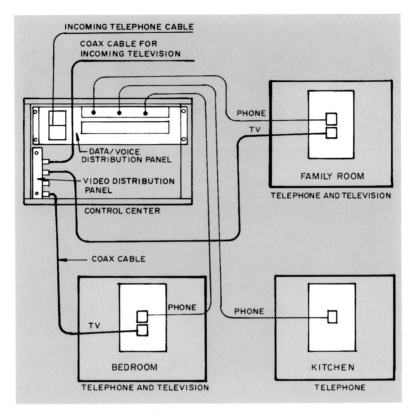

10-8 A typical home cabling system for a small installation involving only television and telephone installations.

for a telephone jack, fax connections, and another for electrical outlets. The structured wiring system will consolidate these into a single wall plate about the same size as the typical electrical outlet wall plate.

Structure wiring allows the installation of services in every room even if at the moment you do not anticipate a need. For example, multimedia outlets could be provided in every room. This could provide access to computers, televisions, telephones, and entertainment in every room.

Typical systems have wiring in several types of unified wiring bundles, such as branch, applications, and communications.

Communications cable includes video coaxial cable and telephone cable.

Applications cable provides for digital data as well as the direct current voltage used by sensors.

Branch cable has a conventional electric power cable and a digital data cable.

Digital signaling wires provide message data and appliance control.

A system controller provides system management, scheduling of various services, and routes data between appliances. The system controller is installed next to the service entrance panel providing the electric power supply, has circuit breakers, surge suppressors, and the ground-fault circuit interrupters. A typical installation is in **10-8**.

A wiring distribution panel provides a central access point for all the systems and

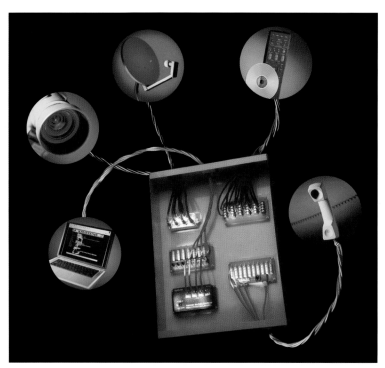

10-9 *This wiring distribution panel uses structured wiring to provide telecommunications, home entertainment, satellite and cable, security, and high speed internet connections.* **Courtesy M & S Systems**

The key to the system is the control panel as seen in **10-10**. It receives and interprets signals received from various types of sensors located at doors, windows, and other areas. The control panel will sound an alarm inside and outside the house and, if you desire, to a central monitoring company that will check to see if the signal was a mistake made by the homeowner. If they get no response from the homeowner they notify the police. The central monitoring company also will call the phones of those you list as backup contacts as a neighbor or relative. The control panel can even send a message to your pager.

The control panel is usually located in a fairly central location within the house. Since it is not large it is often put in a closet or

when using structured wiring makes installation and adding or changing anything electric easier **(10-9)**.

Under development are fiber-optic systems. With such a system, the communications company delivers fiber cable service to each home. A curbside pedestal receives the fiber-optic cable and service to the nearby homes is run from this street location. It will deliver high-speed Internet connections and voice, video, and data.

Home Security

A security system can range from a rather simple installation to a large interior and exterior system.

10-10 *This control panel operates a hard-wired security system. It is located in an automation closet and uses a 120V transformer to supply 24V to the system.*

10-11 *This control pad controls all of the functions of the security system. It is placed near the frequently used entry doors and in other locations as desired.*

storeroom or the automation closet. Remember to include this location on the house electrical plan and if possible have it on its own electrical circuit. Other things on the same circuit may interfere with its operation.

The system is operated by keypads **(10-11)** that are located in any area from which you would like to be able to control the system. One by each exterior door will enable you to arm the system as you leave and disarm it as you enter. Perhaps one in the bedroom area or hall or in the kitchen would be useful.

Security systems manufacturers have various types of keypads. These contain a series of buttons which you push to arm or disarm the system. The system will have a code programmed in it that is a series of numbers. The code series arms and disarms the system. The code can be changed when desired. The keys also serve other functions. These are identified by each button.

The keypads are about the size of a light switch box holding two switches. They are mounted at the same height as light switches.

Usually 55 inches above the floor suits most people. Mount the keypad so it is not subject to direct exposure to sunlight. This may damage the display.

The sensors are units mounted on the doors, windows, glass panes, and other items to be part of the electric control system. The type of sensors used depends upon the type of door or window used in the house. Wood-framed doors have sensors set into holes drilled in them so they are not visible when the door is closed. Vinyl windows require surface mounted sensors.

Motion detectors note activity with the area they scan and activate the alarm when an intrusion is noted. They are mounted high on the wall and usually in a corner **(10-12)**. If the room is large it may require several motion detectors to cover the entire area. Some are used in halls to detect intruders that may have gotten past those in a room.

Aim motion sensors away from heating and air-conditioning vents, air returns, and fireplaces where air currents may activate a false alarm.

10-12 *A motion detector is placed in the corner of the room near the ceiling.*

10-13 *An outside alarm will notify the neighbors when help is needed.*

10-14 *This smoke alarm is on the regular house current so no batteries are needed.*

A typical security system will have inside and outside alarms. A typical residence can get by with one inside alarm. However if the house is large or on several levels additional interior alarms may be helpful. The exterior alarm is placed where a neighbor or passerby can clearly hear it. It should be installed so it cannot be deactivated by someone from the outside (10-13). If your roof has attic roof vents the alarm could be placed behind them for greater security.

The wiring for home security systems is small gauge, low-voltage wire. The keypads and sensors are connected to the control panel with this wire. If you plan to send a signal to a central monitoring company remember to install the telephone wire to the control panel. Most systems also offer smoke detectors so locate these as required and wire to the control panel (10-14).

A Video Entry System

A video entry system uses a pushbutton control inside the house to tilt an exterior camera providing color images of those at the door on a screen on a master video station inside the house (10-15 and 10-16). It also permits you to talk with the person before you open the door.

10-15 *This is a color-video door station that is mounted on the door at the outside. The indoor unit has a tilt control that moves the lens from horizontal up forty degrees, twenty degrees up and down. The unit also has an audio system permitting you to communicate from inside the house with the person or persons outside the house while the door remains closed, before you decide to unlock it.* **Courtesy Aiphone® Corporation**

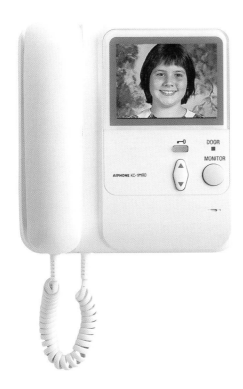

10-17 *The images stored by the picture memory unit have the date and time recorded.*
Courtesy Airphone®Corporation

10-16 *This is the video master station mounted inside the house by the door. The long vertical button controls the angle of the lens on the exterior unit. The handset on the left side is used to communicate with the person outside the door.*

One camera can supply the same image to several monitors located in different rooms within the house. The system not only provides a color or black-and-white picture of the person at the door, but with the addition of a picture memory unit it will store images for replay. The image can include a time and date stamp of the viewing **(10-17)**.

SURVEILLANCE CAMERAS

Surveillance cameras are used to give views of both interior and exterior areas **(10-18)**. They can be connected to the cable TV system, and video from every camera can be displayed on the screen of any TV set in the house. As you plan a system identify the areas you wish to monitor. For example, consider monitoring the bedrooms of small children, an entrance foyer, or a recreation room in the basement. Outside you may want to monitor exterior doors, the swimming pool, and driveway.

Cameras inside should be mounted so draperies do not obstruct them and so natural light through a window does not wash out the picture.

Exterior cameras can be blinded at times by the sun so avoid facing them due west or east. Watch for trees, shrubs, or porch roofs that may obscure their view. The higher you mount the cameras the wider the view. For example, a wide view is desirable for monitoring a swimming pool so the camera will be 10 feet or so above the ground. Inside they are usually installed near the ceiling. At

10-18 *There are many styles of surveillance cameras. Some are small and easily hidden. They provide considerable protection and are used on interior and exterior locations.*

exterior doors 6-feet high is common.

The equipment needed to transmit the images, remotely tilt or pan the area, and record the images is stored in a central area as an automation closet. The space needed will vary depending upon the equipment purchased but a closet designed to hold the equipment is desirable. It should be well-ventilated and an exhaust fan is often recommended.

Manufacturer recommended coaxial cable is used to connect each camera to the control equipment in the closet and to connect it to the television monitors.

REMOTE SECURITY MONITORING SYSTEMS

Electric monitoring systems use a telephone or computer to contact you and tell you what is happening at your home. It transmits a message to your pager. For example, the interior temperature may be dropping and freezing could cause damage. Even if you are many miles away you can increase the setting on the thermostat. Or maybe you did not alarm the system you left. You can enter the password and code by a telephone and set the alarm.

Systems that permit Internet-enabled

home monitoring have you log on to the Internet and access a personalized Web page that will show you the condition of systems connected to the automation system. For example, you can check the thermostat, security system, lights, and other systems.

Security systems are constantly being upgraded with new technology so it is wise to make a careful study of those available to determine what you might need in the way of telephone service and computers.

Whole House Audio/Video

Audio can be distributed to as many areas of the house as desired. The simplest system is referred to as single-zone audio. Your audio source, as a CD player, will distribute the audio to two or more rooms connected to the system. Each room has a control permitting regulation of the volume and shutting off the music **(10-19)**.

A more effective and comprehensive system is a multisource/multizone installation. This permits playing audio from different sources, as a CD player and a tuner, in different rooms at the same time. For example, the tuner could be playing news in the living room while a CD is playing music in the family room **(10-20)**.

With a multisource/multizone audio system the house is divided into listening zones. The zone may be a single room, such as a family room, or a combination of several rooms, such as a bedroom and master bath. Each zone has independent access to the control sources connected to the system. The source can be shared with other zones. When desired, zones can be grouped, such as deciding to provide music to the kitchen, dining room, and living room simultaneously.

The speakers used in entire house audio systems are available in a wide range of sizes and shapes. They need to be matched with the other components in the system. The choice also directly influences the quality of the sound. Generally they are mounted in the wall but this is optional.

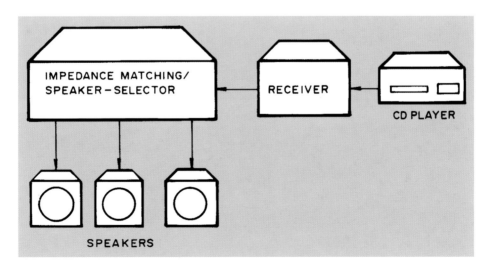

10-19 A typical single-zone whole house audio system provides music to all of the rooms where speakers are located.

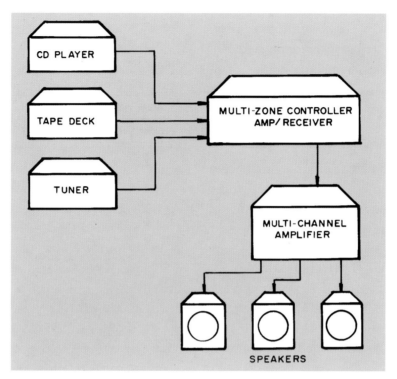

10-20 *A multisource/multizone whole house audio system provides audio from several sources to various designated areas of the house.*

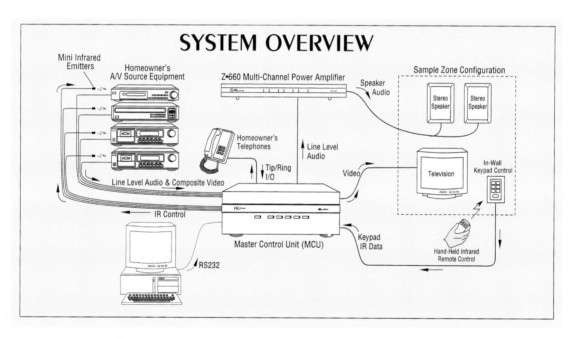

10-21 *This is a plan for a multisource/multizone whole house system that provides audio and video to various designated areas. Notice the source equipment provides both audio and video. The telephone is also integrated into the system.* **Courtesy Elan Home Systems**

10-22 *The master control unit provides for easy expansion of the system providing distribution of audio, video, telephone and other systems. The architecture can be customized by the use of cards adding to the capabilities of the unit.* **Courtesy Elan Home Systems**

Zone ON/OFF	
System OFF	
Source Select	Also turns on a Zone
Zone Volume UP	
Zone Volume DOWN	
Do-Not-Disturb	
Zone Mute	
Whole-House Music ON	
Whole-House Music OFF	

10-24 *Control functions available on one type of keypad. Similar controls are on the remote.* **Courtesy Elan Home Systems**

10-23. There are several types of keypads available and the system designer should be the person to choose the best one for the situation. The control functions of one of these are shown in **10-24**.

10-23 *Two types of keypads and a remote used to issue commands to the master control unit.* **Courtesy Elan Home Systems**

A plan for a multisource multizone audio and video system are in **10-21**. The control of the source equipment is based on the manufacturer's computer system, which learns the commands from the components remote controls in the master control unit **(10-22)** and reissues these commands whenever they are entered by you at a wall-mounted keypad or remote control.

Two keypads and a remote are shown in

10-25 *This LCD touch panel can be moved around the house as needed. It controls audio/video sources from any room in the house.* **Courtesy Elan Home Systems**

10-26 *This LCD remote control is used in a home theater to control the video and audio.* **Courtesy Elan Home Systems**

The telephones in the house can also be integrated into the system. They use the speakers installed for multiroom music to serve as an intercom. This also permits a number of other telecommunication features to be available, such as a two-way door speaker communication connection.

Video can be controlled from a remote control that has an LCD touch screen **(10-25)**. You touch the button labeled DVD and the movie appears on your large screen TV and audio is piped to speakers in the wall. This is ideal for a home theater **(10-26)**. It also controls the audio for the whole house.

This system will control more than the audio/video system. This whole house audio/video system uses a desktop personal computer **(10-27)** to define and program macro commands, system shut off, timed events, and other desired controls. It can automate lights, draperies, gates, sprinklers, home theater projector screens, lifts and other systems.

Telephone Systems

As you plan your house it is important to install a telephone system that will handle your needs now and allow future expansion. In addition to locating telephones where needed within the house, consider the need to connect to the Internet, have a fax and answering machine, and maybe an external ringer or call notification light on the patio or porch. Remember that wireless phones are widely used so plan the location of a base station. Then there are the cell phones you carry with you.

Visit with the local telephone service provider. Typically it will be the service we are all familiar with that brings the service to the house over copper wires. This is a dependable source serving the customer very efficiently. It is an analog voice communication service. In some areas a digital voice communication service is available. It will provide service of two telephone lines over a single installation. Check carefully on the cost and other advantages and disadvantages of each service.

Watch for the possible development of your local television cable service offering telephone service on the same cable. They have developed a device that will split the telephone and cable television transmissions as they enter the house.

Consider at least one phone outlet in the living room and dining room. If you have a family room locate several phone outlets around the room. As the activities develop the need for a telephone in several locations may become necessary. It is important to have a telephone in the kitchen in an area away from the cooking and cleaning up areas. Some have a small planning desk in the kitchen. This is a good place for the phone. Each bedroom needs a phone. They are usually on the bedside table. If you have a home theater locate a telephone jack

in the wall behind the audio/video components so movies coming in over the line may be shown. Of course a home office needs a business phone and one or more wall jacks for computers and other office equipment. It may have several separate telephone lines so full service of equipment is always available. Where else do you need a telephone? Look over the floor plan carefully. Perhaps one in the basement would save some steps. Do you want to answer the phone from the bathroom?

Typically each telephone jack has an individual wall outlet. If you use a structured wiring system it will be integrated in a single outlet box with connections for other services such as cable television or a whole-house music system.

Probably the most commonly installed telephone system is to have the telephone company run one line to the house. Generally this cable (called a quad cable) will have wires for two separate telephone

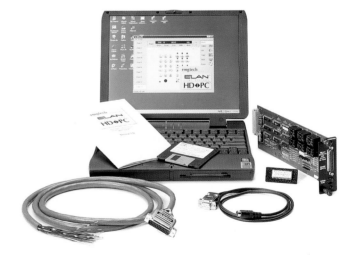

10-27 *This home automation system is used to program commands, which control the operation of all the systems in the house.* **Courtesy Elan Home Systems**

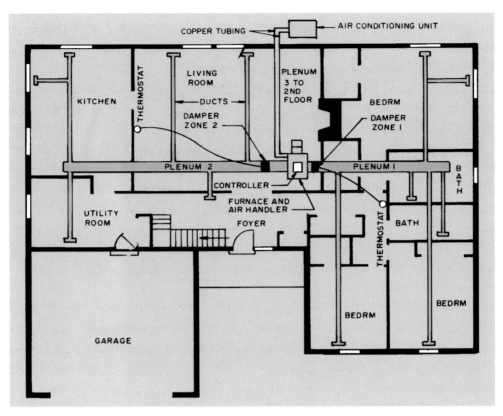

10-28 This is a three-zone heating and air-conditioning system. Each zone is controlled by its own thermostat increasing the efficiency and economy of the system.

lines. From the connection box on the house the electrician runs wires to the location of each telephone jack. This is the easiest and lowest cost system. It works well; however, only one of the telephones can be used at the same time on each line.

Another more versatile system uses a central processor called a key system unit (KSU). It directs the incoming calls to the appropriate telephone. This is especially helpful for those who operate a business from their home. It will automatically separate business calls from personal calls and transfer calls between telephone stations. It can also serve as an intercom. You can have a business phone, modem, and a fax machine on the same line.

The key system unit (KSU) is contained in a small cabinet that can be hung on the wall in an out of the way place, such as a utility room, large closet, or the automation closet. Each telephone is wired to the KSU system box. The outside telephone lines enter the box and are routed through the KSU to the desired telephone. The KSU microprocessor regulates and directs the incoming and outgoing calls. The features offered by various KSU products vary so choose one that will perform all the things you require. Consider one that will allow the installation of additional lines and extensions as needed.

The KSU will enable you to take a business call from any phone on the system, even if it is not in your home office. The basic functions available include hold, transfer, intercom, and paging. Some have caller ID and voice mail.

Heating/Air-Conditioning Control

Using a zoned air distribution system produces efficient temperature control within a house. The conventional warm air heating/cooling system has one main plenum from the warm air furnace from which small ducts branch off to the various rooms.

With this system one thermostat controls the temperature of the air to all the rooms in the house. The only control you have to vary temperatures in each room is to adjust the size of the opening in the heat register.

A zoned system will have two or more plenum ducts running from the hot air furnace to various parts of the house. If the house is to have three zones three plenum ducts will run from the furnace to each area **(10-28)**. In a two-story house this is espe-

cially effective for conditioning the air on the second floor because it will operate on a different thermostat. Then two zones on the first floor and one on the second floor will each have separate thermostats. This means the air temperature in the rooms in each zone can be different. For example the zone for the kitchen, living room, and dining room can have a higher temperature than the zone for the bedrooms. All the rooms in each zone receive air at the same temperature. Each zone has a return air duct back to the furnace.

The air flow to each zone is controlled by mechanical damper mounted in the plenum. They open and close depending upon the heating/cooling requirements for that zone. A separate thermostat controls each damper. The three-zone house will have three thermostats.

Each thermostat is wired to a microprocessor-driven controller that is part of the air handling unit of the furnace. There are a number of different kinds of thermostats that can integrate the heating and cooling system. A programmable thermostat **(10-29)** can be set to change the desired air

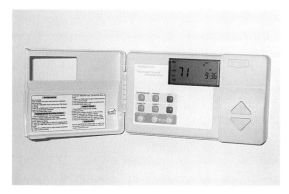 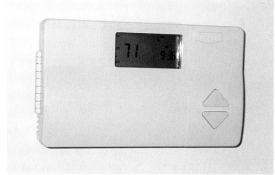

10-29 A programmable thermostat. The buttons to program the times and temperatures are concealed by the cover shown open.

10-30 *These are communicating thermostats that function as a standard thermostat and a processor of remote X-10 or RS232/485 commands to set specific temperature setpoints and modes for the HVAC system. It interfaces through a thermostat control unit via an interface module and cable.*

Courtesy Residential Control Systems, Inc.

temperature at different times of the day. Some controls will let you schedule different requirements for each day of the week. To save energy it could be programmed to lower the temperature in the winter on week days when no one is home, yet automatically schedule it higher on the weekends. To change the settings you must go to each thermostat and make the temperature and time adjustments. It is not part of the home automation system.

Another type of thermostat is the communicating thermostat **(10-30)**. While it controls heating and cooling as just described it can also be tied into the home automation security and lighting systems. When you leave the house a single control is used to set the air temperature, arm the alarm systems, and, when you are away, turn off all lights. When you return it will disarm the alarm, turn on the lights, and regulate air temperature. It permits you to call in by

telephone and change the air temperature setting on the thermostat and turn the security system on or off.

Communicating thermostats are controlled in several ways. One system uses thermostats that listen and respond to X-10 signals. Codes sent to the thermostats result in different preprogrammed set points. For example, an ON signal to a particular HVAC unit may have an ON set point of 75°F and an OFF point of 65°F.

X-10 is a chip permitting the controlling of lights and appliances without having to rewire the home. It uses existing power lines and 60-hertz power as the carrier. Among the functions available are commands such as ON, OFF, Dim, Bright, All Lights ON, and All Lights OFF. Each unit in the wiring system, as a light, has an identity and a command receiver. These receiver modules receive the commands. All of the receiver modules in the system "hear" the command but only those set to the last address sent will respond to the command.

The most technically involved communications link is between an HVAC system and a personal computer. The thermostat is linked to the computer. An image of the thermostat appears on the computer monitor. Changes in the setting of the thermostat are made directly from the computer.

As you plan the heating/cooling system secure information from manufacturers on the features of their products. Many have a complete control system available designed to integrate with the heating/cooling equipment and operate in connection with the home automation system.

Lighting Control

Lighting control systems can control lighting in every area of the house and the exterior surroundings. The possibilities are many and are an important factor to consider as you develop the plans for the house. What do you want from a lighting system? As you make these decisions consider consulting a lighting designer or work with the staff of a local company selling and installing lighting control systems if they have the knowledge needed to do the actual design rather than just sell components.

Make a list of what you think would be desirable for your house. For example, consider having exterior lights that come on when motion is sensed. This is a security feature and also helpful when someone may come by for a friendly visit. Perhaps have a control turn on a couple of interior lights as you unlock a door and enter after dark. Allow the system to dim the lights in the home theater when you turn on the system. If you are on vacation set the system so some lights will turn on and off at predetermined times so it looks as though you are at home. Outdoor lights can be programmed to turn on at sunset and off at sunrise or a predetermined time. Control lights in various parts of the house from several locations with wall mounted keypads.

Another control feature is to program

10-31. This living room has several sources of lighting. The lighting control system can set the "scene" desired by turning some lights off, dimming some, or increasing the intensity of light by the simple pushing of a button.
Courtesy CentraLight Systems

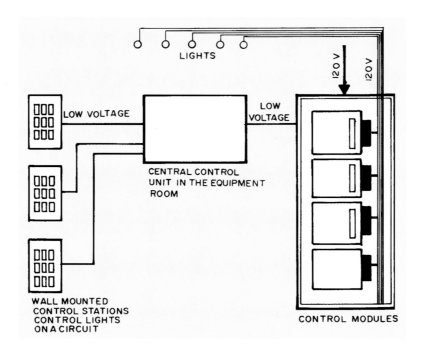

LIGHTS

LOW VOLTAGE

LOW VOLTAGE

120 V

120 V

CENTRAL CONTROL UNIT IN THE EQUIPMENT ROOM

WALL MOUNTED CONTROL STATIONS CONTROL LIGHTS ON A CIRCUIT

CONTROL MODULES

10-32 *This diagram shows the components and connections for a low voltage lighting control system.*
Courtesy LiteTouch, Inc.

the system to produce "scenes" where required. A "scene" involves turning on or off or dimming certain lights in a room to provide the desired atmosphere or lighting conditions **(10-31)**. For example a kitchen "scene" might require the main lights to be on at 100 percent. If you are cooking it could set the below counter lights and stove light at 100 percent and dim the others. In the home theater or family room where a visual presentation is to occur you may program the "scene" to turn off all the lights but leave on one or more table lamps or floor lamps at 15 percent. In the master bedroom the scene as you get in bed could be all lights off and a light in the master bedroom at 15 percent. You could have a "scene" for the entire house where all lights are turned off and hall and bathroom lights are on at 10

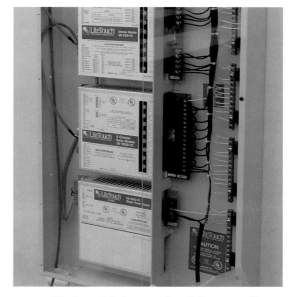

10-33 *The box with the control modules is typically located in an automation closet. These modules are self-contained units that provide actual dimming, relay switching, and peripheral equipment interfacing.*
Courtesy LiteTouch, Inc.

10-34 *These wall-mounted control stations provide control of several lights and scenes.*
Courtesy LiteTouch, Inc.

percent. The arrangements are up to you.

As you consider a lighting control system get the facts about several systems. For new construction a low voltage (LV) lighting control system is diagrammed in **10-32**. It has 120V power entering the box with the

control modules **(10-33)**. The master control panel receives low voltage power from the module box. The wall-mounted switches **(10-34)** also operate on low voltage. They have words on each button identifying their control function. When a wall switch is pressed low-voltage current activates a module directing 120V current to the designated light fixture. All of the lights in the house can be controlled from the master control panel.

Another lighting control system is in **10-35**. The components for this system are in **10-36**. The switching of circuits is performed by solid state relays which are electronic switches. They are mounted in a steel cabinet often installed in the automation closet. Low voltage current is transferred to the master control panel and the wall

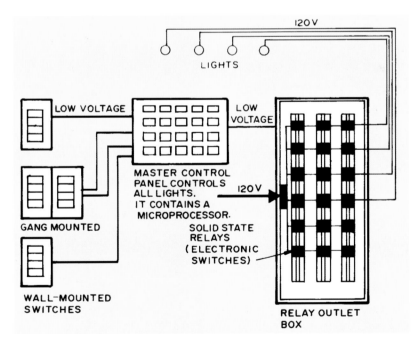

10-35 *This low voltage lighting control system has 120V current supplied to a series of solid state relays, which, when activated, direct the current to the lights. The system is controlled by a microprocessor.*
Courtesy CentraLite Systems

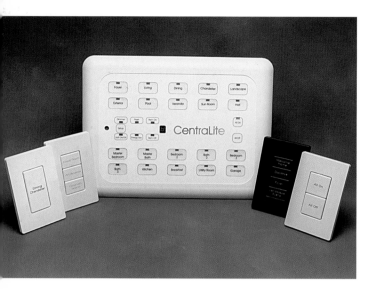

10-36 *The master control panel has a microprocessor that operates the system. It controls all of the lights. The wall switches are mounted as needed to provide control of individual lighting fixtures.*
Courtesy CentraLite Systems, Inc.

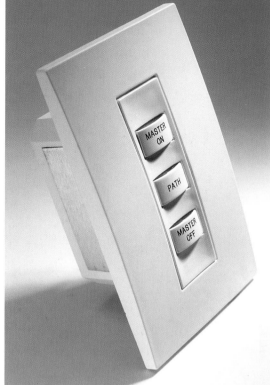

10-37 *This wall switch has the module mounted behind it. It replaces the standard light switch and operates on 120 volts.* **Courtesy LiteTouch, Inc.**

switches. Each button on a switch is designated to perform a programmed action such as turning a light on or off or establishing a scene. The master control panel is located in a place where you want access to all the lights from a single source. The system is controlled by a microprocessor that is contained in the master control panel. It is programmed using the buttons on the front of the panel.

Some lighting control systems not only control the lighting but also can be compatible with controls for other systems, such as audio/video components, security, and thermostats.

A power line carrier (PLC) system is used to add automated lighting control to existing houses. It is difficult to run the many wires required for a low-voltage system in a finished house. This system connects the switches and modules to the regular 120V

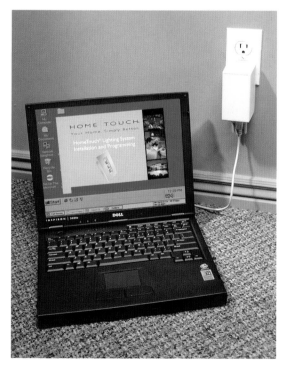

10-38 *The system operating program is fed into the central control unit by a computer.* **Courtesy LiteTouch, Inc.**

*10-41 This home theater uses a motorized drapery track system to operate light-proof draperies over a wall of windows. They also help with the acoustics in the room. **Courtesy Silent Gliss USA, Inc.***

*10-39 This handheld remote controls the entire house lighting system and other existing systems such as security and thermostat control of the heating and air conditioning system. **Courtesy CentraLite Systems***

*10-40 This home entertainment center occupies a room devoted to the enjoyment of multimedia systems. The color, the comfortable surroundings, and sound-proof wall and ceiling construction provide an atmosphere of relaxation and luxury. **Visionaire FX™ Personal Entertainment Center provided Courtesy of Owens Corning***

lighting system. The wall switch used has the control module mounted on the back of the switch as shown in **10-37**. This is mounted in the electric box where the old light switch was installed. The electric wiring carries commands from the pushbutton to smart dimmer switches. The program operating the system is fed into the central control unit from your computer **(10-38)**.

Some systems offer remote control. A handheld remote controller **(10-39)** gives you the ability to control the lighting system as well as the security system, thermostats, and audio/video systems from anywhere in the house.

Home Theater Systems

A home theater can be located in almost any room. Typically a family room or den is used if you do not wish to devote an entire room to this one activity. If a dedicated room is used it has the advantage of being designed to give the very best performance **(10-40)**. For example, it can have heavily sound-

proofed walls and carefully controlled natural lighting using proper draperies or shades **(10-41)**. The draperies can be activated by a wall switch or remote control. The wall upon which the projection screen is located may be enhanced with an attractive frame and curtains **(10-42)**. When not in use the curtains may be lowered hiding the screen. In a dedicated room the projection unit, speakers, and video equipment can be located in the most effective manner.

A home theater involves the use of high-quality video and maximum quality sound. A big screen high-quality video display coupled with the proper projector produce

10-42 *The projection screen has an attractive wood frame and curtains. Notice the door to the room also has curtains adding to the ambiance of the room.* **Courtesy Electronics Design Group, Inc. Piscataway, NJ** *www.edge/line.com*

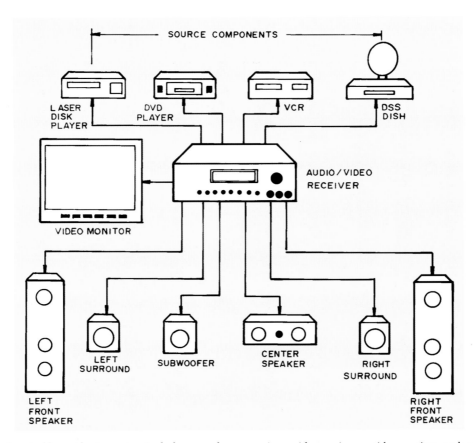

10-43 *A typical home theater system includes several source units, a video receiver, a video monitor, and several speakers.*

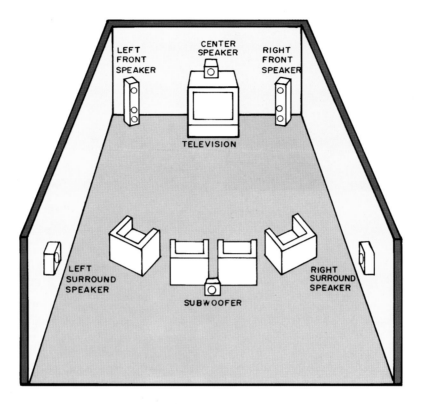

10-44 Place the center speaker on top of the television. The front right and left speakers are spaced an equal distance from the center speaker and directed toward the listeners. The right and left surround speakers are placed above and slightly behind the listeners. The subwoofer is placed in the front of the room about five feet from the wall.

visual images greatly superior to any standard television **(10-41)**. Projectors and sound system components are constantly being improved and new technology is continuously being developed so when you select your components or system make a careful study of what is available.

The design of a home theater system can be very complex. The choice of components from various manufacturers should be carefully analyzed before they are integrated into a viable system. Some people might be better off to choose a complete system offered by a reputable manufacturer or employ the services of a company doing home theater design.

The home theater system is composed of a number of components. The design of the system can be very complex and require the efforts of an experienced designer. The system shown in **10-43** uses an audio/video receiver as the control for the system. The audio/video receiver has a controller, an AM-FM tuner, and five power-amplifier channels to drive the speaker system. It is the simplest way to design a system.

THE AUDIO/VIDEO CONTROLLER

The controller separates 2-channel signals into right, left, center, and surround channels. It receives audio and video signals from source components, as a laser disk, DVD,

10-45 *The video projector projects video images onto the front projection screen.*

DSS, and VHS and selects the one to be decoded and amplified by the audio system and sends it to the video monitor (television).

SPEAKERS

The typical home stereo system has left and right audio channels reproduced by the left and right speakers. These are used to produce the span of sound in front of those in the room.

A home theater system typically provides five channels. Each channel powers a separate speaker. These are located in front on each side of the video monitor, one in front in the center of the room and two surround speakers behind and to the side of the seated listeners **(10-44)**. If a subwoofer is wanted a sixth channel is needed.

The right and left front speakers reproduce music and sound effects. The center speaker reproduces dialogue, music, and some sound effects. The rear surround speakers produce surrounding background sounds. They are placed above and a little behind the listener.

The last speaker used is a subwoofer. It can be placed almost anywhere in the room.

Front and rear locations are often used. However, move it around until you find a location giving the best sound. The subwoofer reproduces low bass frequencies. This is not used on many systems but is a desirable option. If the left and right speakers cannot adequately reproduce low bass frequencies a subwoofer should be used. If a subwoofer is used the controller will need to offer six channels.

SOURCE COMPONENTS

Source components are those that secure information from some storage device, as a CD player, or those receiving a broadcast signal, as an FM tuner. Some frequently used source components include the VHS tape machine that reads video and audio signals on a tape and enables them to be viewed on the video monitor. DVD players and DSS (Digital Satellite System) dish are other audio/video source components. LP turntables, CD players, and FM tuners are audio-only source components.

As you consider source components you should realize new and better technology will produce other source components that will eventually replace these.

VIDEO MONITORS

The video monitor displays the visual images. A conventional television set may be used. It is referred to as a direct-view monitor. Conventional television sets are available in a wide range of sizes. For a small home theater a 32- or 35-inch set is often used.

If you would like a larger picture usually a rear-projection television is used **(10-41)**. This projects the image on to the screen

*10-46 This home theater has a video projector hung from the ceiling. It projects the image on a front projection screen. **Visionaire FX™ Personal Entertainment Center provided by Courtesy of Owens Corning***

through a series of lenses and mirrors. The projector is mounted in a cabinet behind the screen and projects the image upon it. A home theater with a screen over 35 inches will use a rear-projection television.

The very best picture quality is achieved by using a front-projector.

The front-projector is mounted out in the room in front of the screen. It projects the image across the room onto the screen. The distance between the projector and the screen adjusts the size of the projected picture. As with other components the technology of front-projector components is constantly changing and improving in quality. The projection can be mounted on a table or as a motorized unit (**10-45**) or hung from the ceiling (**10-46**).

The front-projection screen directly influences the quality of the image produced. The size of the screen must be

matched to the output of the projector. The selection of the screen and projector must be made as a single decision.

Screens can be mounted directly to the wall, hanging with no permanent mounting and a motorized unit that will roll up when it is not needed. The motorized unit definitely helps change the room from a small theater into the original family or living room.

SEATING

The seating is placed away from the screen a distance about 2 to 2½ times the width of the screen. If a 32-inch television is used the seating should be 64 to 80 inches away. Experiment to find the best distance for your use. In **10-47** the seating provides a number of distances from the screen. This gives the viewer a choice of distances from the screen. Notice the use of motorized draperies to conceal the screen when it is not in use.

*10-47 The arrangement of seating gives the viewer a choice of distances from the screen. The motorized draperies conceal the screen when it is not in use. **Courtesy Silent Gliss, Inc.***

Motorized Television Systems

Motorized television lifts can conceal the television yet bring it into view at the push of a button on a remote control. It can turn a room, as a family room, into a small home theater. The use of a unit for a thin plasma television is ideal for this purpose **(10-48)**. It makes it possible to have a television in any room yet conceal it when not in use. The attractive cabinet serves as a decorative piece of furniture **(10-49)**. A popular installation locates a cabinet at the foot of the bed providing relaxing viewing **(10-50)**. Units are available that can lower television sets from the ceiling yet form an attractive architectural feature when not in use **(10-51)**.

A room planned for daily living yet to serve also as a home theater can have the projector lift in **10-52** installed. When the projector is lowered an attractive table is in view. Dim the lights, pull the draperies, and lower the screen and you are ready to raise

10-49 This handsome cabinet conceals a television that is raised on demand yet is lowered and concealed when not in use. **Courtesy Auton Motorized Systems**

10-50 This cabinet at the foot of the bed houses a motorized television lift. Now you see it. Now you don't. **Courtesy Auton Motorized Systems**

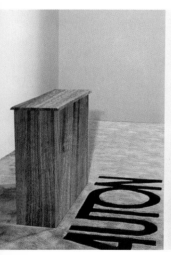

10-48 This thin cabinet is designed to conceal a large plasma television.
Courtesy Auton Motorized Systems

10-51 *This unique ceiling mounted motorized television lift will raise the television up into the cabinet when it is not in use.*
Courtesy Auton Motorized Systems

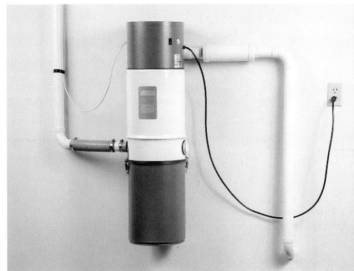

10-53 *The central cleaning power unit operates on 120V current. It is insulated to reduce the sound produced as it operates. It has a large storage capacity and generally needs to be cleaned two or three times a year.* **Courtesy Broan-NuTone, LLC**

10-52 *This motorized projector lift can turn a living room or family room into a home theater yet conceal the projector for regular use.*
Courtesy Auton Motorized Systems

the projector and enjoy a movie. It may also be mounted on the ceiling.

Central Vacuum Systems

A central vacuum system is a good feature to include as you plan your new house. The power unit is more powerful than most portable vacuum cleaners. Therefore more dust and dirt is removed. This makes the house a healthier place in which to live. Since it has excellent dust pickup, furniture requires less dusting.

Central vacuum systems trap the dust and dirt in the central power unit **(10-53)**. Since this is located away from the living area, no particles are put in the air as occur with many portable vacuum cleaners. This is especially helpful for those with allergies.

Since the system has outlets in the rooms all that is needed is to connect the

10-54 *The floor tool is connected to a wall outlet valve with a long hose. Other tools are available such as a dusting brush, upholstery tool, and crevice tool.*
Courtesy Broan-NuTone, LLC

10-56 *The hose is plugged into the wall outlet, which starts the system. The system stops when the hose is removed.*
Courtesy Broan-NuTone, LLC

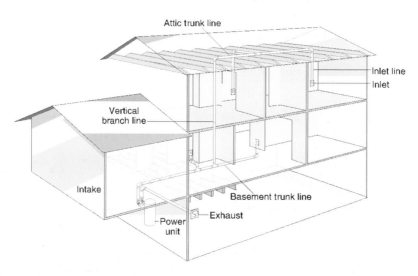

A selection of lightweight thirty-foot hoses gives you complete cleaning access to every corner of your home with fewer inlets. The typical home requires one cleaning inlet per 750 square feet of area.

10-55 *An example of a complete vacuum system. Notice the power unit is in the basement where it is out of the living areas.* **Courtesy Broan-NuTone, LLC**

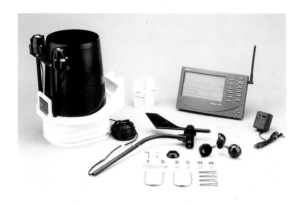

10-57 *A complete home weather station that measures inside and outside air temperature, accumulated rainfall, barometric pressure, inside and outside humidity, and the dew point.* **Courtesy Davis Instruments**

hose to the outlet. It does not require moving a large unit around the room. Also it is quiet because the power unit is installed in an out of the way place, as in the basement or garage **(10-54)**.

A typical system is shown in **10-55**. Here the power unit is located in the basement. The piping from the power unit to the rooms is run in the wall, under the floor, and in the ceiling. It is usually 2-inch PVC pipe. The wall outlet valve is activated by inserting the hose into it **(10-56)**. The system shuts off when the hose is removed. Some systems have an exhaust from the power unit running outside the house.

Home Weather Stations

Weather stations, while widely used in agriculture and industry, are also used by the homeowner to monitor and predict weather conditions locally. They are small and easy to install. Homeowners enjoy following the weather as a hobby as well as using the information for their daily activities. The system is built with a variety of components

10-58 *The components are mounted on a steel pole that can be secured to the building or on a tripod.*
Courtesy Davis Instruments

10-59 *Data are displayed on a console with a LCD display.* **Courtesy Davis Instruments**

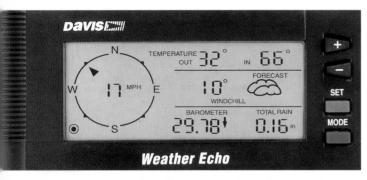

rainfall, barometric pressure, inside and outside humidity, and the dew point. If you are an avid cultivator of flowers or have a vegetable garden or fruit trees this information will be very important to you.

The station is mounted on a galvanized steel pole **(10-58)**. The station operates on an AC-power adapter with a battery backup. It has a radiation shield to protect the temperature/humidity sensor from solar radiation. The data are transmitted to a console with an LCD display **(10-59)**. A wireless system is available that transmits data to a portable receiver **(10-60)**. The wireless transmitter is installed in a convenient outside location and will transmit data to several receivers **(10-61)**.

providing a range of information about the weather. A complete weather station is shown in **10-57**. It measures inside and outside air temperature, wind speed and direction, wind chill, daily and accumulated

DEVELOPING THE FLOOR PLAN

As you work on the floor plan for your new house review the earlier chapters and make some preliminary decisions on the number of rooms, possible room sizes, and a preliminary decision on the furniture to be placed in each room. It is important that you become involved in developing the final floor plan. Even if you hire an architect or residential designer, your ideas and wishes should be clearly presented to them. It is to be your house not theirs.

As you begin to arrange the rooms in relation to each other observe the traffic patterns within the house. Also consider:

Orientation of rooms in relation to a view, the sun, prevailing winds, and privacy. For example, a garage can be placed on the side that will receive heavy cold winter winds and serve as a windbreak.

Observe the setbacks on all four sides of the lot. A setback is a minimum required distance from the sides of the lot. No part of the house can be in the setback.

Slope of the lot and drainage problems.

Location of utilities and ease of supplying them to the house.

Style of houses in the neighborhood and those typical of the geographic area.

The maximum size or cost of the house that is in your budget.

Keep in mind the exterior design including proportion, mass, and possible details. The exterior must be in balance.

Will the house be one story, two-story or a split-level?

Consider any special features that will influence the floor plan such as a swimming pool, patio, or tennis court.

Sources of House Plans

After you have made the preliminary decisions about the rooms to be in the house and you have developed a preliminary floor plan and possible elevation sketches, you need to get a final set of architectural drawings. One way to do this is to take your plans to an architect or experienced residential planner.

Architects & Residential Planners

These professionals will take your preliminary work and review the results. They will visit with you and discuss changes they feel are beneficial. When an agreement is reached they then prepare all the drawings needed to build the house **(11-1)** and write the specifications. Specifications are a written document describing in detail the scope of work, materials to be used, method of installation, and quality of workmanship for

11-1 After the preliminary planning has been completed the architect or residential planner will prepare a complete set of architectural drawings.

Consider changing room shapes and sizes as the plan develops.

Pay special attention to exterior door and window types and locations. Consider natural light and ventilation provided.

Provide space for a water heater, heating/air-conditioning units, and other possible mechanical systems. Will there be a fireplace requiring a chimney? Will the heating unit need an outside vent? These could be major problems if this is to be a two-story house.

Review electrical and plumbing requirements. Consider possible locations for a service entrance panel. There may be a need for a plumbing wall, especially if this is to be a two-story house.

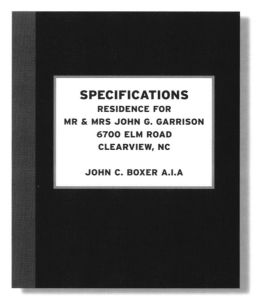

SPECIFICATIONS
RESIDENCE FOR
MR & MRS JOHN G. GARRISON
6700 ELM ROAD
CLEARVIEW, NC

JOHN C. BOXER A.I.A

11-2 Specifications are a written document describing in detail the scope of work, materials to be used, method of installation, and quality of workmanship.

the project **(11-2)**. These plus the architectural drawings form part of the contract for the construction.

The architect and residential designer prepare not only the floor plan and elevations but also design the foundation and structural system. If the structure has some unusual or difficult requirements they may employ a civil engineer to work out these structural details.

The advantage of using an architect or residential planner is that you can have direct input—and get the benefit of their expert advice. You get the house you want while they help eliminate features that may be costly or unsuitable.

Stock Plans

Another source of plans is from companies that have developed many stock plans. They have catalogs showing the elevations and floor plan and giving information about the house **(11-3)**. You select the house you want and they sell you the number of sets of architectural drawings you will need. The plans are complete including structural details. If your lot has unusual features, such as a steep slope, a local designer will have to

INNOVATIVE FLOOR PLANS
While we strive to design homes that maintain a traditional dignity on the outside, our floor plans offer the latest in convenience for contemporary living. Spacious kitchens with island cooktops, rear stairways, lower floor guest rooms, and vaulted ceilings are features common to many of our plans. Upper floor layouts feature spacious Master Bedroom suites, many with adjacent Sitting Rooms. We emphasize open stairwells and provide ample bathrooms for the other bedrooms.

CADDHOME 256A, UPPER FLOOR PLAN

CADDHOME 256A, LOWER FLOOR PLAN

STYLISH EXTERIORS
In this latest edition of Caddhomes we feature new plans with a wide variety of exterior styling, including County Manor homes finished with stone and stucco, traditional New England homes with wide porches and dormers, and Craftsman Revival houses with gabled fronts.

CADDHOME 431A

VOLUME 1 • EDITION 4

11-3 Companies producing stock sets of architectural drawings have catalogs showing the designs and floor plans available. A large variety of building sizes and designs are available. **Courtesy CADDHOMES, Vienna, VA**

11-4 Computer-generated drawings can produce three-dimensional drawings of exterior and interior rooms.
Courtesy CADDHOMES, Vienna, VA

prepare a revised foundation plan. Qualified residential designers and architects prepare them. The company can cite the qualifications of those preparing the plans.

Regardless of how you get the architectural drawings they will eventually be given to the building contractors you select. As

they examine the drawings and prepare a bid they will often come up with suggestions that can save money or improve the plan.

Pay attention to their suggestions and refer back to the architect or residential planner if you wish for an opinion. For example, making the garage just a few inches shorter

Door Schedule

Mark	Quantity	Size	Type	Material
A	2	1 ¾" x 3'-0" x 6'-8"	panel	steel
B	1	1 ¾" x 8'-0" x 6'-8"	sliding	aluminum
C	4	1 ⅜" x 2'-8" x 6'-8"	panel	masonite
D	2	1 ⅜" x 3'-60" x 6'-8"	bifold	pine
E	1	1 ⅜" x 5'-0" x 6'-8"	bifold	pine
F	1	1 ⅜" x 2'-0" x 6'-8"	panel	masonite
G	1	1 ¾" x 3'-0" x 6'-8"	panel	fiberglass

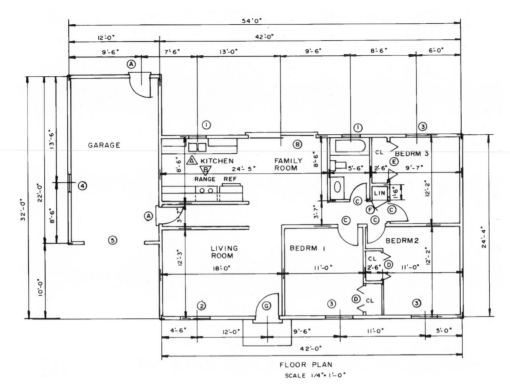

11-5 A typical floor plan for a small house.

could possibly save money if it makes it possible to build with standard size lumber.

Computer-Assisted Design (CAD)

Architects and residential planners generally will prepare their plans using CAD (computer-assisted design) graphics and engineering software. The design is developed on the monitor and is therefore rapidly and easily changed. Three-dimensional images can be drawn of the exterior and room interiors **(11-4)**. They are used to prepare the architectural working drawings from which bids are made and the house is built. The images are stored on disks and can be used to make prints on the printer whenever a copy is needed.

Architectural Drawings

A complete set of architectural drawings will typically include a floor plan, foundation plan, exterior elevations, sometimes interior wall elevations, site plan, landscape plan, wall sections, and details such as fireplace or a stair.

Floor Plans

A typical floor plan for a small house is shown in **11-5**. One such drawing is needed for each floor. It shows the overall room and hall sizes, location and sizes of doors and windows, location of interior partitions, location of electrical switches, light fixtures, wall outlets, appliances, various plumbing fixtures, door swing, and overall outside dimensions.

Foundation Plans

The foundation plan shows the overall outside dimensions, the size and location of each pier, size of all footings, vents or windows and doors in basements, beams and joist sizes and placement, special features, such as a fireplace or chimney footing, concrete slab floor in basement or on a porch above grade, water and sewer line locations, and thickness of foundation wall (11-6).

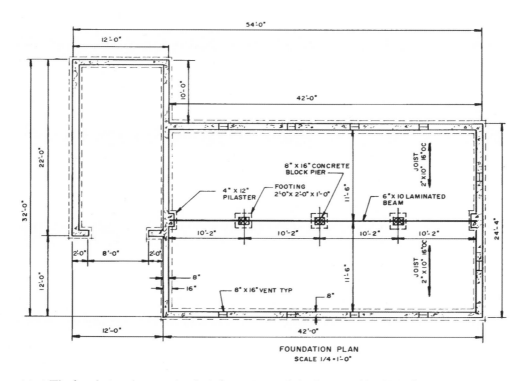

FOUNDATION PLAN
SCALE 1/4 = 1'-0"

11-6 The foundation plan contains the information needed to locate and build the foundation and piers.

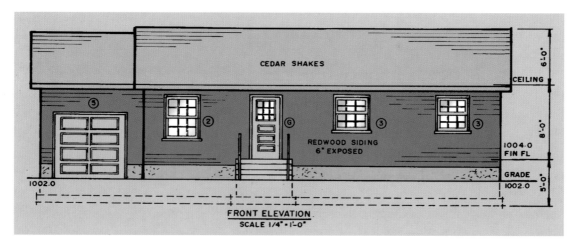

11-7 The elevation drawings show the exterior details including doors, windows, lights, and materials used.

Door Schedule				
Mark	Quantity	Size	Type	Material
1	2	2'-6" x 3'-4"	DH	fiberglass
2	1	2'-6" x 4'-6"	DH	fiberglass
3	3	2'-6" x 4'-6"	DH	fiberglass
4	1	2'-6" x 3'-6"	DH	fiberglass
5	1	8'-0" x 7'-0"	folding	aluminum

Elevations

An elevation is a drawing showing the exterior walls of the house. One is drawn for each exterior wall. This is typically the front, rear, right, and left sides. It shows the location of doors, windows, and porches. Roofing and wall finish materials are noted. The grade is established and the desired slope of the lot is shown. The elevation of the grade at each corner is given. The slope of the roof is shown, as are exterior lights, railings, finish floor, and ceiling and other details (11-7).

Site Plan

The site plan records the legal size of the lot, locates the setback and the outside of the foundation and any porches, decks, or other protrusions. It shows the original slope of the lot and the desired finished grade. Driveways and sidewalks are located and sometimes trees that must not be removed are shown. The location of water and waste lines and their connection to public utilities or a well and septic system are located (11-8).

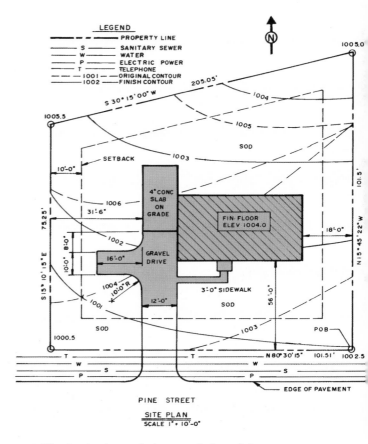

11-8 The site plan locates the house on the lot and shows the original and new contours for the slope of the site.

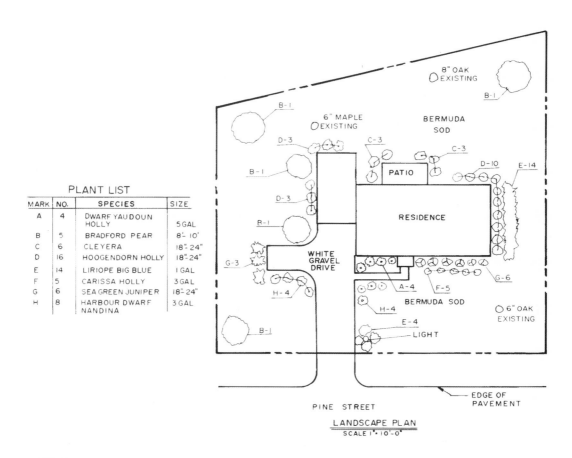

PLANT LIST

MARK	NO.	SPECIES	SIZE
A	4	DWARF YAUDOUN HOLLY	5 GAL
B	5	BRADFORD PEAR	8'- 10'
C	6	CLEYERA	18"- 24"
D	16	HOOGENDORN HOLLY	18"- 24"
E	14	LIRIOPE BIG BLUE	1 GAL
F	5	CARISSA HOLLY	3 GAL
G	6	SEA GREEN JUNIPER	18"- 24"
H	8	HARBOUR DWARF NANDINA	3 GAL

LANDSCAPE PLAN
SCALE 1"- 10'-0"

11-9 *The landscape plan shows the trees to remain on the site and the location, size, and specie of each shrub to be planted.*

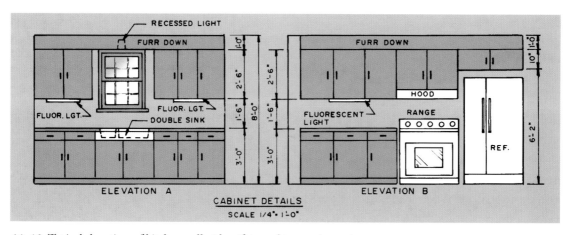

CABINET DETAILS
SCALE 1/4"= 1'-0"

11-10 *Typical elevations of kitchen walls, identifying cabinets to be used.*

Landscape Plan

A landscape plan records the bounds of the lot and shows the outline of the house. It locates the driveway and sidewalks. Trees that must not be removed are identified. New plants are drawn and their species, size, and location are given. The species and size are often lettered on the edge of the drawing and keyed to the actual location **(11-9)**. It is usually made by a landscape contractor who has training in landscape architecture.

Interior Elevations

Whenever there is something special about an interior wall an elevation is often drawn. This might be a kitchen wall or a wall in a den with considerable built-in shelving and cabinets. Basic sizes are given and items are identified **(11-10)**.

Wall Sections

Typically the design and construction of the exterior wall is shown by a section drawing. It contains information about the materials used, the size, and other pertinent details **(11-11)**. Other sections are drawn as needed.

Other Drawings

Frequently the designer will draw a plan and section through a stair. This can show tread

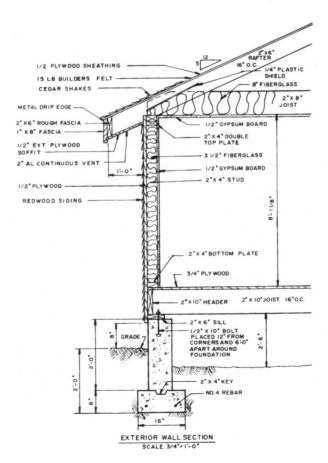

11-11 A typical wall section showing the construction of the exterior wall from the footing to the eave.

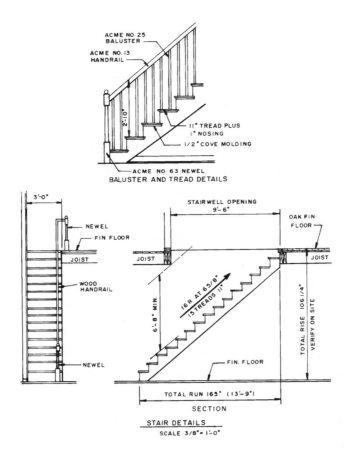

11-12 A typical stair detail, giving the tread and riser size and handrail information.

and riser sizes and construction details. The stair actually built will be sized much like this but may vary some because the final sizes will be decided by the actual total rise of the stair that exists after the house has been framed **(11-12)**.

A fireplace detail will show a section through the firebox and a front elevation. These can be dimensioned, materials identified, and mantel details shown **(11-13)**.

Developing the Final Floor Plan

Possibly the best way to develop an original floor plan containing the rooms you want is to prepare templates for each room at the sizes established during the preliminary consideration of each room and what it will contain. These are best developed on graph paper having ¼-inch squares. Each square represents one foot. If working in metric units use metric graph paper divided into one-millimeter squares with light lines and 5-millimeter squares with dark lines. One-millimeter squares represent 50 millimeters and the 5-millimeter square represent 250 millimeters. See the template drawings in Chapter 2.

Begin by arranging the templates in various ways forming a floor plan. Adjust, move things around and try various positions as shown in **11-14** through **11-17**. As you do this keep in mind the planning principles in the earlier chapters. Sketch traffic flow from room to room, from the front door and garage to various parts of the house and observe the shape of the developing plan. You may not want a long narrow or square house.

Remember to separate the rooms into basic areas. This is called zoning. For example, the bedrooms need to be in a quiet zone where noise from the living area will not intrude. The dining room, living room and kitchen have a natural relationship forming a living zone.

Think about the halls and where to put a stair if it is a two-story house. These are the core of the traffic flow. Where do you plan to have storage and how about the laundry and mechanical systems equipment? Do not forget closets.

Do not be afraid to change the shape and size of the rooms. However be certain they can still function as planned and if enlarged do not increase the price of the house too much. This is the most interesting part of the process.

As you move things around remember it changes the exterior. You can make some exterior sketches on graph paper to see how the changes in the floor plan alter the exterior. Elevation A **(11-18)** is a simple rather plain design for this small house. Elevation B **(11-19)** is a bit more interesting because the living room has been projected

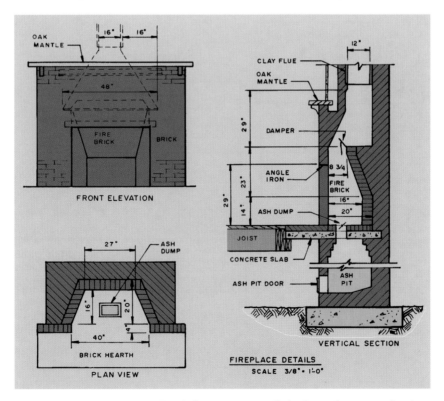

11-13 Typical construction details for a conventionally built, single-opening fireplace.

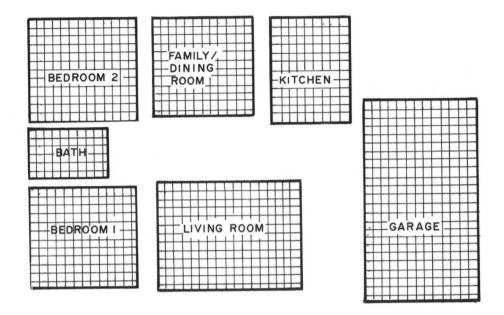

11-14 This is the first attempt to arrange the rooms into a floor plan. Getting from the garage to the kitchen could be a problem. Overall it is a pretty good plan. The flat front wall does not give the best possible elevation.

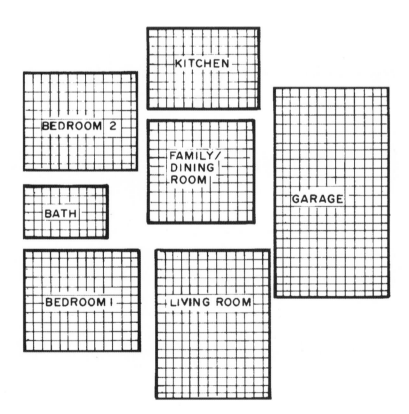

11-15 This is a second arrangement. It tightens up the plan and has better access from the garage to the kitchen but not to the rest of the house. A front entrance is a problem. A good feature is that the living room extends beyond the bedroom, possibly producing a more interesting front elevation.

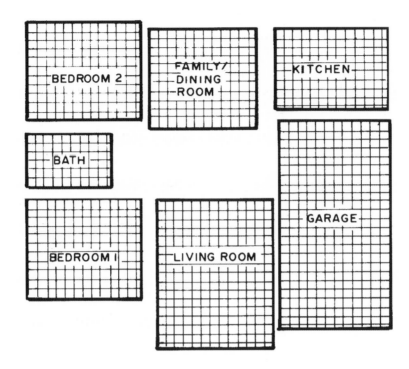

11-16 *The third try moves the kitchen behind the garage giving direct access. The living room could be made larger utilizing some of the open center area.*

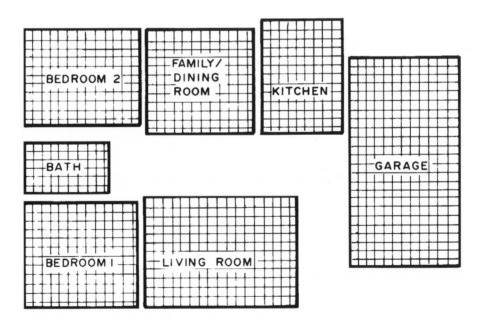

11-17 *This is the plan finally accepted. The access from the garage to the kitchen is adequate. An open area by the living room could be the entrance foyer and passage could be developed providing passage to the bedroom area.*

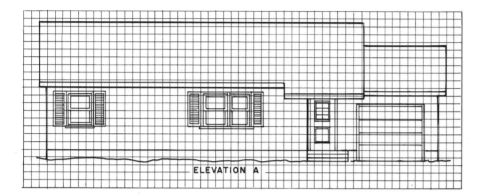

ELEVATION A

11-18 *This elevation shows an efficient but rather boring small house. Consider widening the front entrance, projecting the living room forward, and other floor plan adjustments. All of this cost money so keep account of the cost.*

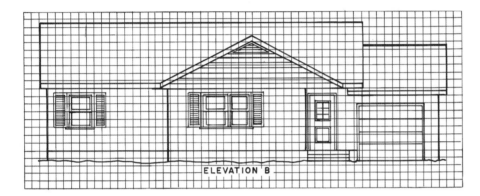

ELEVATION B

11-19 *This elevation is a bit more attractive. The living room was extended beyond the front wall and a gable roof was framed over it.*

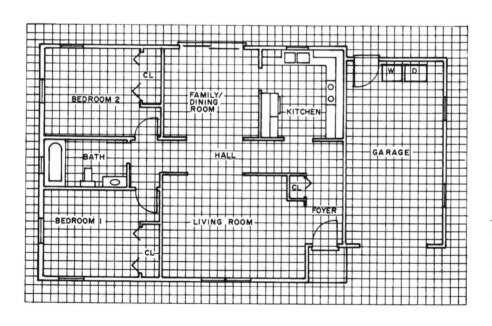

11-20 *After reaching what seems to be a satisfactory solution the room placement is drawn on graph paper. At this time wall thicknesses are drawn, closets worked in, the hall is sized and located, the foyer is established, and doors and windows are located. Recheck the rooms for furniture placement and make necessary revisions in the bathroom and kitchen. The size of the rooms is adjusted as needed.*

beyond the front wall permitting a gable end to be built making the elevation somewhat more attractive.

Once the plan seems to have reached a possible final solution sketch it on graph paper (11-20). Here you have to include the thickness of exterior and interior walls which will decrease floor area or you will enlarge the house. The typical interior partition is 4 ½ inches (114mm) thick. Exterior wood-framed walls with wood, vinyl, or cement board siding are typically 6-inches thick (152mm). If brick veneer is used, the exterior wall will be 10-inches thick (216mm).

Locate doors and windows watching for traffic flow, furniture placement, natural light, and ventilation. Check again if this changes the exterior elevation. Again it may be necessary to make some changes. New layouts may be needed. You can place a sheet of vellum over the layout, copy the parts that will not be changed, and draw on the changes. Eventually a solution will be reached and you can prepare a final layout. Take this to your architect or residential planner to have the final architectural drawings prepared. If you have had contact with a builder you might be able to get a "ballpark" estimate of the possible cost before making the final architectural drawings. The architect could also give an estimate.

Now you can begin to make visits to appliance dealers, electric supply houses and select light fixtures, kitchen cabinets, plumbing fixtures, floor-covering materials, paint colors, wallpaper, and other such decisions that have to be made.

11-21 It is an exciting experience to watch the construction of your house. Visit the site often. Check the work with the plans.

Check the completed architectural drawings to be certain it is as you want things. Then multiple sets can be run. These are given to the Building Planning and Inspections Department of the local government for approval. They check to see if they meet the codes. Often a community will have an Architectural Review Board that checks the exterior design and material choices to see if they meet local approval. Additional copies are given to building contractors you want to consider to build the house. They will give a bid usually on the completion of all the work shown on the architectural drawings and agree to meet the requirements in the specifications. Once the local government approves, you get a building permit. Once you reach agreement with a builder and you sign a contract construction may begin (11-21).

BUILDING
THE
HOME

CHOOSING & PURCHASING A BUILDING SITE

The Building Site

The choice of a building site is an important part of the process of building a house. Many factors depend upon this decision. Even the eventual design of the house can be influenced by the site. The shape, size, and contours are important in addition to the satisfaction of finding a site in a location you want. Do not forget the cost. There are a number of legal matters to be handled as well as possible financing.

One of the first things generally considered when choosing a site is the location.

Things to check are the value of other sites and homes in the area, schools, shopping, medical facilities and ease of access. Are there undesirable things nearby, such as polluting industries, a swamp, an airport, or noisy recreational activities? What type of police and fire protection is available (**12-1** and **12-2**)?

The availability of municipal water and sewer service, electricity, telephone, and cable television are important. If water and sewer service are not available conditions for drilling a well must be investigated and the soil must be checked with a percolation test to see if a septic tank and drain field will work. Local government agencies will have information on these and can make recommendations and grant approvals. Check the site to ascertain the subsurface water level. A high water table can cause major problems and if they cannot be handled the site should not be used. The quality of the bearing soil should be checked. The local building inspection

12-1 This beautiful church establishes a pleasant and restful atmosphere in the neighborhood; but do you want to build your house next door or across the street?

department can possibly advise if there have been problems in the area. Soils can be tested to ascertain their load-bearing capacity. Soils with low-bearing capacity will require special consideration when the foundation is designed. Of course be certain the site is not in a flood-prone area **(12-3)**. If it is in a wetlands construction will be prohibited. If on the coast get a record of hurricanes and storm damage not only about the sites on the water but sites inland that may still be flooded during seasonal storms. How about heavy snows and access in the winter? Are the roads kept open? Is help nearby? Visit with realtors about sites for sale and get prices so comparisons can be made. As you explore the area are there many for sale signs **(12-4)**? If so what is the matter? Would a visit with people living in the neighborhood maybe bring some things into focus?

If the site is in a development try to get some information about the developer and the project. Is the project stable and ade-

12-2 This well-kept group of small retail shops provides local access to shopping; but would you buy a lot next door or across the street?

12-3 This site has a large area that will have standing water after a heavy rain. The soil is often water-logged and spongy.

12-4 Are there a number of "for sale" signs in the neighborhood? Check around to see what might be the problem.

quately financed? Will things promised, such as a clubhouse, actually be built? What quality streets are being built? Are the sites selling and new houses under construction **(12-5)**? What does the local bank tell you about loaning money for construction? What are the taxes on the site and the houses in the area?

Finding a Site

Building sites can be bought directly from the owner. These are typically in areas already developed. They may be in older areas where the new house fills in a lot that for some reason never was built upon. These are generally offered for sale by local realtors. Some tend to specialize in sites as well as houses and advertise lists of available locations with addresses. You can drive by these before the realtor is contacted or let the realtor drive you around to visit those that might meet your requirements. Prices will vary considerably and negotiations sometimes reduce the price quite a bit.

Another source of building sites is in a planned development often referred to as a subdivision. Here the amenities are clearly spelled out and prices vary depending upon the size of the site and its location. For example, a site on a golf course will cost considerably more than a similar site that is backed up to a lot where a house will be constructed. The contours of the site may also influence cost. Such developments typically have covenants and building restrictions detailing the minimum size of the house, materials that are acceptable, minimum landscaping, fence regulations, and a host of other restrictions. Read these carefully before buying the site **(12-6)**.

Sometimes the developer is also a builder and will bid on and build a house for you. This does not mean other builders cannot build it.

In either case, a development site or a direct purchase of a lot in the community, the process of planning the house is a major project and involves study and inquiry and can be interesting and fun if you do not try to rush it. Careful consideration will get the house you desire in a desirable location and hopefully at a price you can afford.

Purchasing the Site

Once a building site has been chosen a contract of sale of real estate is prepared. Generally, the sale will be handled by a realtor, who will have a sales contract prepared. It

12-5 This nice slightly sloping site is high and dry. Notice a great home has been constructed on the next lot. This would appear to be a good location to be considered.

12-6 This entrance to a residential development adds to the ambiance of the neighborhood.

is wise to have a lawyer who works with real estate transactions to review the contract before signing it. The contract must contain all the terms and conditions of the sale. Of importance is the type of deed. You want a full covenant and warranty deed. Also consider having the title of the property insured. If there is something wrong with the deed the insurance protects the purchaser from loss.

TYPES OF OWNERSHIP

It is useful to be aware that there are several types of property ownership. These include Fee Simple or Fee Simple Absolute, Fee Simple Determinable or Qualified, Fee Simple on Condition, and Life Estate.

Fee Simple or Fee Simple Absolute ownership is the highest type of ownership. If you want to have unconditional control of the property and the right to sell it when you wish and use it as you see fit within the zoning regulations you should have Fee Simple ownership. The other three types have qualifications limiting what you may do. For example, Fee Simple Determinable or Qualified puts a limit such as you have ownership of the property unless you do something banned such as start a dog kennel on it. If you do this, the original owner regains ownership. The Fee Simple on Condition states how you must use the property. For example, it may require you to build a children's playground or the original owner may repossess the property. The Life Estate condition means you own the property until you die after which it goes to some designated source, such as a local church or hospital.

Contracts

A contract of sale of real estate should include the following:

The contract must be written and signed by the seller and purchaser.

The parties to the sale must be competent and clearly identified.

A statement indicating the seller agrees to the sale and the purchaser agrees to buy.

A complete, detailed description of the property involved in the sale.

The price, down payment and other terms of the sale.

An agreement to convey the title upon completion of the terms and the type of deed to be offered.

A fixed date for closing the sale after which the seller must deliver the deed and the buyer must pay the price.

An explanation of the encumbrances on the property. An encumbrance is a right to the property by a third party. Examples include, but are not limited to, deed restrictions, easements, a mechanics lien for work performed or materials used on the property.

Conditions related to a default after the contract is signed.

Making an Offer to Purchase

Should you decide after examining the property and reviewing all aspects, including encumbrances, to purchase it, make an offer to purchase. The real estate agent handling the sale typically prepares this. It should clearly include all the factors to be in the contract of sale. Usually the real estate agent collects a cash deposit held in escrow until the sale is closed or a decision to not accept it has been made. If the seller rejects the offer the earnest money is returned. If the offer to purchase is accepted a formal contract of sale is presented to the buyer. It should contain all the features mentioned in the offer to purchase. It is a good idea to have your lawyer review the contract of purchase and the contract of sale before signing them.

It is recommended that the contract of sale have a deadline for which the seller must accept the sale or the contract is automatically void and the money in escrow is returned to the buyer. If the seller rejects the contract of sale the money in escrow will be returned. Escrow is money deposited with the realtor by the buyer indicating the buyer wishes to purchase the property. It is held in a special escrow account that holds all such deposits from all sales in progress. Escrow money must be kept in a special account and must not be mingled with other accounts of the real estate firm or the law office.

Should the seller accept the signed contract of sale and you fail to proceed with the sale the money in escrow can be retained by the seller.

The amount of the initial deposit is usually negotiated between the seller and buyer. Typically 10 percent of the sale price is used.

Sales Commissions

A fee is paid to the realtor handling the sale. It is usually a percentage of the sale price. Generally it is paid by the seller of the property. A person looking to buy property may pay a fee to the realtor for finding the property wanted. Fees typically range from 5 to 10 percent. Remember, if you are the buyer, the realtor handling the sale is representing the seller and is going to try to make the best deal for their client. You must bargain with them to get the best price because they are not going to easily reduce the value of the sale. The dollar amount of their commission depends upon the sale price they can get you to accept.

Conditions of a Default

A default occurs when either the buyer or seller cannot meet the conditions of the signed contract. For example, the seller may not be able to present a clear title to the property or the buyer may not be able to get a loan and complete the purchase. The contract should clearly state the conditions to be taken in case of a default. Otherwise a legal action will most likely be taken.

Deeds

A deed is a document used to transfer ownership of a property. When properly written, executed, and delivered it transfers the sellers right, title, or interest to the property to the buyer. The document must have the signatures witnessed by a notary public or other authorized official.

While the deed transfers ownership it is not proof of a marketable title. The title may have defects. The title must be checked before making the purchase.

A deed has a number of critical elements that must be accurate. If this is not the case it may be declared invalid or challenged in court. The deed must be checked by an attorney who works with real estate to be certain it is properly drawn.

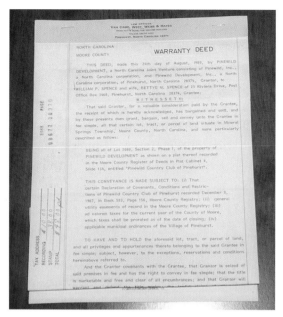

12-7 A warranty deed gives a buyer protection against all claims made against the property. The seller defends the buyer.

Types of Deed

There are a number of different types of deeds. What they offer in terms of legal rights and guarantees can differ so the type of deed offered when you buy property needs legal consideration.

A Warranty Deed with Full Covenants is usually referred to as a Warranty Deed. It indicates that the seller will defend the buyer against all claims made against the property. This gives the buyer a high degree of protection **(12-7)**.

A Bargain and Sale Deed without Covenants against the Grantor's (sellers) Acts conveys all rights, title, and interest in the property to the buyer but does not contain specific covenants protecting the buyer.

A Bargain and Sale Deed with Covenants against Grantor's (sellers) Acts is the same as the previous deed but the grantor indicates that he/she has done nothing to encumber the property while he/she was the owner of it.

A Quitclaim Deed is used to remove some type of encumbrance on the deed that will affect the title to the property. It asks someone who has a claim to the property to release (quitclaim) this interest.

Other types of deeds found occasionally include a Tax Deed, a Sheriff's Deed, a Referee's Deed, and a Trustee's Deed. These are used to convey the title to a property that is sold pursuant to court orders related to foreclosure proceedings against the property. This includes things as taxes due, unpaid mortgages, or legal judgments placed against the property.

Deed Restrictions

The deed may contain restrictions that were placed in the deed by the current owner. These are in effect when the property is sold. This can include things like setting the minimum size house allowed, maximum building height, restricting the use of certain specified building materials, as vinyl siding, and many other such factors. These are in addition to the restrictions established by the local zoning ordinances that are produced by the local government.

Be absolutely certain you are aware of the restrictions in the deed as well as local governing restrictions.

Liens

A lien is a claim held by a creditor against the property for a debt. The debt must be paid before the property can be sold. The lienor (the person holding the lien) may be entitled by law to sell the property to settle the debt even if the owner of the property does not agree to the sale.

There are many types of liens. The most common lien is a mortgage lien. This is agreed to by the property owner when a loan is taken out on the property. The loan is secured by a mortgage lien held by the agency providing the loan. If the property owner defaults on the loan the lien holder can secure a court order to foreclose the loan and sell the property.

Municipalities tax property, provide water and sewer services, and sometimes levy assessments to raise funds for some improvement, as improving the street or sewer system. The local government will give the delinquent property owner a notice to pay the due balance. Should it not be paid a judgment is levied against the property and it is sold to pay the unpaid debt.

Mechanics liens can be filed against your property by anyone who has contributed labor or materials toward its construction and who has not been paid for the work performed or the materials supplied. The lien is attached to property to which the labor or materials were used. The lien applies to any work or materials that improved the value of the property. For example, if a number of windows were delivered and they had broken glass or a broken sash, payment would not be due so a lien could not be filed.

The lien is filed in the office of the county clerk. The notice of lien is notarized under oath by the lienor. The organization providing the loan on the house will check for liens before releasing any funds to pay

for a section of construction completed. Your attorney can insert a clause in the contract you sign with the general contractor to protect you against liens filed against your property due to failure of the contractor to pay bills as they come due. You can also check with local material suppliers and subcontractors to see if the general contractor you are about to hire has a record of not paying the bills.

Titles

The title to the property conveys the right of ownership. The holder of the title has the right of possession and control of the property and the right to sell it and transfer the ownership. The documents related to the title must be recorded in the Registry of Deeds in a designated public office in the county where the property is located.

Title Search

To search a title means going through the public records to review the names of all persons who have an interest in the property and look for defects that may hinder getting a clear title to the property. Usually a professional such as a representative from a title insurance company or a lawyer makes the title search. They are familiar with the records and know how to conduct a search. The title searcher finishes the search and prepares an abstract of title, that is, a history of all the documents in the public record related to the title.

Generally the lawyer for the seller will prepare a current abstract of title and give it to the buyer's lawyer for examination. Then a certificate of title can be issued if all is in order.

Title Insurance

A title insurance policy is issued by a title insurance company after it searches the title. If all is clear, the title insurance company will sell the insurance to the buyer. The policy in general will reimburse the buyer if there are losses due to defects in the title. The policy provisions can vary so a careful reading is recommended **(12-8)**.

Mortgages

If you cannot or do not wish to pay cash for the site or the cost of construction it becomes necessary to get a mortgage. A mortgage is a legal agreement between the person borrowing the money and the lending institution, such as a bank. The property to be bought with the mortgage is used as security for the loan.

The things to consider as you review the mortgage agreement include the principal, as well as the rate of interest, the length of the repayment period, points, equity, other closing costs, and the size of the required down payment.

The monthly payment required depends on the principal and interest. The principal is the amount borrowed and is the amount of the total cost of the project minus the down payment. The interest is the charge made by the lending institution. It is a fee charged for lending the money stated as an annual percentage rate (APR).

The money is to be repaid over a period of years, which is the repayment period. The down payment plus the amount of principal paid back each month is the equity you have in the property. The building of equity thus reducing the debt through the

12-8 Title insurance protects the buyer from losses that may occur due to defects in the title.

monthly payments and interest is called amortization. Points are changes made by the lending institution as an extra cost for processing the loan. One point is equal to one percent of the loan values. Be certain to inquire about points because they are another cost of closing the loan.

The length of the repayment period affects the size of the monthly payment and the total interest costs over this period. The longer the repayment period, then the smaller the monthly payments and the greater the amount paid for interest. If you can handle large monthly payments considerable savings in interest costs will be made.

It is smart to get a mortgage that has a prepayment privilege. This allows the borrower to make cash payments that are then applied directly to the principal, thus reducing interest costs. If the mortgage has a due-on-sale clause, it means that the loan balance must be paid as soon as the property is sold.

There are many types of mortgages available and it is wise to review each before deciding on the one to use. Some are conventional loans made by a private lender with no government or other backing. Insured loans can be provided, such as those by the Federal Housing Agency and the Veterans Administration or a private mortgage company. The lender is guaranteed payment if the loan holder defaults. There are adjustable rate (ARM) loans where the monthly payment is adjusted occasionally depending on the market interest rate. When interest rates drop the monthly payment drops and when they rise the monthly payment is increased. A fixed-rate mortgage has the established interest rate in effect for the entire length of the loan. Shop around and explore other types of loans available. Get full information on each before signing anything.

Closing the Sale

The closing process occurs with a meeting between the buyer and seller, the real estate broker and the attorneys. The title is transferred as the seller gives the property deed to the buyer. All financial transactions are settled at the closing.

There are various closing costs that will occur. While these vary depending upon the situation they can include prorating property taxes, fees for the title search, attorneys fees, surveyors fees, points by the lending agency, homeowners insurance premium, and any local or state transfer fees.

BUILDING THE HOUSE

The following description is for a typical wood-framed house. You have selected the building site (see Chapter 12) and have developed an accurate and complete set of architectural drawings and specifications. The local building officials have approved these and you have accepted a bid from one of the several building contractors you had bid on the job. Now construction can begin. The contractor has received a building permit and arrives at the site **(13-1)**. The building permit is displayed in a weatherproof cabinet at the street side of the site **(13-2)**.

Building regulations require that erosion control barriers be built to keep soil erosion and blowing debris from getting on adjoining lots and into the street. The building inspector will require these and check during each site visit to make certain they are erect and effective **(13-3)**.

After the trees that must be removed are cleared away and the stumps dug out the site is rough leveled **(13-4)**. It is not accurately graded to the contours shown on the landscape plan but prepares the site for digging the foundation. See Chapter 11 for a landscape plan. As the site is graded the area to be occupied by the house receives additional earth removal and leveling. Since soil is needed for backfilling around the foundation and final grading of the site, all soil removed during the initial grading and digging is stockpiled for future use **(13-5)**.

Building the Foundation

Now the foundation is staked out with chalk lines **(13-6)**. The lines are established using a

13-1 *The building site as purchased will have many trees and often brush that must be cleared away. Examine the landscape plan to find the trees to remain. Mark them with a colored ribbon. Notice this site had the electrical transformer and telephone and cable television boxes available.*

13-3 *Before disturbing the lot very much install }barriers on any side where erosion control is necessary. This barrier has metal posts and a thick plastic sheet material. Be certain soil and debris do not flow on neighboring lots or into the street.*

13-2 *One of the first things the general contractor will do is post the building permit.*

13-4 *After the unwanted trees have been removed the site is rough graded in preparation for locating the foundation.*

13-5 *Soil removed during the initial grading is stockpiled for future use as backfill. It must be placed in an out-of-the-way place so it does not interfere with the construction process.*

13-6 *The outside of the foundation is located with chalk lines running between batter boards. It is leveled with a level transit or laser level.*

13-8 *Footings are typically dug with a backhoe that can cut them rapidly, accurately, and level.*

13-7 *A laser level is used to establish level (horizontal) and plumb (vertical) lines.*

level transit that is used to lay out and measure horizontal and vertical angles, distances, and directions and establishes the levelness of the line of sight. Another tool used is a laser level used to establish level (horizontal) and plumb (vertical) lines **(13-7)**.

Now that the foundation is laid out the footings can be dug. In warm climates where the footings can be just a foot or so below the surface of the ground they are often dug by hand. When they have to go deeper a small backhoe is used **(13-8)**. It can dig rapidly and the depth can be accurately controlled. The depth must be deep enough to get the bottom of the footing below the frost line and it must be level. Since the backhoe can pivot, the soil can be placed a distance away from the footing. It is then moved to a stockpile with a tractor with a bulldozer blade as shown in **13-4**.

In soft, sandy soil the footings should have forms installed as shown in **13-9** because the dirt walls collapse. If the soil has enough clay so the sides of the footing trench will stand **(13-10)**, the concrete can be poured without forms as those shown in **(13-11)**. It is important that the footings be level. The footings for the piers are dug and poured in the same manner. A house with a crawl space will generally use 8 × 16 inch concrete blocks to form the pier. The foot-

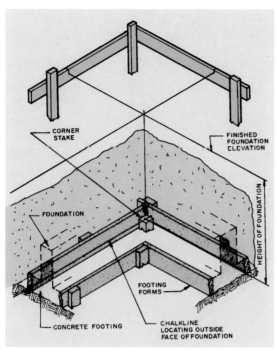

13-9 *When the sides of the dug footing trench will not stand, forms should be used. This shows how the chalk lines are used to locate the corners and sides of the foundation.*

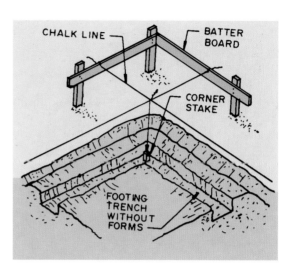

13-10 *If the sides of the dug footing are firm enough to stand, the footing can be dug and poured without forms.*

ing is typically 16 × 24 inches and 8 inches thick **(13-12)**. If a basement is to be built steel columns are used instead of concrete blocks **(13-13)**.

13-11 *These footings were poured without forms.*

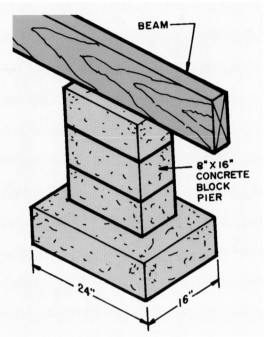

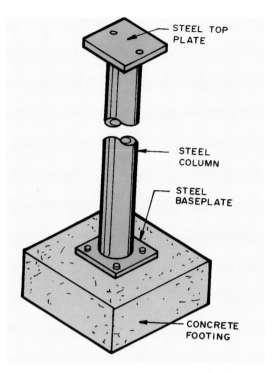

13-13 *Steel columns are used to support floor beams when the house has a basement.*

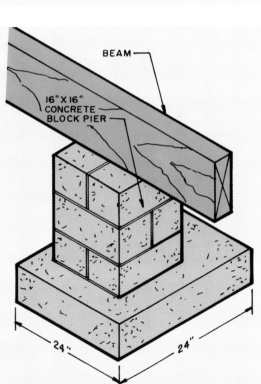

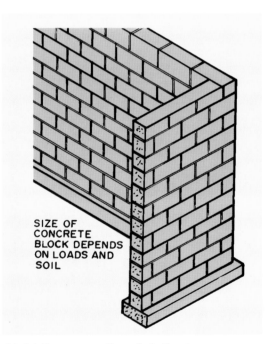

13-12 (ABOVE TOP AND BOTTOM) *Concrete blocks are typically used to build piers on wood-framed houses having a crawl space.*

13-14 *Basement walls can be built using concrete blocks. Be certain they are designed to withstand the pressure from the earth.*

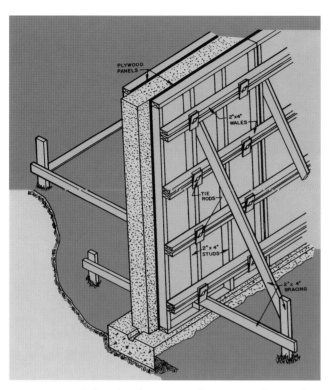

13-15 *Cast-in-place concrete basement walls provide the strongest watertight basement wall. These have been built with wood forms.*

13-17 *These piers were built using two 8 x 16 inch concrete blocks for each layer. Notice their direction is alternated on each layer.*

13-18 *This concrete block foundation has been covered with a layer of brick. This greatly improves the appearance.*

13-16 *This foundation and piers are made from concrete blocks. The area to be below grade has been waterproofed and a gravel bed has been laid around the outside. The exposed block usually has a layer of rich cement toweled over it to improve the appearance. This is called parging.*

When the house has a basement the foundation wall can be laid up with concrete blocks **(13-14)** or formed up and poured with concrete **(13-15)**. Crawl space foundation walls can also be concrete block or cast-in-place concrete **(13-16)**.

After the footings have cured the foundation and piers are built **(13-16** and **13-17)**. In **13-18** notice the concrete block foundation

13-19 *This porch area will be exposed to the weather so it will have a concrete floor. It has been filled with soil providing support for the concrete floor as it is poured and gains strength.*

13-20 *The floor beams are set on the piers and foundation and leveled.*

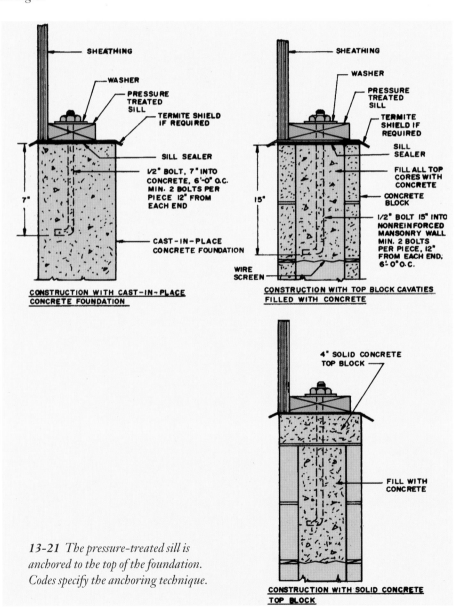

13-21 *The pressure-treated sill is anchored to the top of the foundation. Codes specify the anchoring technique.*

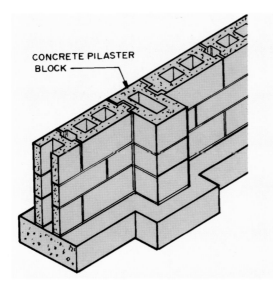

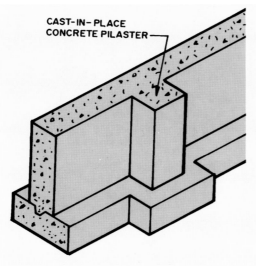

13-22 *Floor beams can rest on pilasters built as part of the foundation wall. Pilasters also add stability to the wall.*

has been covered with a layer of bricks. If the exterior siding is to be wood or anything but brick this will make the exposed foundation more attractive than if the concrete block was left exposed. If the exterior walls are to be brick they will be built upon this row of brick. In **13-19** the area that will be a large porch with a concrete floor has been filled. It will be

13-23 *This floor beam is supported by a wood column. The wood I-joists rest on the beam.* **Courtesy Truss Joist**

tamped and prepared to receive the concrete later during construction.

Framing the Floor

Now the beams supporting the floor are set and leveled **(13-20)**. The sill is bolted to the top of the foundation **(13-21)**. At the foundation a pilaster is built upon which the beam is supported **(13-22)**.

The floor joists are placed on the beams and foundation sill **(13-23)**. These may be solid wood joists or a manufactured joist called an I-joist (**13-24** and **13-25**). Another manufactured joist is a truss joist **(13-26)**. It can span long distances. After the floor

13-24 *This floor has been framed with I-joists.*
Courtesy Truss Joist

13-27 *Before the subfloor is placed on the floor joists a bead of adhesive is laid along the joist. This reduces the tendency of a floor to squeak as the house ages.* **Courtesy APA—the Engineered Wood Association**

13-25 *This shows how the I-joists are secured to the beam with metal joist hangers.*
Courtesy Willamette Industries, Inc.

13-28 *The subfloor is pulled against the previous sheet and nailed or screwed to the floor joist.*
Courtesy APA—the Engineered Wood Association

13-26 *These truss joists will span long distances and form a strong floor.*

joists are placed, leveled, and secured the subfloor is installed. First a layer of adhesive is laid along the top of each joist **(13-27)** and then the sheathing is lowered in place and nailed or screwed to the joists **(13-28)**. After the floor is covered **(13-29)** the walls and partitions can be built on the floor deck.

13-29 *The subfloor completely covers the floor joists and forms the platform upon which the walls and partitions are framed.*

13-30 *The studs forming the exterior wall are laid out on the floor and nailed together.*

13-31 *This exterior wall had this window opening framed into it as it was assembled on the floor.*

Erecting the Exterior Walls

Now the exterior walls and interior partitions are assembled and lifted into place. They are laid out on the subfloor and nailed together **(13-30)**. The necessary headers and openings for doors and windows are framed **(13-31)**. The wall is then lifted into place **(13-32)** and secured to the subfloor

13-32 *The assembled walls are lifted into place.*
Courtesy Truss Joist

13-33 *The walls are nailed to the floor joists.*

13-35 *Oriented strandboard sheathing encloses the building and produces a very strong exterior wall.*

13-34 *As the walls and partitions are set in place they must be secured with temporary bracing.*

13-36 *This house was sheathed with a rigid foam polystyrene sheathing and has been covered with housewrap.*

and floor framing below it **(13-33)**. As the walls and partitions are erected considerable temporary bracing is used to hold them erect and plumb **(13-34)**. The sheathing is secured to the exterior wall as shown in **13-35**. This house is sheathed with oriented strand board sheathing. It produces a very strong wall and keeps it from racking. Other

types of sheathing include a rigid foam poly-styrene sheet with a moisture resistant facing **(13-36)**, a fiberglass sheet with a foil facing **(13-37)**, and an asphalt impregnated fiber-board panel **(13-38)**. When these sheathing materials are used the exterior wall framing requires bracing be installed as specified by the codes. They provide no structural strength but have good insulating properties.

After the exterior walls and interior partitions have been erected the ceiling joists are installed on their top plate **(13-39)**. Like the floor joists these can be solid wood, I-joists, or truss joists **(13-40** and **13-41)**.

13-39 The ceiling joists rest on the top plate of the exterior wall and interior load bearing partitions.

13-40 These truss joists frame the ceiling and serve as joists for the second floor.

13-37 This fiberglass sheathing has an aluminum foil facing. **Courtesy Celotex Corporation**

13-41 I-joists are used as ceiling joists and can span long distances. **Courtesy Willamette Industries, Inc.**

13-38 Black asphalt-impregnated fiber sheets are another type of wall sheathing.

Building the Roof

Building the roof is next. This is a difficult task and requires experienced carpenters especially when rafters are to be used. They must be designed and cut to fit accurately **(13-42)**. The ridge is set and the rafters are run from it to the top plate on the exterior wall **(13-43)**. The amount of rafter overhang is shown on the architectural drawings. This is the key to forming the cornice **(13-44)**. A typical cornice detail is in **13-45**. It is important to install aluminum vent strips in the soffit so the air in the attic can be changed constantly **(13-46)**. Collar beams are

13-42 This roof is being built with solid wood rafters. Roof framing is a difficult project and must be carefully and accurately completed.

13-44 The rafter tails are overhanging the exterior wall. They will be cut to length and the fascia nailed to them.

13-43 The ridge board has been set and the hip rafters on the end are in place. The common rafters are being run from the ridge board to the exterior wall.

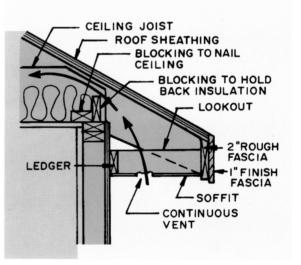

13-45 This soffit detail drawing shows the amount of overhang required and how the fascia is to be constructed.

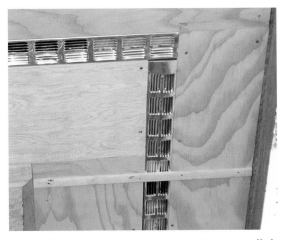

13-46 *Continuous aluminum vent strips are installed in the soffit.*

13-49 *The roof sheathing is covered with builders felt. This roof has 2 by 4 members nailed to the sheathing. These serve to give the roofers a footing and are a vital safety device.*

13-47 *Collar beams tie opposite rafters together to help them resist uplift in high winds.*

13-50 *The finish roofing material is laid over the builders felt. This roof has fiberglass asphalt shingles.*

13-48 *This roof has been sheathed with oriented strandboard. It ties the rafters together and greatly strengthens the roof structure. The sheathing on the walls has been covered with housewrap.*

installed between the rafters providing a cross tie reducing the stress on the outside walls and help the roof resist uplift in high winds (**13-47**). Now the roof sheathing is installed which greatly strengthens the roof (**13-48**). Before it is installed the roof framing is usually temporarily braced. Next, builders felt is nailed over the sheathing (**13-49**). It protects it from the weather and serves as an underlayment for the finished shingles. The finish roofing can now be

13-51 *Natural slate roofing tiles provide a durable but heavy finish roofing. The color is an important part of the overall appearance of the house.*

13-52 *Clay tile roofing has been used on buildings around the world for centuries and is virtually indestructible. It is heavy so rafters must be sized to carry the weight.*

13-53 *Various types of metal roofing are available. This is a sheet roofing with standing seams. This type of roofing has been used on residential construction for many years. It is available as shingles and tiles.*

13-54 *These are wood shakes. They are typically cedar. Shakes are split from logs giving the rough irregular shape. Wood shingles are similar but are sawed and are therefore smooth.*

installed **(13-50)**. Commonly used finish roofing materials include fiberglass asphalt shingles **(13-50)**, slate **(13-51)**, concrete and clay tile **(13-52)**, metal roofing **(13-53)** and wood shingles and shakes **(13-54)**.

Another way roofs are frequently built is with factory-assembled trusses **(13-55)**. The truss is designed by specialists at the plant where they are manufactured. The parts are assembled with plates having prongs bent at

13-55 *This roof has been framed with a scissors type wood truss. It spans the entire width of the house.*

13-57 *These wood trusses have been delivered to the site and are ready to be installed.*

13-56 *The members making up a wood truss are joined with metal plates.*

90° to the plate and are forced into the wood members under pressure (13-56). They span wide distances and on most houses run from one exterior wall to the other. This frees up the interior planning because none of the partitions have to be load bearing and several rooms can open into each other without a dividing partition.

The trusses are assembled in a manufacturing facility and delivered to the site with several banded together with metal strapping (13-57). They must be handled carefully so they do not twist or bend causing some of the connections to come loose.

I-joists can also be used for rafters (13-58 and 13-59). They are available in long lengths and are lightweight compared to solid wood rafters. This makes them easier for the carpenters to handle.

The carpenters can also trim the cornice. The rake, fascia, and soffit can be installed (13-60).

Painting the Exterior

As soon as exterior wood that will be permanently exposed to the weather, such as the cornice or wood siding, is installed the

13-58 *I-joists are also used as rafters.*
Courtesy Boise Cascade Corporation

13-59 *I-joist rafters can span long distances.*
Courtesy Boise Cascade Corporation

13-60 *This soffit has the fascia and rake boards installed and is ready for the soffit and vent strip to be set in place. Notice the framing for the soffit.*

13-61 *The rough opening for the window is flashed and the housewrap is folded over the sides and nailed to the studs.*

painters should appear and apply a prime coat to seal it. The final coats can be applied at some later time. Exterior latex enamels are often used. They are made with a water vehicle which suspends the pigments and evaporates as the paint cures. Brushes and power spray guns can be cleaned with water.

The 1970 Clean Air Act establishes National Air Quality Standards. These limit the amount of volatile organic compounds (VOC) emitted by anything such as paint and automobile exhaust. Solvents in various coatings are one of the largest sources of air pollution. VOC is specified in grams per liter or pounds per gallon. Architectural coatings are limited to 250 grams per liter or 2.09 pounds per gallon. This regulation will influence your choice of finishing material.

Finishing the Exterior

Meanwhile the carpenters are covering the exterior wall with housewrap **(13-48)**. This

13-62 The window is set in the opening and the flange is nailed to the sides of the rough opening.

13-63 The window flange is sealed to the window wrap with a special adhesive tape.

13-64 The gable end and wall around the windows have been covered with wood siding. The second gable end is ready for a layer of builders felt and then the wood siding.

seals any air leaks and provides some protection of the wall should moisture penetrate the exterior siding. Windows and exterior doors can be installed (**13-61, 13-62, 13-63**). After they are in place the exterior siding can be installed. Many types

13-65 This gable end has been finished with fibrous cement shingles.

13-66 The brick veneer is being installed over the housewrap and around the window.

13-67 This stone veneer provides a beautiful, durable finished wall.

13-68 The plumbers have installed the hot and cold water lines for a lavatory and the waste disposal pipe.

of exterior finish materials are available. Among these are wood siding **(13-64)**, vinyl, aluminum, cement products **(13-65)**, brick **(13-66)**, and stone **(13-67)**.

Plumbing, Electrical & Heat/Air-Conditioning

As soon as the building is weather tight plumbing, as well as the electrical system and heating and air-conditioning systems can be installed. This can be done before the exterior siding is in place.

The Plumbing System

The plumbing system will include installing hot and cold potable water pipes to the various fixtures and waste disposal lines. In **13-68** is an installation for a bathroom lavatory.

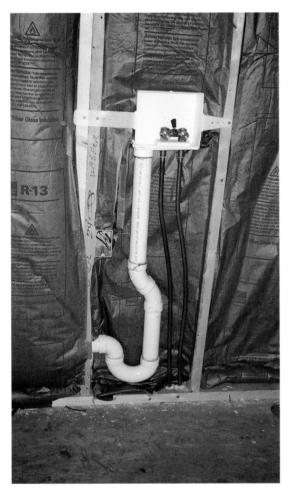

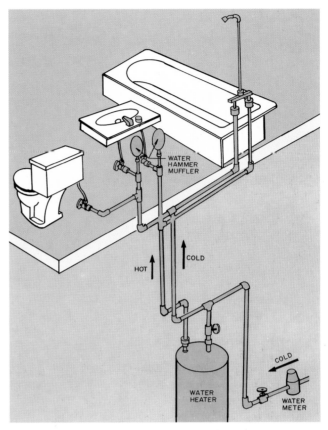

13-71 *A typical piping arrangement for a bathroom.*

13-69 *This installation provides hot and cold water and a waste disposal pipe for a clothes washer.*

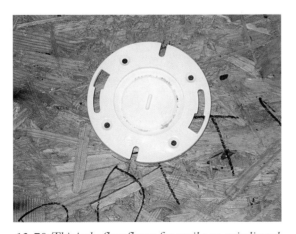

13-70 *This is the floor flange for a toilet or, as indicated on the subfloor by the plumber, the "potty."*

The plumbing for a clothes washing machine is shown in **13-69**. A toilet requires a cold water line and a floor flange on the floor for the waste disposal **(13-70)**. A typical piping diagram is in **13-71**. As the process continues connections with the city water and sewer are made or a well is drilled and a septic tank and drain field is installed and connected to the system within the house.

If a whirlpool **(13-72)** or a large built-in shower **(13-73)** are required some framing is necessary. Then the plumber must provide the water and waste lines as needed. The electrician will supply the electric line

13-72 *This framing is sized to hold the whirlpool. Hot and cold water, a waste disposal pipe, and electricity are required.*

13-74 *This electric water heater is located in the crawl space. It is the center of the hot water distribution system and should be located to keep the runs to the faucets as short as possible. Gas-fired water heaters are also available.*

13-73 *This is framed for a built-in shower. A bench has been built. Notice the raised drain in the center.*

to run the pumps on the whirlpool. The water heater must be located, plumbed, and an electric circuit provided (13-74).

The Electrical System

The electrical system requires good planning and a design and materials to meet the electric code. After the floor plan has been

13-75 *The electrician has to route the wires through the floor joists and up walls and in the attic to supply power where needed.* **Courtesy Truss Joist**

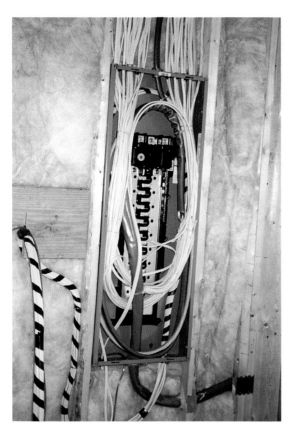

finished the location of electrical outlets, lights, and appliance connections are noted. The electrician has the job of getting the power to the places indicated and installing the wire size large enough to carry the required current (13-75). It is also necessary to divide up these requirements into circuits. Each circuit is designed to carry only so much current and planning must be done so the circuit will not be overloaded. Typical amperage capacities of several wire sizes are in **Table 13-1**.

One decision is locating the service entrance panel. The power from the electric utility enters the house here and all circuits

13-76 The service entrance panel receives the power from the public utility. It is divided into circuits that are then routed as needed through the house. Each circuit has a circuit breaker cutting off the power if there is a short in the circuit.

Table 13-1 Typical Amperage Capacities for Several Wire Sizes

Amperage	Voltage	Wire Size	Capacity	(Volt-Amperes) = 125% of permissible load or 80% of Capacity
15	120	#14	1800	1440
20	120	#12	2400	1920
30	120	#10	3600	2880
40	120	#8	4800	3840
50	120	#6	6000	4800

Note: Compute residential 240V circuits as two 120V circuits added together.

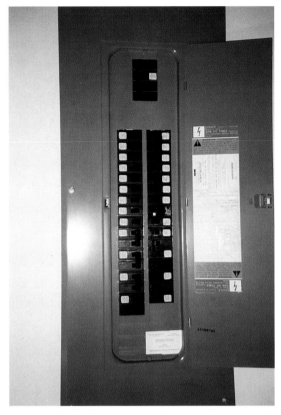

13-77 The finished circuit breaker has a heavy metal protective casing and door. Notice the individual circuit breakers.

13-79 This is an installation for a recessed light.

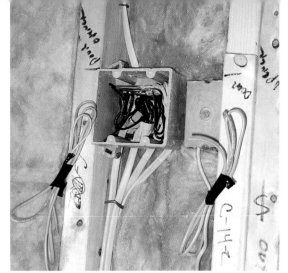

13-78 This electric box will contain switches controlling lights. Notice the notations on the framing made by the electrician noting features related to the installation.

are run from it (13-76 and 13-77). Boxes are installed that hold light switches and outlets (13-78) and various types of lights (13-79). Having a good electrical contractor is very important.

The Heating/ Air-Conditioning System

Warm air heating and air-conditioning systems require that the ducts be installed below the floor or in the attic and register openings be cut in the subfloor (13-80). There are a number of different systems available. In southern states the heat pump is commonly used. It consists of an outdoor unit (13-81) that has a compressor, fan and heat exchanger coil, and an indoor unit called an air handler that has a refrigerant coil, resistance heating coils, and a blower. When in the heating cycle an air-to-air heat pump takes heat from the outside air and discharges it into the house (13-82). The cooling cycle reverses the flow of refrigerant and takes heat from the air inside the house and discharges it to the outside air. Other types of heat pumps are available.

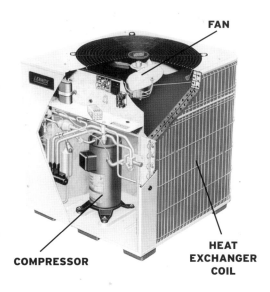

FAN

COMPRESSOR

HEAT
EXCHANGER
COIL

13-80 *This heavily insulated flexible heat duct is*
connected to a floor register.

13-81 *The outdoor heat-pump unit contains a*
compressor, heat-exchanger coils, and a fan.
Courtesy Lennox Industries

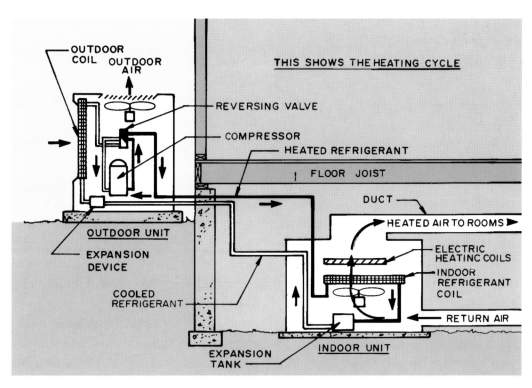

13-82 *The heating cycle for an air-to-air heat pump. In the heating cycle heat is taken from the outside air and*
discharged into the house through ducts. In the cooling cycle the flow of refrigerant reverses and takes heat from
inside the house and discharges it to the outside air.

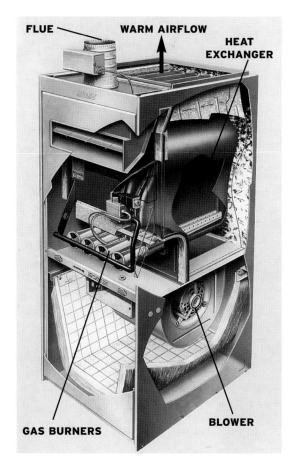

FLUE — WARM AIRFLOW — HEAT EXCHANGER

GAS BURNERS — BLOWER

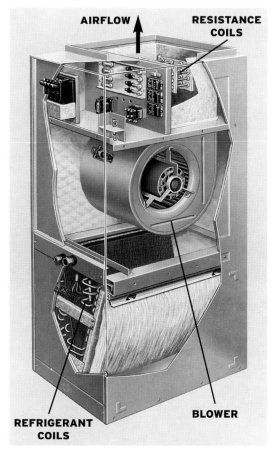

AIRFLOW — RESISTANCE COILS

REFRIGERANT COILS — BLOWER

13-83 A typical forced-air, gas-fired warm-air furnace. The blower moves air over a heat exchanger that is heated by the gas burners. The heated air is moved through the ducts to the room.
Courtesy Lennox Industries

13-84 This electric warm-air furnace has resistance heating coils in the top and air-conditioning refrigerant coils in the bottom. The blower pulls air from the house over these coils to heat or cool the house.
Courtesy Lennox Industries

One places the outdoor coil in water as a well or large pond or lake. The heat is taken from the water to provide heat and in cooling heat is discharged into the water. Another type buries the outside coil in the earth and takes heat from the earth or discharges heat into the earth as required for heating or cooling.

Another warm-air mechanical unit is a furnace that heats using natural gas or propane **(13-83)** or electric resistance heating coils **(13-84)**. Another type of warm-air

furnace is oil-fired **(13-85)**. The oil is burned in a combustion chamber heating the heat exchanger. All warm-air furnaces have a blower that moves the warm air through ducts to the floor registers in each room **(13-86)**.

Warm-air systems have chilled evaporator coils mounted in a housing on top of the mechanical unit **(13-87)**. The furnace blower moves the air from inside the house over these refrigerant coils cooling the air that is then moved through the ducts into the

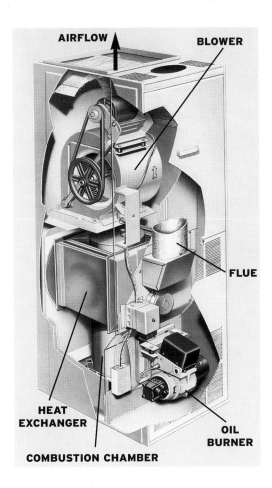

AIRFLOW **BLOWER**

FLUE

HEAT EXCHANGER

OIL BURNER

COMBUSTION CHAMBER

house. The refrigerant passes through the condenser outside the house where the heat is discharged to the outside air.

Another heating system used in more expensive homes in the northern states is a hot water system. Basically the heating unit is a boiler that may be oil or gas fired (**13-88** and **13-89**). The heated water is moved by pumps through pipes to radiators in the various rooms. These systems are called hydronic systems. While there are several piping systems in use the two-pipe hydronic reverse-return system (**13-90**) is a good one and does a good job of balancing the amount of heat available at each register.

13-85 A typical oil-fired warm-air furnace burns the fuel in the combustion chamber, heating the heat exchanger. The blower moves the warm air into ducts to the rooms. **Courtesy Lennox Industries**

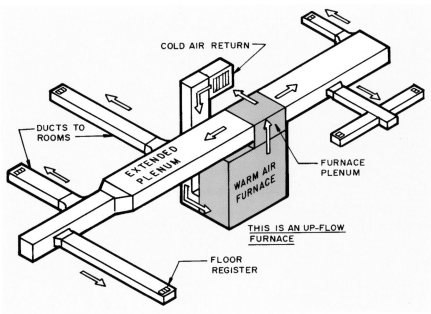

COLD AIR RETURN

DUCTS TO ROOMS

EXTENDED PLENUM

WARM AIR FURNACE

FURNACE PLENUM

THIS IS AN UP-FLOW FURNACE

FLOOR REGISTER

13-86 A typical system for distributing warm or cool air from a forced air system. The furnace plenum is extended the length of the house and ducts to the various rooms are taken off as needed. Notice the cold air return that moves air inside the house back to the furnace.

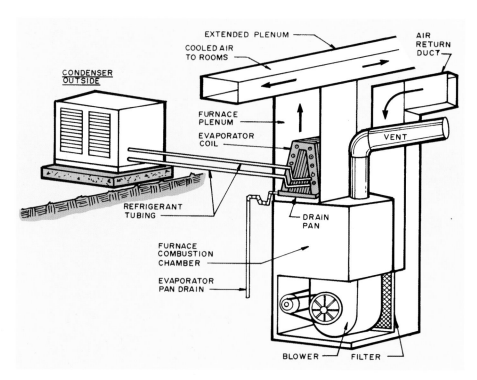

13-87 A typical central air-conditioning system installed on a forced warm-air furnace. It uses the furnace blower to move air over the chilled evaporator coils and into the house through the ducts. The refrigerant disposes of the heat picked up in the house through the condenser located outside.

13-88 This is an oil-fired hot water boiler. The burner assembly on the lower right side sprays atomized fuel oil into the combustion chamber. It is ignited by a voltage electric spark.
Courtesy Burnham Corporation

13-89 This gas-fired hot water boiler heats the water with a gas burner. **Courtesy Burnham Corporation**

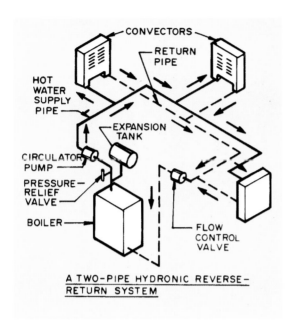

A TWO-PIPE HYDRONIC REVERSE-RETURN SYSTEM

13-90 *The two-pipe reverse hot-water heating system feeds the hot water to the convectors from the boiler with one pipe and returns the cooled water to the boiler in a second system of pipes.*

13-91 *Typical cast-iron freestanding radiators and a section of a baseboard radiator.* **Courtesy Burnham Corporation**

13-93 *This is a ceiling vent installation that will contain an electric fan and a ceiling light.*

Typical radiators in use are in **13-91**. With this system of heating an entire duct system must be installed to provide summer cooling.

Power Ventilation & Supplemental Heating

Power ventilation is another important planning function. Typically power vents are built in the kitchen **(13-92)** and the bathroom. The installation of a room ventilation, such as used in bathrooms, is in **13-93**. It shows the metal box containing the fan and

13-92 *This kitchen has a large hood over the cooking unit. It is designed so it matches the cabinets.* **Courtesy Wellborn Cabinet, Inc.**

13-94 *After the venting unit is installed and wired and the ceiling is in place it is covered with this attractive fixture. The fan pulls air in through the slots around the edge. The dome is a light providing general illumination.* **Courtesy Nutone, Inc.**

13-96 *These radiant heat lamps will warm anything the infrared radiation strikes. They are excellent for use just outside the shower.*

13-95 *This ceiling mounted unit has resistance heaters for quick spot heat and a ceiling light.*

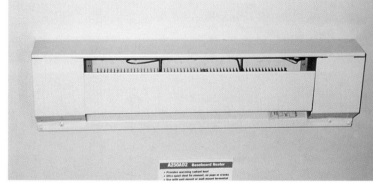

13-97 *This electric baseboard heater is mounted on the wall near the floor. It is used to increase the temperature of the air in the room.*

the flexible duct carrying the exhaust out of the house. This unit also has wiring for a ceiling light so one switch turns on the fan and light **(13-94)**. The lighting fixture is integrated with the venting unit. Each can be wired to a separate switch so the fan will not run every time you turn on the light. Supplemental heat in the bathroom is also important. The ceiling mounted unit in

13-95 has an exhaust fan, a light, and an electric heater. In **13-96** is a ceiling mounted unit that has radiant heat lamps to give instant heat as you leave the shower. In **13-97** is an electric baseboard heater that provides a quick general source of heat. The electrician must know how much power they need so the proper size wire is run to them and the circuit breaker at the service entrance panel is the right size.

Installing Insulation

After the plumbing, electrical, and heating/air-conditioning systems are installed the insulation can be set in place. Proper choice and placement of insulation is a major factor in building an energy efficient house.

WHERE TO INSULATE

All heated/air-conditioned areas should be insulated. Typically this includes the floor, ceiling, and exterior walls **(13-98)**. Cantilevered areas especially need insulation because they are directly exposed to the weather. The floors of rooms over unheated spaces, as a room over a garage or porch must be insulated **(13-99)**. Insulate the

13-99 Rooms over unheated spaces, such as over a garage, should have the floor (garage ceiling) insulated.

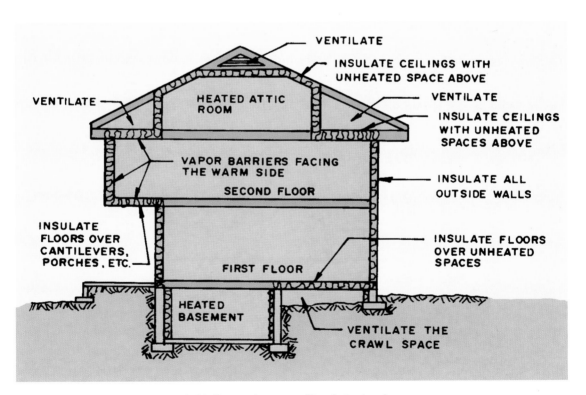

13-98 Proper placement of insulation in a home.

Table 13-2 Typical R-Value per inch thickness of Selected Insulation Materials

RIGID PANELS	R-Value (customary units)*	R-Value (metric units)**
Fiberglass Board Panels	4.30	30
Extruded Polystyrene Rigid Panels	5.00	35
Polyisocyanurate Rigid Panels	6.00	40.5
Polyurethane Rigid Panels	6.25	43
Wood Fiber Rigid Panels	2.80	19
GRANULAR INSULATION		
Vermiculite	2.1 to 2.3	14 to 16
Perlite	2.6 to 3.5	18 to 24
BLANKETS		
Fiberglass	2.09 to 2.75	14.6 to 19.25
Cellulose	3.30	23.10
Mineral Fiber	3.40	23.80
INJECTED FOAM		
Urethane Foam	6.1	42.7

* R-Value (customary units) hr ft degree F/BTU

** R-Value (metric units) m K/W

Consult manufacturers' data for exact values for their products.

foundation wall of crawl spaces **(13-100)**. This is especially important in cold climates. Then cover the ground in the crawl space with a thick plastic sheeting. If a floor is over a heated basement it need not be insulated.

Concrete slab floors need insulation around the perimeter **(13-101)**. If this is not insulated the cold from freezing temperatures will penetrate into the house through the edges of the floor slab.

Kinds of Insulation

Insulating materials are available in a number of forms and made from several materials as shown in **Table 13-2**. The choice of which to use depends upon where they are to be used in the house, exposure, effectiveness, and cost as compared to future energy savings. Insulation materials are rated by their ability to resist the flow of heat, which is indicated by their R-value. Some typical R-values are in Table 13-2. These are indicated on the insulation material so it is easy to compare products on their insulation value.

Insulation batts are available in 15- and 23-inch (380 and 584mm) widths and are 4 feet (1.2m) in length. They are available in thicknesses from 3 to 10 inches (76 to 254mm).

Insulation blankets are the same as batts except they are in rolls often 40 feet or longer. Both are typically fiberglass or rock wool fibers. They are stapled to the studs as shown in **13-102**. Some types have an aluminum foil facing which faces the inside of the building. It reduces the transmission of vapor into the wall. They are also used to insulate floors, attics, and roofs.

Blown-in insulation is typically fiberglass or a cellulose fibrous product that is placed in wall cavities. The product is blown into a cavity created by stapling a strong plastic vapor barrier over the studs. The vapor barrier should be strong enough so that it will not bulge when the insulation fibers are compressed behind it. The cavity is filled by cutting a small opening in the vapor barrier and inserting the hose from the blowing machine into the wall cavity. Consult the manufacturer of the system for specific details.

Loose-fill insulation is available as a loose fibrous or granular material. Fibrous insulation may be cellulosic fibers obtained from waste materials (wood chips and newsprint), glass fibers, mineral wool, and cotton

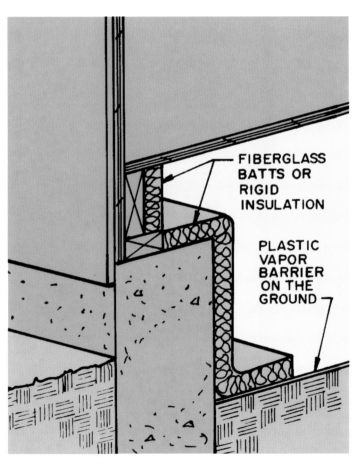

FIBERGLASS BATTS OR RIGID INSULATION

PLASTIC VAPOR BARRIER ON THE GROUND

13-100 In cold climates insulate the foundation walls or crawl spaces. This can be blanket insulation or rigid foam insulation sheets.

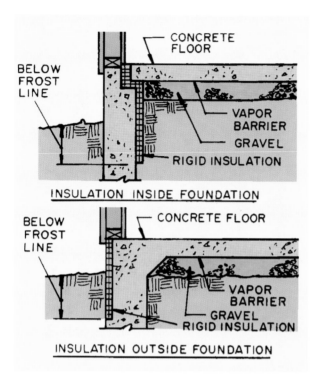

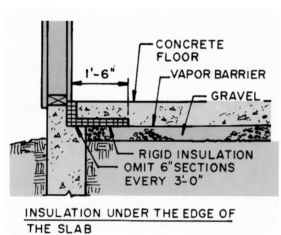

13-101 *Typical ways to insulate concrete-slab floors.*

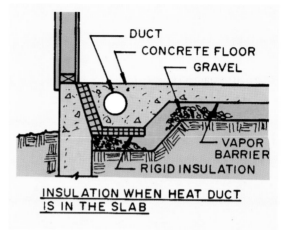

13-102 *The insulation blankets are stapled to the studs.* **Courtesy CertainTeed Corporation**

fibers. It is available in bags and can be poured or sprayed over the area to be insulated.

Granular insulation is typically perlite (expanded volcanic rock), vermiculite (expanded mica), cork, and expanded polystyrene. It is poured into the cavities to be insulated.

Reflective insulation is usually a copper or aluminum foil in sheets or rolls. The rolls are 24 and 48 inches wide and up to 500 feet long. Reflective insulation is available as a single thickness or a multilayer batt that has dead air spaces between the layers.

Reflective insulation is bonded to the face of some blankets and gypsum wallboard sheets.

Rigid insulation board is made from organic fibers (wood, cane), mineral wool fibers, glass fibers, corkboard, and various types of expanded plastics. It is used on all parts of the building such as the roof, ceiling, walls, floor, and foundation.

Rigid insulation panels are available in thicknesses from one to three inches and up to 48 × 96-inch sheets. Actual sizes vary with the material used to form the panel.

Foamed-in-place insulation is a creamy mix that is pumped through a hose into cavities needing insulation. It is generally a polyurethane or phenol-based compound. After it is in place it hardens into a rigid cellular mass. The foam can also be sprayed onto surfaces such as roof decks, where it hardens. The finished roof is laid over the hardened foam.

Vapor Barriers

A vapor barrier is a material used to keep moisture in the air from passing through the surface upon which it has been installed. It is applied to the walls, ceiling, and floor of rooms and faces the heated area. Moisture generated inside the room (such as from cooking) is stopped from penetrating the wall, floor, or ceiling and getting into the insulation. Materials frequently used are plastic films, aluminum foil, and asphalt-laminated paper.

Vapor barriers are compared based on their perm ratings. The perm rating is a measure of the material's resistance to vapor penetration. Codes require vapor barriers have a perm rating not exceeding 1.0. For example, 15-lb. asphalt felt paper has a perm rating of 1.0, 6-mil polyethylene sheeting has a perm rating of 0.06, and aluminum foil vapor barrier is rated at 0.00.

The vapor barrier is installed as part of the insulation process. When insulation blankets are used the vapor barrier can be bonded to one side (13-103). This provides insulation and a vapor barrier in one step. If unfaced blankets are used a heavy plastic sheet is stapled over the insulation providing the vapor barrier (13-104).

13-103 This blanket insulation was supplied with a vapor barrier on one side. The vapor barrier faces the warm side of the wall.

Finishing the Interior Walls

After the insulation has been installed the work finishing the interior walls can begin. Typically this is with gypsum wallboard or some type of wood, plywood, or fiberboard paneling. Another good wall finish is a veneer plaster installed over gypsum baseboards.

13-104 *This is unfaced insulation. After installation plastic sheets are stapled over the wall providing a vapor barrier.*

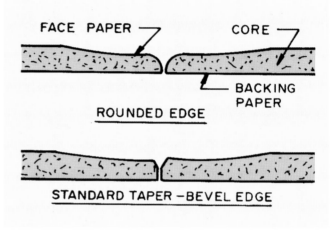

13-105 *Two of the types of tapered gypsum wallboard panel edges.*

Table 13-3 Data for Various Types of Gypsum Wallboard			
Type	**Thickness (in)**	**Width (ft)**	**Length (ft)**
Regular	½, ⅜, ⅝	4	6-16
Type X (Fire-Resistant)	½, ⅝	4	6-16
Moisture-Resistant	½ reg., ⅝ type X	4	6-16
Flexible	¼	4	8 & 10
High-Strength Ceiling	½	4	6-16
Predecorated	½	4	8, 9 & 10

Gypsum Drywall

There are several types of gypsum wallboard available. Consult the manufacturers catalogs for technical information about the sizes, properties, and recommended uses. In **Table 13-3** is basic data about the types commonly available.

Regular drywall panels have a paper covering on each face and on the long edges. The long edges have a taper enabling the joint to be covered and have a flush finish **(13-105)**, for use on walls ½-inch and ⅝-inch (12.7 and 16mm) thick. Ceiling drywall panels are high strength ½-inch and ⅝-inch thick. They are for use on the ceiling. It has

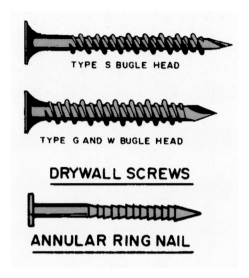

13-106 *Fasteners used to secure gypsum panels to wood framing.*

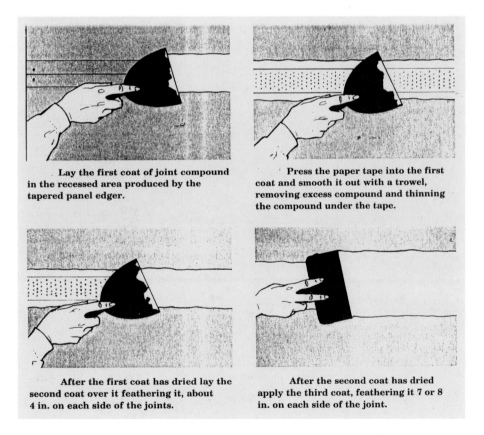

Lay the first coat of joint compound in the recessed area produced by the tapered panel edger.

Press the paper tape into the first coat and smooth it out with a trowel, removing excess compound and thinning the compound under the tape.

After the first coat has dried lay the second coat over it feathering it, about 4 in. on each side of the joints.

After the second coat has dried apply the third coat, feathering it 7 or 8 in. on each side of the joint.

13-107 *The four steps typically used to apply joint compound and tape to gypsum wallboard joints.*
Courtesy National Gypsum Company

13-108 *This gypsum wallboard has the joints taped and smoother with drywall compound. Each nail was set in a dimple and covered with drywall compound.*

13-110 *The drywall compound is being sanded with an electric disk sander.*

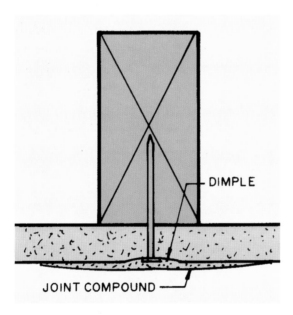

DIMPLE

JOINT COMPOUND

13-109 *The nail head is set in a slight dimple so it can be covered with joint compound.*

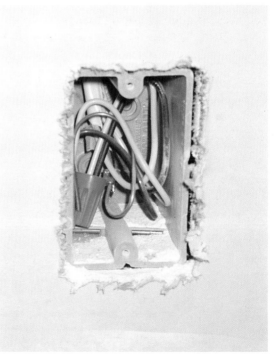

13-111 *The drywall compound seals the opening on three sides of this electrical box but a gap was left on the right side. This should be sealed with caulking.*

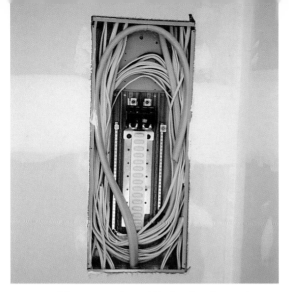

13-112 *The gypsum drywall is fitted to the service entrance panel.*

a special treated core that helps the panel resist sagging over time. Type X fire-rated drywall has a specially formulated gypsum core containing additives that enhance its fire resistance properties. It is used on walls and ceilings where the building code requires a higher fire rating than that of regular drywall. Moisture-resistant drywall is used on walls and ceilings in areas where there will be high moisture levels in the air. Typical applications are in the kitchen and bathroom. It is not used where direct exposure to water or excessively high moisture will occur. A cementitious tile backer board is used in these areas. Flexible dry wall is a ¼ inch (6.4mm) thick gypsum panel with heavy paper faces that will bend around concave and convex walls. Predecorated drywall panels are covered with a decorative material as they are made. This is generally a fabric or vinyl sheet. They are installed with nails colored to blend in with the colors on the panel.

The wallboard panels are secured to the studs with special nails or screws **(13-106)**. The joints are covered by laying on a layer of joint compound and pressing a paper tape in the compound over the joint. After the compound hardens the joint may be lightly sanded and additional coats of joint compound are applied as shown in **13-107**. Another technique is to use a self-adhesive fiberglass tape. It is pressed over the joint and bonds to the wallboard. Joint compound is troweled over it as described for paper tape. Notice in **13-108** that the joints between the panels have a wide band of joint compound. The nails and screws are installed so they have a slight dimple in the board but do not break the paper **(13-109)**. Between coats the compound is carefully sanded. Both hand and power sanding are used **(13-110)**.

It is important that the wallboard fit closely around things that open through the wall, such as electric boxes **(13-111)** and the service entrance panel **(13-112)**. When the wall is taped these should be tightly sealed to block air infiltration into the house from inside the wall. Openings around these will let a lot of outside air infiltrate the house reducing energy efficiency.

Another thing to consider is the finish on the wallboard. If it is to be painted or covered with wallpaper **(13-113)** the paper

13-113 *This gypsum drywall was covered with wallpaper that requires a surface free from dents or rough areas.*

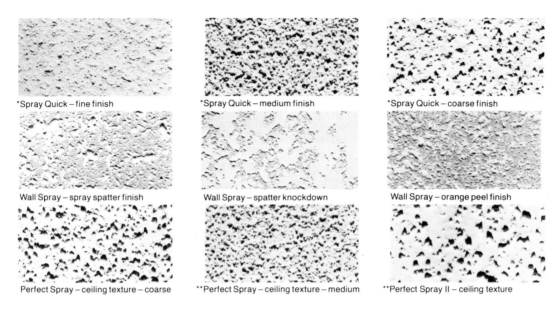

*Spray Quick – fine finish	*Spray Quick – medium finish	*Spray Quick – coarse finish
Wall Spray – spray spatter finish	Wall Spray – spatter knockdown	Wall Spray – orange peel finish
Perfect Spray – ceiling texture – coarse	**Perfect Spray – ceiling texture – medium	**Perfect Spray II – ceiling texture

*Spray Quick medium is most commonly used. Spray Quick fine and coarse are available only in certain areas.
**Perfect Spray medium and Perfect Spray II available only in certain areas.

13-114 *These are some of the textures recommended by the manufacturer of gypsum drywall panels and supplies.*
Courtesy National Gypsum Company

covering provides a satisfactory surface. However, consider the possibility of texturing the ceiling and in some cases a wall. This provides an interesting appearance and can be painted **(13-114)**.

Wood Paneling

Paneled walls provide another good choice for a wall finish. In **13-115** the rich redwood paneling was applied vertically. Subdued lighting gives it a rich light honey to darker brown tones. Paneling can also be applied horizontally or on a diagonal as shown in **13-116**. This cedar paneling shows the great variance between the color of various cedar boards providing a most interesting finish wall. Paneling is also available in plywood sheets having a hardwood outer veneer with V-grooves cut into it to simulate boards.

13-115 *This rich redwood paneling provides a warm, private, subdued atmosphere.*
Courtesy California Redwood Association

13-116 *This cedar paneling has been applied on an angle directing attention to the glazed opening and the scene outside.* **Courtesy Pan Abode Cedar Homes**

13-117 *This natural wood wainscot has been tied into the durable resilient floor covering by a baseboard and molding on the top having a coordinated color.* **Courtesy Congoleum Corporation**

Consider using a wainscot to finish the lower wall. In **13-117** a wood wainscot was built around the walls of the bathroom and a top border of wallpaper. The wainscoting is coordinated with the cabinet doors by

using the same material. The durable, moisture-resistant floor provides a pleasant finishing touch.

Veneer Plaster

Veneer plaster wall finish provides a hard, durable high-quality wall finish. It is built by first securing gypsum baseboards to the studs. It is formulated for use with various types of finish plaster. The special finish plaster is troweled over the baseboard. One and two coat systems are available. The finish coat can be smooth or textured (**13-118**).

During the wall finish process the plumber will arrange to install the bathtubs and showers. Some install them before the gypsum wallboard is in place. The toilet often is installed after the bathroom finish floor is in place. Either way some cooperation is required.

Ceramic Tile

Once the cabinets are in place and the bathtub and shower are installed the walls can be covered with ceramic tile. A water-

13-118 This is a hard, durable, textured veneer plaster surface on gypsum veneer plaster baseboards secured to the studs. It provides protection against damage along the stair.

*13-119 Ceramic tile has been installed over water-resistant gypsum wallboard above the sink. This protects the wall and adds much to the attractiveness of the kitchen. **Courtesy Crossville Ceramics Company***

resistant gypsum wallboard can be in areas where there might be some moisture, as around a sink **(13-119)**. In areas where water will fall directly on the tile, as a bathtub with a shower, cement board panels should be used on the wall.

Installing Cabinets & Fixtures

After the interior walls have the finish material installed the subfloor is usually a mess, especially from the cutting, taping, and sanding of the drywall. Now is the time to clean the subfloor and install the cabinets and plumbing fixtures.

Cabinets have been chosen and the order placed. The cabinet supplier will have been to the job and measured the walls to receive cabinets. Even though room sizes are on the drawings an on-site measure is essential because things sometimes change a little. The cabinets will arrive on the job just before they are to be installed. They should not be delivered before the gypsum drywall has been finished. The dust and considerable moisture developed as the joint compound cures could damage the cabinets. There is also the problem of theft. Anything not bolted down is a candidate for theft. Even after instal-

13-120 These kitchen cabinets have arrived and have been placed in the kitchen. Notice the walls have been primed before the cabinets are installed.

lation some things may disappear. The cabinets will arrive carefully packed **(13-120)** and must be stored in a dry clean environment.

Painting & Papering the Interior

After the gypsum wallboard has been taped and sanded the painters will appear and prime the walls for the finish paint or seal for wallpaper. They also will stain and finish the baseboard and door and window casing or paint it usually with a semi- or high-gloss latex interior paint. The walls might also be painted with a latex interior paint. It has a water vehicle carrying the pigments so water can be used to clean brushes and rollers.

Wallpaper could be applied after the interior walls and trim have been painted. This is often done before the finish flooring is installed.

The Finish Floor

After the cabinets are in place the finish flooring can be installed. Now is the time to really clean the subfloor. The flooring con-

tractor may have to sand the subfloor if it has become wet before the roof was on and has a raised grain. Some flooring materials, such as ceramic tile and resilient coverings, will require an underlayment be installed. A good underlayment for ceramic tile floors is ⅜- or ½-inch (9.5 or 12.7mm) cement board. A plywood or particleboard underlayment is used with resilient flooring. It is also used with carpet if the subfloor is in bad shape. The ceramic tile and resilient floors are installed in bathrooms before the toilet is set **(13-121)**.

Ceramic Floor Tile

Ceramic tile floors are an excellent choice for use in rooms in addition to bathrooms

13-121 The ceramic tile floor in the large bath sets the color and tone for the fixtures and wall covering.
Courtesy Crossville Ceramics Company

13-122 *This family room has a ceramic tile floor that is durable and attractive. The color is similar to a gray mountain stone.* **Courtesy Crossville Ceramics Company**

Solid Wood Flooring

Solid wood flooring is available in several species, including oak, beech, birch, hard maple, and pecan. It is available as solid wood strips, planks **(13-124)** that are wider than strips, in laminated strips and planks, and parquet wood blocks. Laminated flooring is made by gluing together thin layers of hardwood. Parquet blocks are square and have tongue-and-grooved edges **(13-125)**.

The solid wood flooring is installed over the subfloor. The subfloor is covered with an asphalt-saturated building felt that serves to repel moisture from below the house and seal any joints allowing dust to

13-123 *This earth-colored ceramic tile has been installed in a sunroom. It will withstand moisture from plants and foot traffic.*

and kitchens. They are excellent in family rooms **(13-122)**, dining rooms, recreation rooms, and other activity areas **(13-123)**.

Ceramic tiles are available in a number of sizes and shapes. Typically 4 x 4-inch, 6 x 6-inch, 8 x 8-inch, and 12 x 12-inch tiles are widely used. Ceramic wall tiles are not suitable for use on floors.

13-124 *This beautiful wide plank solid wood oak flooring dominates the room and provides a warm atmosphere. The interesting open grain of the oak gives a secondary feature of interest.* **Courtesy Harris Tarkett, Inc.**

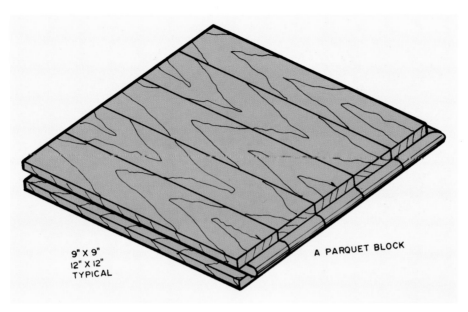

9" X 9"
12" X 12"
TYPICAL

A PARQUET BLOCK

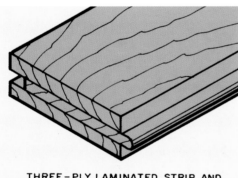

THREE-PLY LAMINATED STRIP AND PLANK FLOORING

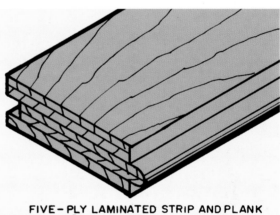

FIVE-PLY LAMINATED STRIP AND PLANK FLOORING

13-125 Typical strip, plank, and parquet wood flooring.

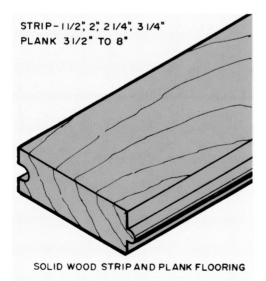

STRIP-1 1/2", 2", 2 1/4", 3 1/4"
PLANK 3 1/2" TO 8"

SOLID WOOD STRIP AND PLANK FLOORING

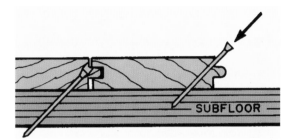

13-126 *Tongue-and-groove strip and parquet floor-ing is nailed through the back of the tongue and the nail set below the surface.*

13-127 *These inlays were made with walnut, quartered oak, and several other species. They provide an eye-catching border and are a great decorating feature.* **Courtesy Kentucky Wood Floors**

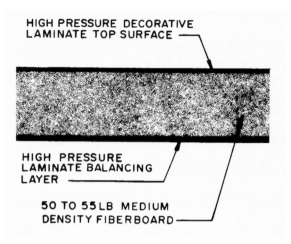

13-128 *Laminate floor covering is made with a high-pressure laminate on the top and bottom and a medium-density fiberboard core.*

13-129 *Laminate floor covering is joined on the edges with a tongue-and-groove joint. This is a patented joint used to secure the edges of the panels.* **Courtesy Wilsonart International**

13-130 *Laminate floor covering is laid in wide strips with the edges and end joints glued. It is laid on top of a foam pad.* **Courtesy Wilsonart International**

penetrate. The wood flooring is nailed through the tongue as shown in **13-126**.

Some wood floor manufacturers produce exquisite inlaid flooring that provides a decorative border around the perimeter of the room (**13-127**). Inlays can also be out in the open area of the room.

Laminate Flooring

Laminate flooring is made by bonding a high pressure plastic laminate to a medium density fiberboard (**13-128**). The panels are

13-131 Laminate flooring provides a beautiful seamless floor. It is available in a number of wood species of different shades. **Courtesy Wilsonart International**

joined on the edges with a tongue-and-groove joint **(13-129)**.

The flooring is installed using a floating concept. It is not nailed or glued to the sub-floor. Instead the subfloor is covered with a foam padding. The laminated flooring is laid on top of this and the edge joints are glued **(13-130)**. In effect the floor is a single large room size panel that floats on the foam pad. The laminate surface is available in a variety of wood species and colors **(13-131)**.

Resilient Floor Coverings

Resilient floor coverings most commonly used in residential construction are of vinyl composition. They are available in tiles **(13-132)** and sheet products **(13-133)**. They are durable and easy to keep clean.

The choice of colors and patterns is great. Resilient floor coverings are used in every room in the house.

Carpeting

Carpet is used in just about every room in the house. The choice depends upon the activities to be held in the room. The living room might use a lush, deep carpet while the recreation room a short pile carpet made with a very durable fiber.

The choice of fibers includes natural fibers such as wool, and synthetic fibers such as acrylic, mod-acrylic, nylon, polyester, and polypropylene (Olefin). Acrylic fibers have good resistance to mildew, aging, sunlight, moths, and chemicals. Modacrylic fibers are soft, resilient, dry rapidly, and are

13-132 This textured resilient floor covering simulates tiles of several shades of brown in several shapes. **Courtesy Manning Resilient Floors**

13-133 This bathroom floor is covered with a seamless sheet, resilient flooring. It is durable and water resistant and available in a wide range of patterns and colors. **Courtesy Congoleum Corporation**

abrasive and flame resistant. Nylon fibers are very strong and resist staining. They are also resistant to mildew, aging, and abrasion, and they are low in moisture absorbency. Polyester fibers have good resistance to mineral acids, and resist mildew, aging, and abrasion. They are not as durable as nylon fibers. Polypropylene fibers (as referred to as Olefin), has the lowest rate of moisture absorption of all the fibers. It resists abrasion, mildew, sunlight, aging, and common solvents. It is lightweight, strong, and soil resistant, and it is less expensive than nylon.

As you consider your choice of carpet realize they are constructed in several different ways. Consider the backing used and how the pile yarn is woven or bonded to the backing.

Carpet is installed over a cushion, which increases the life of the carpet, absorbs noise, and provides a softer, resilient finished installation. Carpet cushions are available made from urethane, fiber, and rubber. They are made in two classes. Class 1 is for light and moderate traffic and Class 2 is for heavy-duty traffic. Some carpets are made with a foam cushion attached to the back. Carpet may be installed over a separate cushion, with a cushion attached to the carpet, or directly to the subfloor **(13-134)**.

Other Things

As a house is constructed many other things have to be built as part of the overall structure. They occur at different times during the construction process and the general contractor has to work out a schedule to get each subcontractor to come at the proper time. Other things occur and are built along with the general carpentry work. Following

1. Carpet installed over separate cushion. This can be done by stretching the carpet in over tack strip, or by glueing the cushion to the floor and the carpet to the cushion.

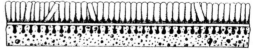

2. Carpet with attached cushion.

3. Direct glue down: carpet cemented directly to the floor without any cushion.

13-134 Types of carpet cushion. **Courtesy Carpet Cushion Council**

are examples of some of the "other things" that have to be accomplished.

Fireplaces

The fireplace may be a masonry built unit that burns real wood and presents a great appearance **(13-135)**. The foundation is poured when the footings and pier footings are poured. The carpenters have to frame an opening in the floor through which it will be built **(13-136)** and an opening in the roof for the chimney. After the roof is on the masons can build the fireplace.

Metal-framed fireplaces are also widely used **(13-137)**. These are like a metal box in which the fire is built. It has a metal chimney, which after it rises above the roof is often boxed in with a wood enclosure. While this is not the best looking situation it

13-136 This masonry fireplace has been built up from the footing on the ground below. The firebox has been completed and it is ready for the chimney to be built.

13-135 This masonry fireplace serves as the focal point of the room and is a great architectural feature.
Courtesy Pan Abode Cedar Homes

13-137 This is a prefabricated metal firebox set on the subfloor. The vent is formed with a metal pipe. All of this must meet local building codes.

13-138 *This ventless fireplace has an attractive wood surround and mantel. It uses a gas log requiring no outside vent. Notice the beautiful multilamp pendant fixture that provides general illumination.*
Courtesy Thomas Lighting

13-139 *The stair stringers are cut from 2-inch stock and must meet building codes. This installation runs to a landing.*

does get a fireplace at less cost. Then there are metal box fireplaces that use gas logs. Many of these are ventless **(13-138)**. The logs are supposed to burn the propane so efficiently that no vent is needed. If you have one install a carbon monoxide alarm and watch your windows and walls for the formation of condensation.

Stairs

The rough stringers are cut and installed as shown on the architectural drawings. In **13-139** temporary 2-inch thick lumber has been nailed to serve as treads so the trades can get to the second floor. After the drywall has been installed the finished treads and risers are installed and protected from damage **(13-140)**. This is not done until

13-140 *The finished treads and risers have been installed after the drywall has been finished. These are protected while other trades are still in the building.*

most of the trades are finished and out of the house. When the carpet is laid the stairs can be carpeted if this is desired **(13-141)** or the finished natural wood tread and riser can be uncovered **(13-142)**.

Decks

At some point during the construction process the deck is built. Often this is a contractor specializing in decks rather than the framing carpenters. Since it is actually a separate structure it can be scheduled at a convenient time for the subcontractor and general contractor **(13-143)**.

*13-141 These finished treads and risers have been overlaid with carpet. **Courtesy Arcways, Inc.***

*13-142 These hardwood treads and risers have a tough, durable clear finish applied. They can withstand normal use without damage. **Courtesy Arcways, Inc.***

13-143 Decks are a major feature on many homes, especially those with a great view of the countryside. This is made using polyvinyl chloride components.
Courtesy Brock Deck'Systems

13-144 *A sunroom is installed after the house is basically completed. The floor can be built as the house is framed and concrete is poured.*

Sunrooms

After the construction has been basically completed the sunroom can be installed. It can be on a concrete slab on the grade or on a raised floor that may be either wood or concrete similar to a porch **(13-144)**. Additional information is in Chapter 7.

Special Cabinets

In addition to the cabinets for the kitchen and bathrooms cabinets of various kinds are used in other rooms. For example, the living room may have cabinets for books and displays. The den will have cabinets for books and records or a large foyer may have an impressive cabinet. As you choose these consider the detailed features available from cabinet manufacturers and how these fit in with your furniture. A few examples of great detailing are in **13-145,** below and opposite.

13-145 (ABOVE AND OPPOSITE) *Cabinets available can have many outstanding details making them an important part of the ambiance of the room.* **Courtesy KraftMaid Cabinetry**

13-145 (Continued) *Cabinet details.*
Courtesy KraftMaid Cabinetry

13-146 This soil was removed and piled when the foundation was dug. It will be used to fill around the foundation and bring low areas up to the level recommended.

13-149 The side forms have been staked and the concrete sidewalk has been poured.

13-147 Often soil must be brought in to raise the level of the yard to the desired contour.

13-150 The driveway is a big job. It is staked and poured in sections with expansion joints between the sections.

13-148 As the soil is brought in it is graded to the contours indicated on the landscape plan. The idea is to slope the land away from the house so surface water drains away and will not penetrate the foundation.

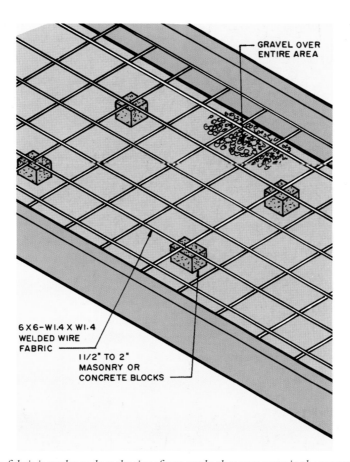

GRAVEL OVER ENTIRE AREA

6 X 6 – W1.4 X W1.4 WELDED WIRE FABRIC

1 1/2" TO 2" MASONRY OR CONCRETE BLOCKS

13-151 Welded wire fabric is used to reduce the size of any cracks that may occur in the concrete slab.

Sidewalks, Driveways & Landscaping

After all the trades have finished their work and hauled away the debris and no longer drive their trucks all over your yard, it is time to do the finished yard work.

The landscape contractor will have a copy of the landscape plan, as shown in Chapter 11, page 282 (**11-9**). The first step is to grade the site to the contours on the plan. This may mean moving earth from one side of the site to another and moving around any soil that had been stockpiled when the foundation was being dug (**13-146**). Often it is necessary to bring in soil to raise the level of the finished yard to the desired contour (**13-147**).

The soil is then graded to the required contour (**13-148**). Once the grades are established the concrete contractor will stake and pour the sidewalk (**13-149**) and driveway (**13-150**).

The soil below the concrete should be compacted. It is best if a bed of crushed rock is laid and compacted. Then welded wire-reinforcing mesh is laid on top and raised an inch or so above the gravel. The wire mesh will not keep the concrete from cracking but will reduce the size of any cracks that may occur (**13-151**).

Now the landscape contractor can work the soil around the foundation and plant the shrubs as indicated on the landscape plan. It is important that the holes are properly prepared and any soil treatment materials recommended for that area be used. The shrubs should also be the size specified on the drawings. If you pay for a five-gallon shrub be certain the one installed is that size **(13-152)**. If a sprinkler system is to be added it can be installed at this time. Finally the yard can be sodded or seeded to start the lawn **(13-153)**.

Many landscape plans call for trees to be planted and shrubs clustered in areas out in the yard. Also driveways and sidewalks often are bordered with plantings. An excellent finished installation is shown in **13-153**.

13-152 The shrubs are planted as indicated on the landscape plan. Be certain they are watered as recommended.

13-153 An excellent finished landscape with a healthy growth of grass and large, well-located shrubs.

Certificate of Compliance
Village of Pinehurst, North Carolina

_____ August 14 _____ , 19 90 _____

This is to certify that _____ D. Adams Const. Co., William Spence _____, having filed an

application on the ___ 13th __ day of _____ February ___, 19 90 _____ to construct

__X__, remodel_____, install _____, repair _____, a ___ Residence _____

at _ Lot 2080, Pinewild Dr., Pinewild _____ Street (Blvd., Ave.), said application having

been duly approved and thereof granted, and said structure now being completed and the

undersigned being satisfied after an inspection of the same that said structure was in full

compliance with the permits granted thereof and with the Pinehurst Zoning Ordinance and the

North Carolina State Building Codes, permission is hereby granted to use the same for the

following purposes: ___ Residence _____

_____

Building Inspector _Taylor Barkley_____

13-154 *When the certificate of occupancy or certificate of compliance is issued you can move into the house.*

Final Inspection

During the construction process the building inspector has checked the construction and installation beginning with checking the location of the foundation on the site, through construction of the foundation, walls, roof, mechanical and electrical systems, finish walls and floors, and finally the finish grades and landscaping. When all is approved a certificate of occupancy is issued. This is sometimes called a certificate of compliance (13-154). This permits the utilities to make the connections in your name and allows you to move into the house. It is also time to change the insurance policy from the builder's risk to a homeowner's policy. A tax assessor will appear, evaluate the value of the house, and send you a notice with the assessed value. If you think the assessment is too high an appeals process is available. The certificate of occupancy is needed to get the final payment on a construction loan and a long-term mortgage.

WOOD-FRAME CONSTRUCTION

There are several structural systems used to construct residences. This is another choice that must be made as the house is planned. As the design process continues consider the cost of each system and the advantages and disadvantages. Possibly some are not commonly built in your area so a contractor might be hard to find. The architect can advise you on this based on his/her experiences building in the local area. Consult various building contractors for their opinions. The local building inspection department staff will also have opinions.

Wood-Framed Construction

This is the most commonly used system for residential construction. It was used in Chapter 13 as the example for how the

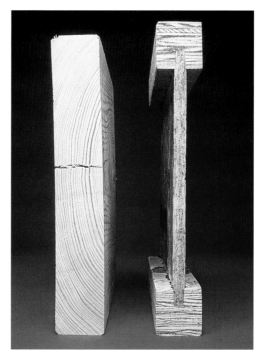

14-1 This shows an I-joist and a solid wood joist.
Courtesy Truss Joist

14-2 *Wood-framed floor joists have long spans.*

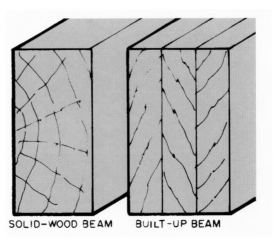

SOLID-WOOD BEAM   BUILT-UP BEAM

14-4 *Solid wood and wood built-up beams are used in floor and ceiling construction.*

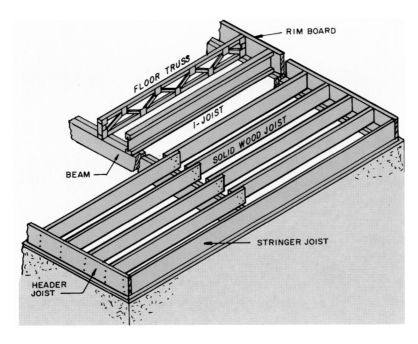

RIM BOARD

FLOOR TRUSS

I-JOIST

SOLID WOOD JOIST

BEAM

STRINGER JOIST

HEADER JOIST

14-3 *I-joists, truss joists, and solid wood joists are used for floor and ceiling construction.*

building is built. Following are additional construction details. The size and placement of the members is determined based on the loads they are to carry and the load-carrying capabilities of the wood used.

Floor Construction

The floor structure consists of 2-inch (51mm) thick wood joists, I-joists, or wood-framed floor trusses (**14-1** and **14-2**). Also see photos in Chapter 13. They span from the foundation wall to beams on the interior of the building (**14-3**). While the joists are typically spaced at 16 inches on center (406mm) other spacings are sometimes used. The beams may be solid wood or built-up

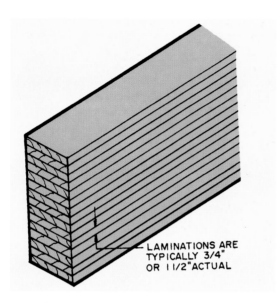

14-5 *Glulam beams are made by bonding solid-wood laminations face to face.*

14-6 *Parallel strand lumber is made by bonding long wood strands with a waterproof adhesive. It is then pressed and cured using microwave energy.*

14-7 *Steel beams are available in a wide range of sizes and types. Their load-carrying capacities are accurately determined by the manufacturer.*

wood **(14-4)**, glulam **(14-5)**, parallel strand lumber **(14-6)**, or a steel beam **(14-7)**.

The joists rest on a pressure-treated wood sill that is bolted to the foundation. The subfloor is laid over the joists and should be glued and nailed or screwed to the joists **(14-8)**. Bridging is placed between the joists. It stiffens the floor, holds the joists straight, and distributes any load on the floor over several joists **(14-9)**.

The subfloor is usually APA-plywood sheathing or APA-Rated plywood Sturd-I-Floor or oriented strand board (OSB). OSB panels are made by bonding wood wafers or strands with a moisture-resistant adhesive. Sheathing grade OSB is used for subflooring. If additional strength and stiffness are wanted use OSB Structural 1 sheathing. Another type available is Single Floor OSB, which is a combination subfloor and underlayment.

Framing the Walls

The wood-framed exterior wall typically uses 2 × 4 or 2 × 6 studs. They are usually spaced 16 or 24 inches (406 or 610mm) on center. The choice of sheathing and interior wall finish material must be able to span

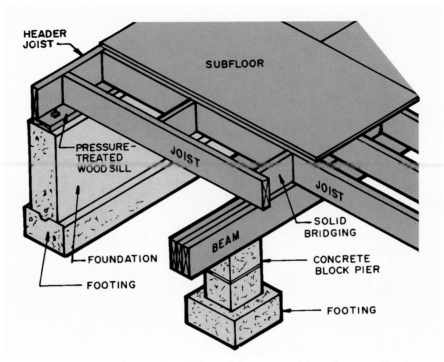

14-8 *The parts of a typical wood-framed floor using solid wood joists and headers.*

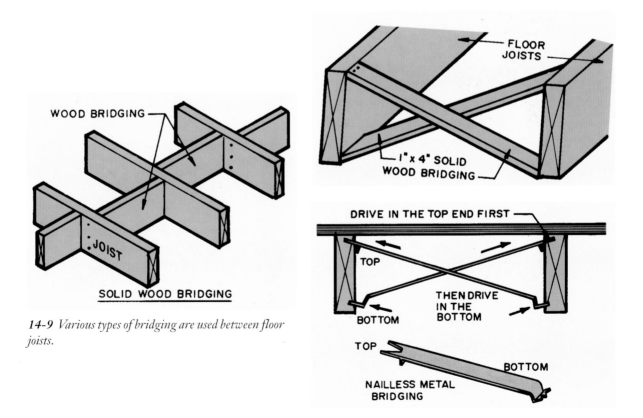

14-9 *Various types of bridging are used between floor joists.*

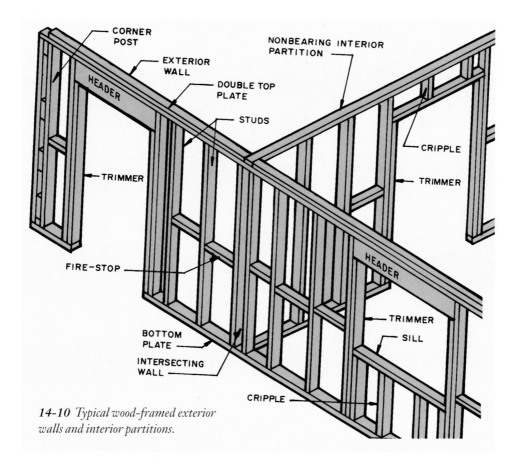

14-10 *Typical wood-framed exterior walls and interior partitions.*

these distances **(14-10)**. Notice the wall has a bottom plate and a double top plate. Nonload-bearing interior partitions can have a single top plate. Openings for doors and windows require a header and trimmer studs. The size of the header depends upon the width of the opening. See Chapter 13 for some photos.

There are two framing methods in use for two-story residences, platform framing and balloon framing.

Platform Framing

Platform framing is the technique most commonly used. The first floor walls are built on the subfloor. The ceiling joists serve

as floor joists for the second floor **(14-11)**. Then the second floor walls are built on the second floor platform in the same manner as those on the first floor **(14-12)**. The roof rafters or trusses rest on the top plate of the second floor wall.

Balloon Framing

Balloon framing uses a continuous stud running from the sill on the foundation to the top plate on the second floor **(14-13)**. The weight of the roof and second floor is transmitted directly to the foundation through the studs. The sill is two-inch-thick material anchored to the foundation.

The first floor joists rest on the sill on the

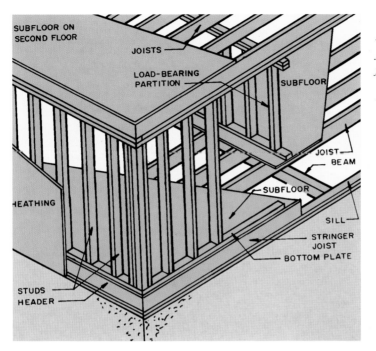

14-11 *Platform framing starts by building the first floor walls and second floor joists in the normal manner. The second floor is covered with the subfloor.*

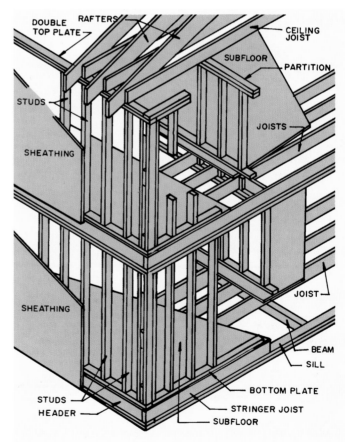

14-12 *With platform framing the second floor walls are built on the second floor subfloor and raised into place. The ceiling joists are installed and the roof is framed.*

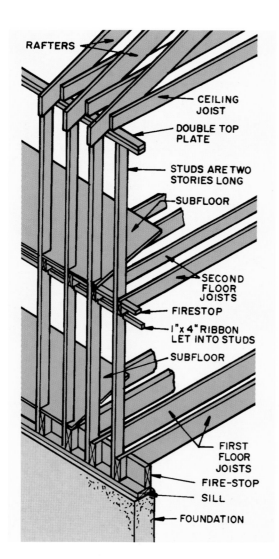

RAFTERS

CEILING JOIST

DOUBLE TOP PLATE

STUDS ARE TWO STORIES LONG

SUBFLOOR

SECOND FLOOR JOISTS

FIRESTOP

1" x 4" RIBBON LET INTO STUDS

SUBFLOOR

FIRST FLOOR JOISTS

FIRE-STOP

SILL

FOUNDATION

14-13 Typical balloon frame construction.

foundation. The second floor joists rest on a wood ribbon let into the studs. The rafters or trusses rest on the double top plate.

Framing the Roof

The roof is framed using wood rafters, I-joists, or trusses. Since there are many types of roofs the design of the structural members varies to suit the type of roof, the span, and the ability to carry the weight of the finish roofing. For example, a clay tile or slate roof will require larger structural members than fiberglass-asphalt shingles because they are heavier.

Framing a Flat or Shed Roof

Framing details for a flat or shed roof are shown in **14-14**. Since most houses are too wide for a rafter to span the distance an interior partition serves as a load-bearing wall.

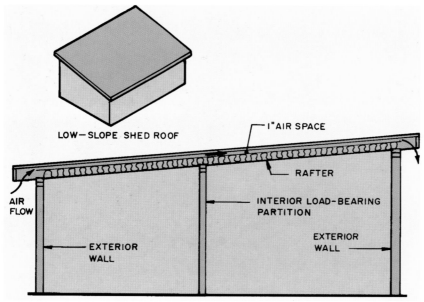

LOW—SLOPE SHED ROOF

1" AIR SPACE

RAFTER

AIR FLOW

INTERIOR LOAD-BEARING PARTITION

EXTERIOR WALL

EXTERIOR WALL

14-14 Typical framing for a shed or flat roof. A flat roof has to have some slope.

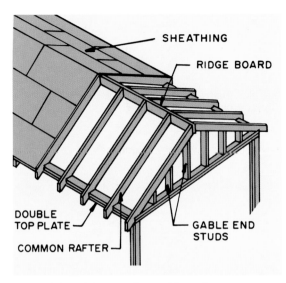

14-15 *Typical framing for a gable roof.*

Framing the Gable Roof

The gable roof is the most frequently used type. The rafters often run from the ridge to the double top plate on the exterior wall (**14-15**). The rafters meet the ridge with a plumb cut and have a bird's mouth cut so they sit on the double top plate (**14-16**). A framing job is shown in **14-17**. Part of the roof has the sheathing applied. See the photos in Chapter 13 for more information.

When some overhang is wanted at the gable end the roof can be framed as shown in **14-18** and **14-19**. A finished installation ready for the sheathing is in **14-20**.

Framing with Trusses

Framing in a gable roof with trusses is rapidly accomplished because the trusses are

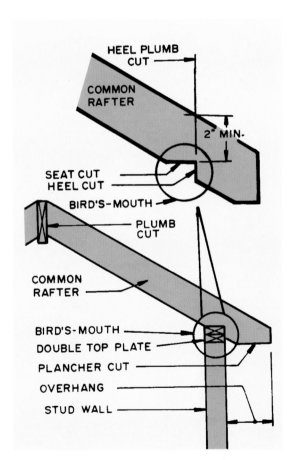

14-16 *The parts and cuts on a common rafter.*

14-17 *This roof has a gable on the front and a hip roof showing on the left side.*

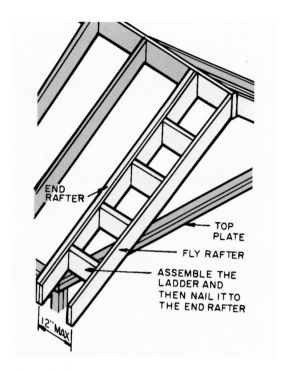

14-18 *Ladder-type construction can be used when the roof overhang on the gable end is less than 12 inches.*

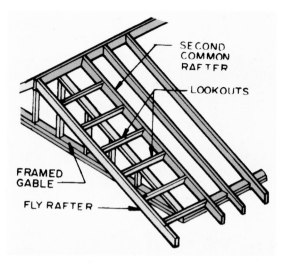

14-19 *Gable-end roof overhangs greater than 12 inches are constructed using lookouts. They rest on top of the gable end top plate framing, which replaces the end rafter.*

14-20 *A finished gable end overhang that is ready for the sheathing to be installed.*

assembled in a factory and shipped to the site. Refer to Chapter 13 for more details. The trusses span the entire width of the building. Therefore no load-bearing interior partitions are needed. They rest on the double top plate and are secured to it (**14-21**). There are many different truss designs. The one chosen by the architect in consultation with the truss manufacturer should be the best design for carrying any roof loads. This can vary by geographic areas because in the northern states snow loads can be considerable and in other places wind loads from hurricanes and seasonal storms are considered. Two frequently used trusses are in **14-22** and **14-23**.

Framing a Hip Roof

Framing for a hip roof is shown in **14-24**. The hip rafters on each end connect the corner of the exterior wall with the ridge.

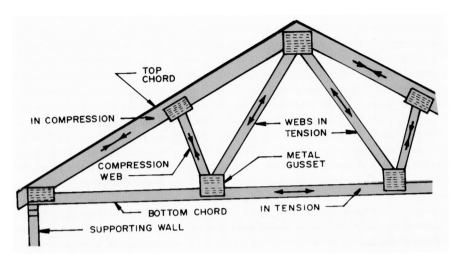

14-21 The parts of a typical W-truss also called a Fink truss.

14-22 A typical W or Fink truss. The bottom chord serves as the ceiling joist.

14-23 A scissors truss produces a sloped ceiling commonly referred to as a cathedral ceiling.

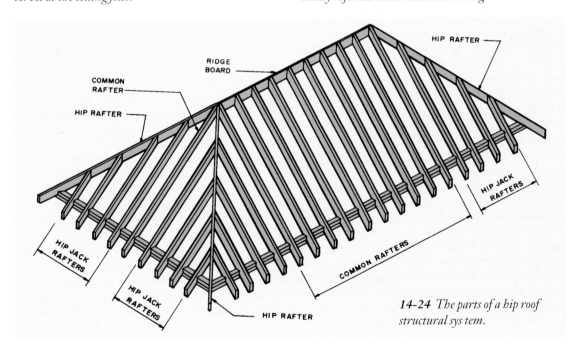

14-24 The parts of a hip roof structural sys tem.

14-25 *Two hip rafters have been connected to the side of the ridge board and one common rafter to the end.*

14-26 *The hip jack rafters have been installed between the top plate and the hip rafter.*

14-27 *The intersection of roofs forms a valley.*

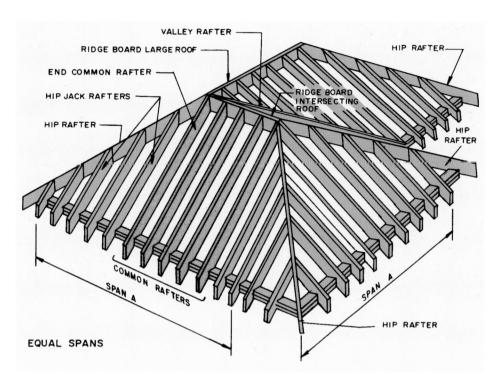

14-28 Typical framing for intersecting roofs for an L-shaped house when the roofs have the same span.

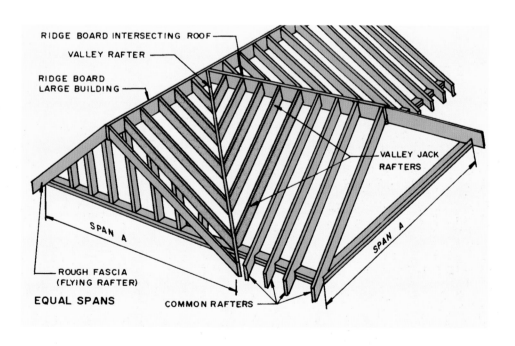

14-29 These intersecting gable roofs on an L-shaped building have the same span.

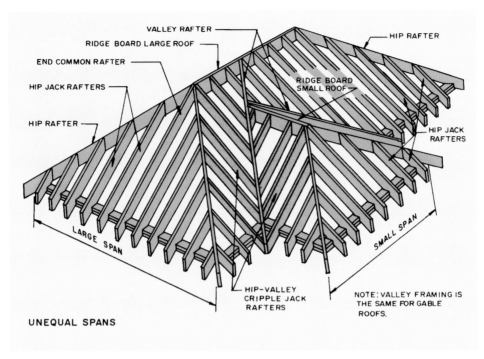

VALLEY RAFTER

RIDGE BOARD LARGE ROOF

END COMMON RAFTER

HIP JACK RAFTERS

HIP RAFTER

HIP RAFTER

RIDGE BOARD SMALL ROOF

HIP JACK RAFTERS

LARGE SPAN

SMALL SPAN

HIP-VALLEY CRIPPLE JACK RAFTERS

NOTE: VALLEY FRAMING IS THE SAME FOR GABLE ROOFS.

UNEQUAL SPANS

14-30 These intersecting hip roofs on a T-shaped building have unequal spans. Framing for intersecting gable roofs would be similar except there would be a gable-end instead of a hip.

Hip jack rafters run from the double top plate to the hip rafter and meet it with a plumb cut. The rafters in the center of the house are common rafters as described for gable roofs. Framing for a hip roof is shown in **14-25** and **14-26**.

Framing Roof Intersections

Framing for intersecting roofs presents the carpenters with additional challenges **(14-27)**. Intersecting roofs over rooms extending out from the main body of the house provides a means of increasing the attractiveness of the exterior. They are constructed as described for gable and hip roofs but require valley rafters to provide the tie in to the main roof. Three typical types of intersections are shown in **14-28**, **14-29**, and **14-30**.

OTHER RESIDENTIAL CONSTRUCTION METHODS

As you plan the residence consider the many ways the structure can be built. Chapter 14 describes typical wood-frame construction often referred to as "stick-built." Following are some other construction methods widely used. Some offer the opportunity to have an exterior that is quite different and that projects a unique image. Note the advantages of each and the use of various materials.

Structural Insulating Panel Construction

Structural insulating panel construction replaces conventional stud wall framing and roof framing. Structural insulating panels, also referred to as SIPs, are composed of a continuous core of rigid foam insulation that is laminated between two

15-1 Structural insulated panels have a rigid foam core bonded between two layers of oriented strandboard. The core on this panel is polyurethane.
Courtesy Murus Structural Insulating Panels

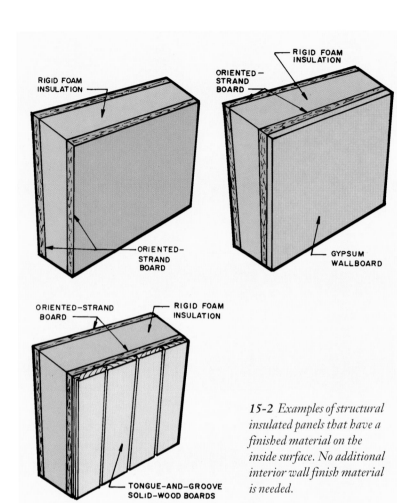

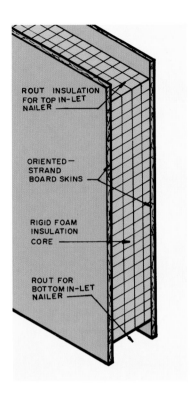

15-2 *Examples of structural insulated panels that have a finished material on the inside surface. No additional interior wall finish material is needed.*

15-4 *Each wall panel has the foam routed out on the top and bottom edges.*

15-3 *The interior face of the structural insulating panels used on this roof was covered with tongue-and-grooved solid wood paneling.*
Courtesy Murus Structural Insulating Panels

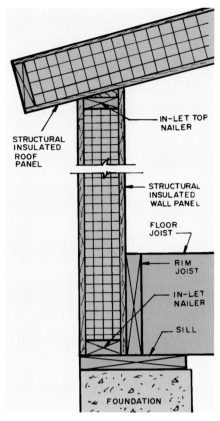

STRUCTURAL
INSULATED
ROOF
PANEL

IN-LET TOP
NAILER

STRUCTURAL
INSULATED
WALL PANEL

FLOOR
JOIST

RIM
JOIST

IN-LET
NAILER

SILL

FOUNDATION

15-5 The wall panel requires a 2-inch nailer at the top and a 2-inch nailer at the bottom.

layers of oriented strand board. They are bonded together under pressure with an adhesive forming a single solid panel **(15-1)**. The outer layers are called "skins."

SIPs vary from one manufacturer to another so it is important to check the properties of each before you choose. Check things like the type of core material, fire resistance, R-value, density of the plastic core, flame spread rating, shear and tensile strength, and other properties found in the manufacturer's literature. The less costly panel does not necessarily have the same properties as a more expensive product. Since they form the structure and provide the major insulation qualities of the house careful consideration of each property is important.

The core material used is usually polyurethane or polystyrene. Each has definite advantages and disadvantages. A choice must be made. For example when exposed to fire polyurethane will char but remains solid. Polystyrene melts and forms a liquid. The char tends to reduce the burning and, when removed from the flame, will self-extinguish. Both types of panels have had to pass rigorous fire endurance tests as required by national codes and meet these requirements.

While the panel in **15-1** shows oriented strand board skins, manufacturers offer a wide range of additional laminations. These include assemblies that have solid wood tongue and groove paneling on one side providing a finished interior surface. Others include a finished plywood panel and gypsum wallboard **(15-2)**. One type has pressure treated plywood on both sides for use in moist conditions. Another has gypsum moisture-resistant wallboard on one side. This is used where ceramic tile is to be installed on the wall. The ceiling in **15-3** used panels with solid wood tongue and groove paneling on the interior face. Other skins are available so consult the manufacturer's literature.

Wall Construction

As the wall panels are prepared for installation, several things need to be done. Each panel needs the insulation routed out on the top and bottom edges **(15-4)**. Two-inch thick inlet plates will be secured in these grooves as the panels are installed in the walls. In **15-5** it shows these plates in place in a finished installed wall.

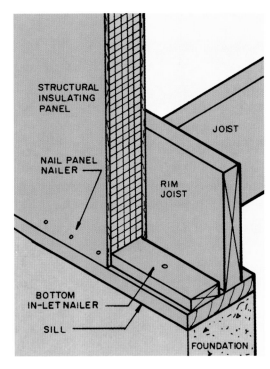

15-6 *The inlet nailer for the bottom of the panel is nailed to the sill. The panel is placed over the nailer and nailed to it.*

15-8 *As the panels are erected they are plumbed, eveled, and braced. The top inlet nailer is installed.*
Courtesy Murus Structural Insulating Panels

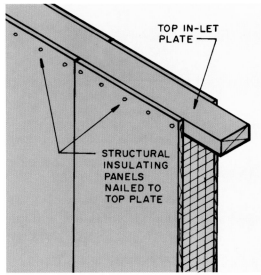

15-9 *The routed opening on the top of the panel has the top inlet nailer installed and the skin is nailed to it.*

15-7 *The wall panels are placed over the bottom inlet nailer and raised into position. They are then nailed to the nailer.*
Courtesy Murus Structural Insulating Panels

The inlet plate at the floor is nailed to the sill **(15-6)**. The panel is placed over it and nailed to it **(15-7)**. As the exterior wall panels are installed they are checked for plumb and levelness and braced **(15-8)**. The top inlet plate is set in place as the panels are erected tying together the tops of the panels **(15-9)**.

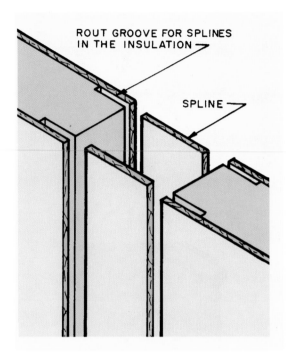

15-10 *Splines set in grooves in the insulation are used to connect the edges of the panels.*

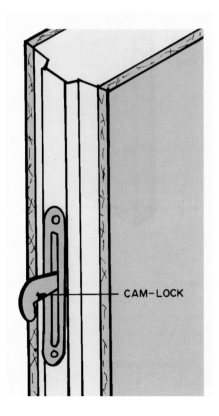

The wall panels are connected on the edges by a number of different joints. One type uses wood splines that are set into grooves cut in the insulation **(15-10)**. The skins are nailed to the splines. Another system has a tongue and groove edge joint and the panels are joined and tightly pulled together with a cam-lock **(15-11)**. Other joint designs are available.

If a panel has to have an opening for a door or window the opening is cut in the panel, the insulation is routed back, and a 2-inch wood insert is nailed in place framing

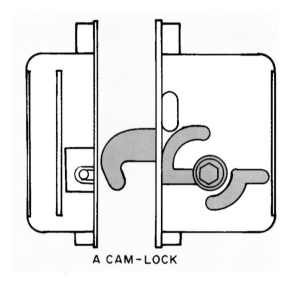

15-11 (LEFT AND ABOVE) *A cam-lock is used to pull these panels together and permanently join them.* **Courtesy Murus Structural Insulating Panels**

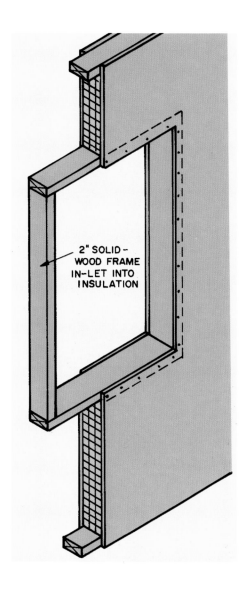

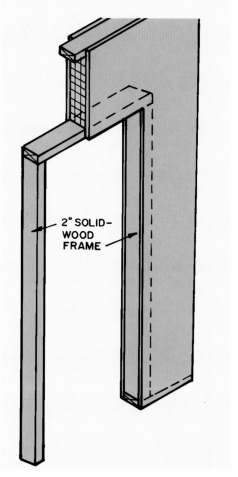

the opening **(15-12)**. If the load on the wall requires a header over the wall opening it can be framed as shown in **15-13**.

Installing a Second Floor

If a second floor is to be built a second plate is installed on the top of the panel. It should cover the entire width of the panel. One such installation is in **15-14**. There are other framing techniques recommended by panel manufacturers.

15-12 (ABOVE LEFT AND RIGHT)*Openings for windows and doors are cut through the panel. The insulation is routed, and a 2-inch solid wood frame is installed.*
Courtesy Murus Structural Insulating Panels

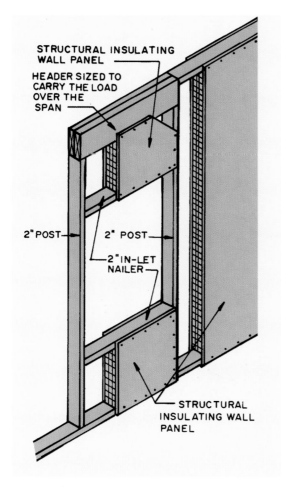

15-13 *This is one way a header can be installed over an opening in a wall panel.*
Courtesy Murus Structural Insulating Panels

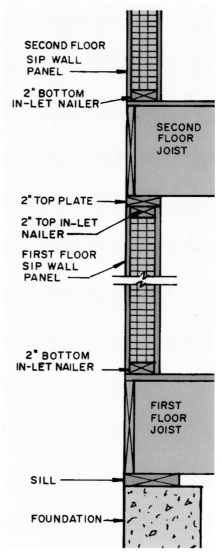

15-14 *Typical framing when a second floor is to be added. Notice the installation of a top plate on the first floor structural insulating wall panel.*
Courtesy Murus Structural Insulating Panels

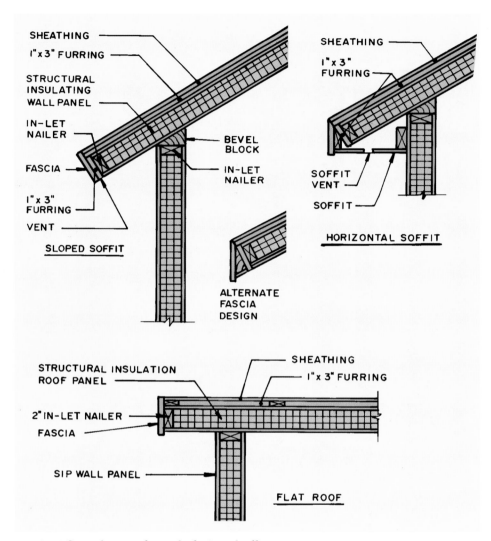

15-15 *Several ways to frame the fascia and soffit. **Courtesy Murus Structural Insulating Panels***

Installing a Roof

The roof rests on the top inlet plate as shown in **15-15**. The fascia and soffit can be framed in a number of ways typical of those used on stick-built houses. The framing at the ridge can take several forms. One is shown in **15-16**. The roof panels can be installed over standard rafters or over roof trusses **(15-17)**. They are applied vertically to the rafters and secured to them with long panel nails or screws.

Wiring

Structural insulating panel manufacturers provide electrical wiring chases and instructions as to how to prepare holes in the insulation for the chases and wiring. One manufacturer of wall panels has chases that are one-inch cardboard tubes that are foamed in place in the wall panel in which wires are run. In **15-18** a chase has been installed behind the 2-inch inlet nailer and provides a channel for the wire to an electric

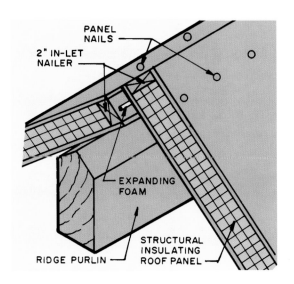

15-16 *One way to frame the roof at the ridge.*
Courtesy Murus Structural Insulating Panels

15-17 *The structural insulating panels can be installed over standard rafters or trusses.*
Courtesy Murus Structural Insulating Panels

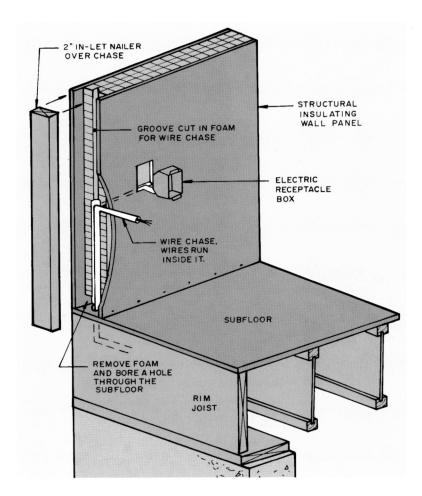

15-18 *Wall outlets have electric power run to them through wires in electric chases in the insulation.*
Courtesy Murus Structural Insulating Panels

15-19 *This large post-and-beam residence uses massive beams and posts for the structural system. They are left exposed and finished a natural brown providing an unusually attractive interior.*
Courtesy Habitat Post & Beam, Inc., 800.992.0121

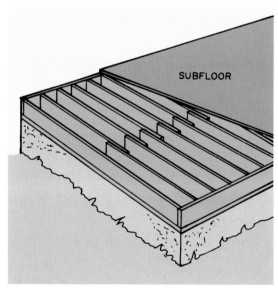

SUBFLOOR

15-20 *This is a floor framed with standard 2-inch-thick wood joists.*

receptacle box. The chase can run vertically to reach switch boxes and in the attic to reach ceiling and exterior lights.

Post-&-Beam Construction

Construction using wood posts and beams has been used for hundreds of years. Early buildings had hand-hewn wood members joined by wood joints.

Currently there are a number of companies manufacturing and erecting these structural systems. Examples of these houses are in Chapter 1, pages 18, 41, 55, 67, and 109. Notice the design of the structural system permits the heavy beams, rafters, posts, and wood planking to be seen and become part of the beauty of the finished interior **(15-19)**.

The design of the structural system can vary considerably depending upon the circumstances. Following are just a few of the possibilities.

Floor Systems

Floor systems are built in several ways. Following are typical examples. The manufacturer of the post-and-beam home you choose can advise you on what works best with their framing methods.

The floor system used could be framed with standard wood joists as described for wood-framed houses earlier in this chapter **(15-20)**. With this construction the floor is usually built using plywood or oriented strand board subfloor. The post-and-beam frame is erected upon this.

A floor system using heavy timber bent girders and timber joists will have the joists spanning between the bent girders. In **15-21** is only one example of how this floor could

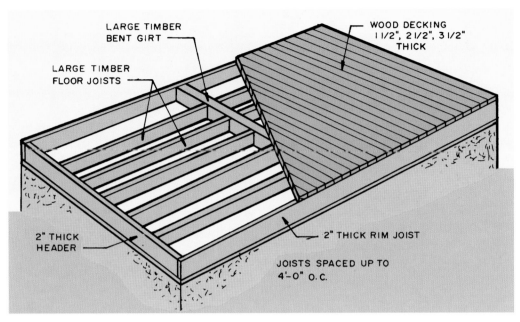

15-21 *One way to frame a floor using heavy timber bent girders, floor joists, and heavy wood decking.*

15-22 *The second floor joists are heavy timbers. They are exposed to the room below forming an attractive ceiling.*

Courtesy Blue Ridge Timberwrights

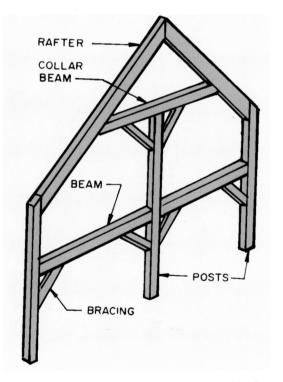

15-23 *A typical timber bent, which is an assembly of posts, beams, rafters, and bracing. They are assembled in a horizontal position and lifted into place with a crane.*

be framed. The design used will depend the span, loads, and location of load bearing interior posts. Framing for a second floor is in **15-22**. These floor beams will be exposed to the room below. Heavy wood floor decking will form an attractive wood ceiling **(15-19)**. The ceiling could also be finished with gypsum wallboard as shown in **15-31**.

Frame Systems

As with floor systems there are a number of ways to build the frame. One system uses bents that are included in an assembled unit containing the posts, horizontal members and timber rafters **(15-23)**. The building is framed by installing a series of bents. They are lifted into place with a crane and secured

15-24 The assembled bents are lifted into place on the foundation forming the wall and roof structure.
Courtesy Blue Ridge Timberwrights

to the foundation **(15-24)**. A series of timber purlins are placed between the bents **(15-25)**. These support the roof decking and finished roofing material. They are often left exposed on the inside of the house providing an interesting architectural detail.

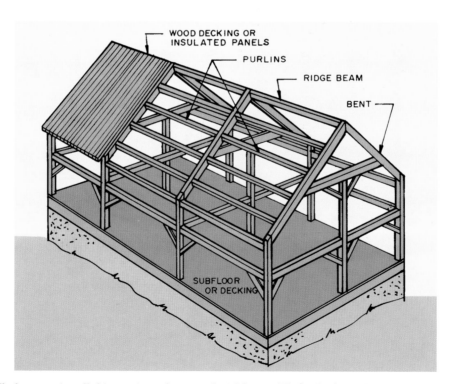

15-25 The bents are installed in a series and connected with beams. The roof is framed with purlins over which the roof decking is applied.

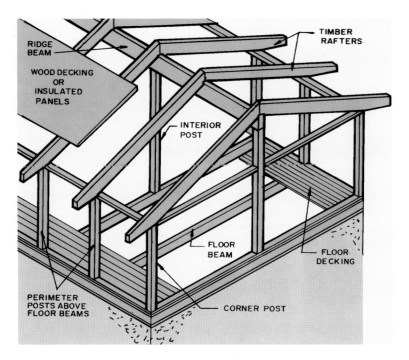

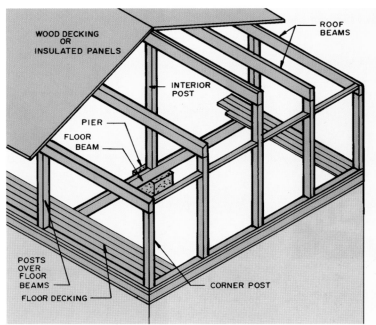

15-26 *This post-and-beam structure has large timber rafters running the width of the building.*

15-27 *This type of post-and-beam construction uses roof beams running the length of the building with the roof decking installed perpendicular to them.*

Another way post-and-beam houses are sometimes framed is shown in **15-26**. Here the floor beams run the width of the structure. The rafters are large timbers spanning from a ridge beam to posts mounted on the outside wall. The roof decking runs perpendicular to the rafters. The rafter spacing is determined by the loads and span capabilities of the roof decking to be used. Another variation is in **15-27**. Here roof beams are

*15-28 The completed heavy timber frame for a one-story home. **Courtesy Blue Ridge Timberwrights***

*15-29 This two-story home is having part of the roof framing set in place. The heavy timbers will be exposed on the interior providing an attractive decorative feature. **Courtesy Blue Ridge Timberwrights***

run the length of the building and the roof decking is run perpendicular to them.

A finished one story home is in **15-28**. Notice the bracing on the wall framing and the roof trusses. Framing for a two-story home is in **15-29**.

The roof is enclosed by installing solid wood decking or insulated panels. The span capabilities of the decking or panels establish the spacing of the purlins. Typically they are from 4 to 8 feet apart. Notice the ceiling in the house in **15-19** and photos in Chapter 1 and the section in this chapter discussing insulated wall and roof panels.

Connections

Generally the joints are some variation of a pegged mortise and tenon **(15-30)**. The mortise and tenon are machine cut and drilled for the wood pegs securing the connection. Some are cut with square cut, which should help transmit the load onto the post. Various types of mortise and tenon and other connectors cut on the wood members produce a smooth looking joint with the method of connection hidden **(15-31)**. There are a

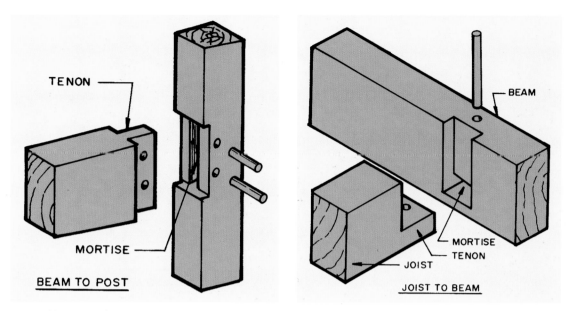

15-30 *Two types of wood joints used to connect wood posts, beams, and joists. Many other types are required such as for roof framing and installing braces.*

15-31 *Connections made with mortise and tenon joints and other cut connections produce a smooth finished installation.* **Courtesy Blue Ridge Timberwrights**

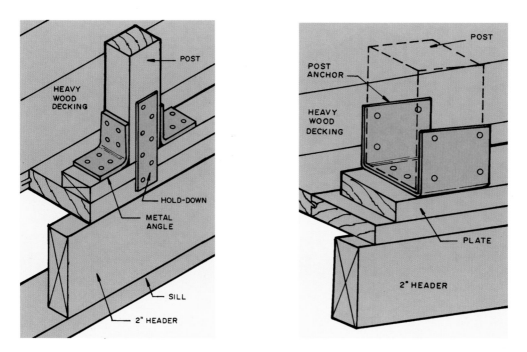

15-32 *One way to connect posts to wood floors or beams is to use metal angles. The hold-down helps the structure resist lifting in high winds.*

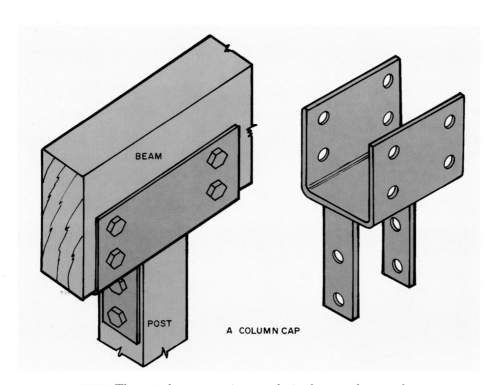

15-33 *The post to beam connection securely ties these members together.*

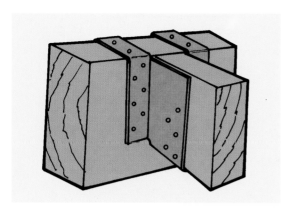

15-34 *A typical beam-to-beam connector. There are a variety of connectors available for beams of various materials.*

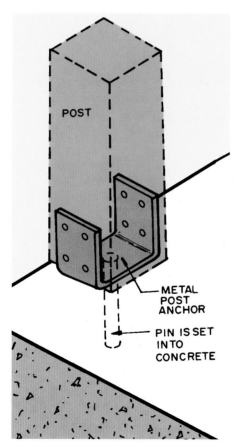

15-35 *Posts are anchored to concrete floors, piers, or foundations with a base connector that is set into the concrete as it is poured.*

number of metal connectors available for post-to-floor (15-32), post-to-beam (15-33), and beam-to-beam (15-34) connections.

Choice and applications are made by those with the engineering background to calculate the loads and stresses. Posts can also be mounted on concrete floors or on concrete piers (15-35).

Finishing the Exterior

There are several ways to apply an exterior finish wall over the post-and-beam frame. One system uses foam-core panels consisting of a core of urethane or expanded polystyrene with a skin of oriented strand board laminated on each side. These are found in

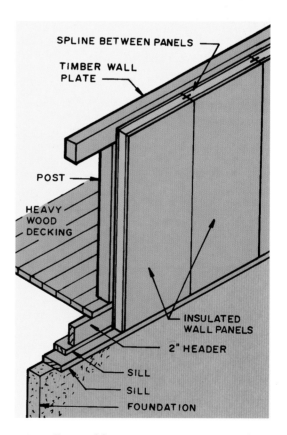

15-36 *Post-and-beam construction can use insulated panels to enclose the exterior walls.*

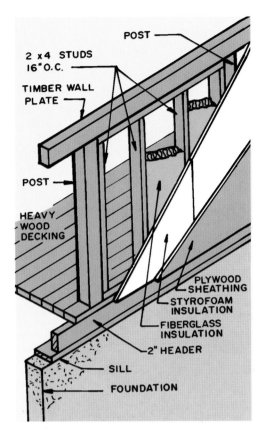

15-37 The space between the posts on the exterior wall can be in-filled with a wall built using 2 by 4 studs covered with sheathing.

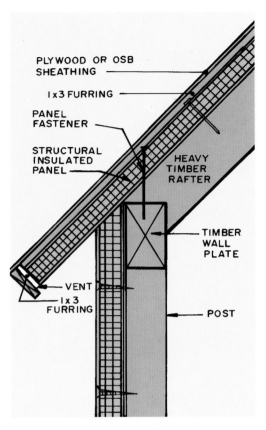

15-38 One type of installation using structural insulated panels over heavy timber rafters. Other fascia and soffit designs can be used, as shown in 15-25.

detail in the section of this chapter. These panels are in large pieces and are energy efficient. The large pieces cover the wall and roof framing rapidly and have fewer joints than when small sheathing panels as 4 x 8 foot plywood or oriented strand board sheets are used. The panels are connected on the edges by splines or other types of joint **(15-36)**.

Openings are cut in the panels for doors and windows. The foam core is cut back allowing 2 x 4 lumber framing to be installed forming the rough opening. The wall panels are then secured to the posts with long screws. The exterior siding can now be installed.

Another technique used is to infill between the posts with a stud wall having openings framed for doors and windows as in conventional wood-framed construction **(15-37)**. The studs are then covered with Styrofoam insulation and oriented strand board or plywood sheathing is placed over this. The exterior siding is applied to the sheathing. Insulation blankets are installed between the studs and the interior wall surface can be finished with drywall or wood paneling.

Other types of exterior wall construction are used by various manufacturers and builders. One big consideration is energy producing a beautiful natural wood ceiling **(15-39)**. The decking is covered with foam insulation and plywood sheathing to which the shingles are nailed **(15-40)**.

Instead of using heavy rafter beams the roof can be framed with standard 2-inch thick rafters, insulated, and have gypsum wallboard or tongue-and-groove wood boards installed forming the ceiling **(15-41)**.

Each of these systems has advantages and disadvantages. Consult the manufacturer of the building, your builder, and your architect as you decide. While differences in cost may be a factor possibly the most energy efficient system would be the best choice.

15-39 *This beautiful ceiling was built using 2-inch tongue-and-groove cedar decking to sheath the roof.*
Courtesy Habitat Post & Beam, Inc., 800.992.0121

efficiency when you select a design. The roof may be sheathed with structural insulated panels, heavy wood decking, or plywood or oriented strand board. Structural insulated panels are secured to the rafters with manufacturer supplied panel nails or screws **(15-38)**. The finish roofing is applied over the panel.

A popular choice for roof decking is the use of solid wood decking. The interior side and rafter beams are left exposed and finished

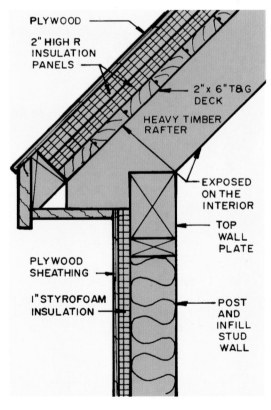

15-40 *This heavy timber framed roof has 2-inch tongue-and-groove solid wood cedar decking remaining exposed, forming an attractive wood ceiling.*

Concrete Masonry Construction

Exterior walls made of concrete masonry units produce a strong, fire-resistant wall that will carry loads many times that of a wood frame wall. Since they are bonded to the foundation with concrete and reinforcing steel they provide excellent protection from high winds. Concrete will not rot nor will it be damaged by termites. Since the wall has considerable mass it also provides resistance to sound transmission making the home a quieter, more peaceful place.

15-42 This concrete masonry has the exterior walls built with concrete block and surfaced with hard, durable Portland cement plaster applied directly to the surface.
Courtesy Portland Cement Association

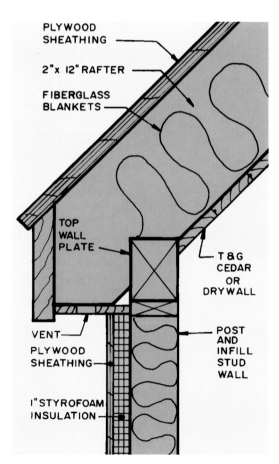

PLYWOOD SHEATHING

2"x 12" RAFTER

FIBERGLASS BLANKETS

TOP WALL PLATE

T&G CEDAR OR DRYWALL

VENT

PLYWOOD SHEATHING

POST AND INFILL STUD WALL

1"STYROFOAM INSULATION

15-41 This roof was framed with standard 2-inch rafters. The ceiling can be finished with wood paneling or drywall.

15-43 The exterior walls on this house were constructed with concrete masonry units with a brick veneer applied over them.
Courtesy Portland Cement Association

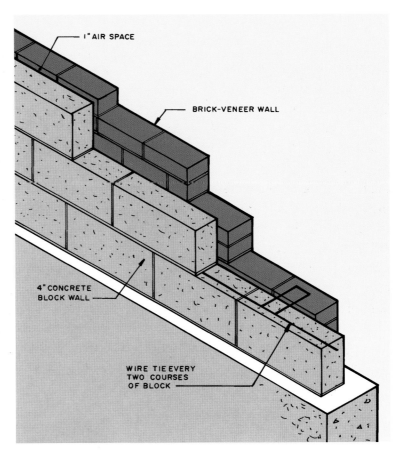

1" AIR SPACE

BRICK-VENEER WALL

4" CONCRETE BLOCK WALL

WIRE TIE EVERY TWO COURSES OF BLOCK

15-44 *A typical masonry wall detail in which brick veneer is applied over a concrete block wall. This design leaves a one-inch cavity between the two materials.*

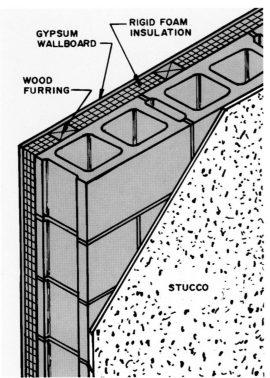

GYPSUM WALLBOARD

RIGID FOAM INSULATION

WOOD FURRING

STUCCO

Concrete masonry block is available in many shapes, colors, and surface textures. A company making blocks can custom build them to designs prepared by the architect.

Typical exterior finishes for concrete masonry walls include applying Portland cement stucco directly to the block **(15-42)**. Split face blocks have a textured surface giving a rough, rock-like appearance. The standard concrete masonry unit can also be faced with a brick or stone veneer or covered with fiber-cement siding **(15-43)**.

A typical wall construction detail is in **15-44**. This shows the use of a 4-inch

15-45 *This exterior wall is built with an 8- or 10-inch concrete masonry unit. The exterior is finished with a Portland cement stucco. It has been insulated by placing rigid foam panels between wood furring and finishing the wall with gypsum wallboard.*

15-46 *Eight-inch thick concrete masonry units were used to lay up these walls. They can be finished with Portland cement stucco or any other siding chosen. The second floor has been stick-built with wood framing.*
Courtesy Portland Cement Association

(101mm) thick concrete masonry unit and a standard size brick veneer. A one-inch air space is left to provide a place for water that may form on the inside surfaces to drip down and weep out of the wall. Instead of a cavity wall it can be laid up with an 8- or 10-inch concrete masonry unit **(15-45)**. The core can be filled with granular insulation. If additional strength is needed the core can have reinforcing bars inserted and then filled with concrete. A house that has been built this way is in **15-46**. The exterior can be finished with Portland cement stucco or some other type of siding. The very large three-story home in **15-47** is built with a structural steel frame carrying the concrete block in-fill walls. This provides the advantages of solid masonry construction and a strong, carefully engineered structural frame.

The wall can be insulated by filling the cavities in the blocks with a granular insulation as perlite, vermiculite, or expanded polystyrene. Another technique is to secure wood furring strips to the inside of the wall, installing rigid insulation between the strips and applying gypsum wallboard over the wall **(15-45)**. This is also a good way to finish the interior walls. It permits installation of gypsum wallboard and wood, plywood, and hardboard paneling.

INSTALLING THE FLOOR & ROOF

The roof is installed as described for wood-framed buildings. A wood plate is anchored to the top of the wall and the rafters are framed to it in the normal manner **(15-48)**.

15-47 *This very large home has a structural steel frame. The concrete block in-fill provides a fireproof wall and greatly reduces penetration by outside noise.*
Courtesy Portland Cement Association

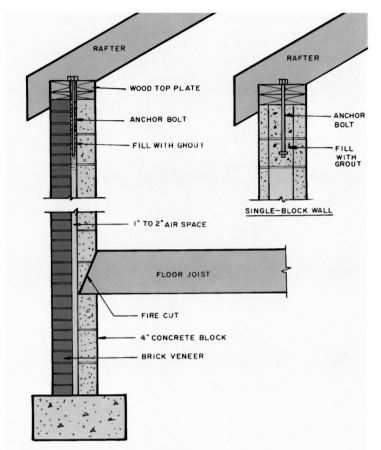

RAFTER

WOOD TOP PLATE

ANCHOR BOLT

FILL WITH GROUT

RAFTER

ANCHOR BOLT

FILL WITH GROUT

SINGLE-BLOCK WALL

1" TO 2" AIR SPACE

FLOOR JOIST

FIRE CUT

4" CONCRETE BLOCK

BRICK VENEER

15-48 This is one way to install floor joists and set rafters on concrete masonry exterior walls.

Cast-in-Place Concrete Homes

While concrete homes are not as widely built as other types they do have some outstanding features to be considered. Obviously concrete floors and walls will not rot or be attacked by termites and other insects. Since concrete does not burn it produces a fire-resistant structure. The mass of concrete is an excellent sound retarder so the outside sounds do not penetrate the interior as readily as with other types of construction. When properly built it produces an energy efficient home. Air infiltration is greatly reduced minimizing the drafts that often occur with other types of wall construction. The thermal mass of the walls conserves heating and cooling energy resulting in lower utility costs.

Cast-in-place concrete homes may be built using the traditional large metal or wood forms or with the newer insulating concrete forms (ICFs).

Cast-in-place walls made using metal forms are cast just like basement walls have been for years. The metal forms are secured to the concrete footing and stacked upon each other forming a cavity into which the concrete is passed (15-49). Steel reinforcing bars are placed in the cavity. After the concrete has hardened the forms are removed. Openings for door and windows

15-49 Metal forms are widely used to form cast-in-place concrete walls.

15-50 *Insulating concrete forms are stacked to form the cavity for the concrete wall. They are secured and braced as recommended by the manufacturer.* **Courtesy Portland Cement Association**

15-52 *This insulated concrete form is reinforced with Diamond-Snap ties.* **Courtesy AMF R-Control**

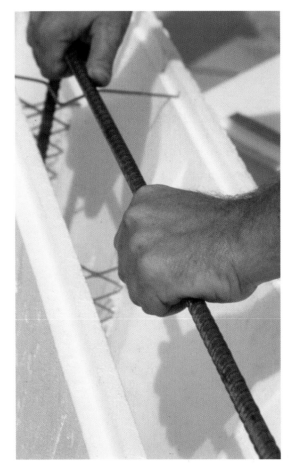

15-51 *Steel reinforcing bars are placed in the cavity in the form.* **Courtesy Portland Cement Association**

are formed from wood members and placed in the form.

ICFs are composed of polystyrene, which is an excellent insulator. The forms are placed on the footing and stacked forming the wall **(15-50)**. The wall cavity has steel reinforcing bars inserted **(15-51)**. The forms have metal crossties that give additional strength. One system shown in **15-52** and **15-53** provides snap-tie connectors that fit on the expanded polystyrene form. They hold the forms the correct distance apart and reinforce them when the concrete is poured. They remain in place after the concrete has hardened providing permanent reinforcing.

As the walls are built they have exterior bracing installed to hold the forms in place as the concrete is poured **(15-54)**.

Openings for doors and windows are framed in wood and inserted in the form **(15-55)**.

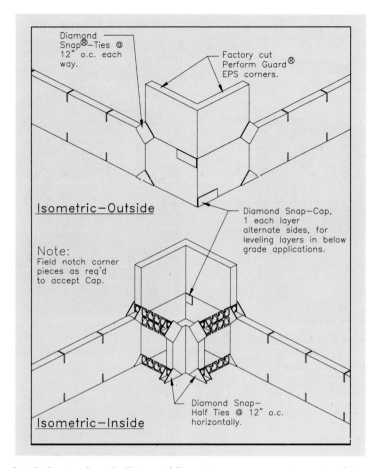

Diamond Snap®–Ties @ 12" o.c. each way.

Factory cut Perform Guard® EPS corners.

Isometric–Outside

Diamond Snap–Cap, 1 each layer alternate sides, for leveling layers in below grade applications.

Note:
Field notch corner pieces as req'd to accept Cap.

Diamond Snap–Half Ties @ 12" o.c. horizontally.

Isometric–Inside

15-53 *Installation details showing how the Diamond Snap tie connects across the cavity of the insulated concrete form providing permanent reinforcing.* **Courtesy AMF R-Control**

15-54 *After the forms are set and braced they are ready to have the concrete poured in the cavity.*
Courtesy Portland Cement Association

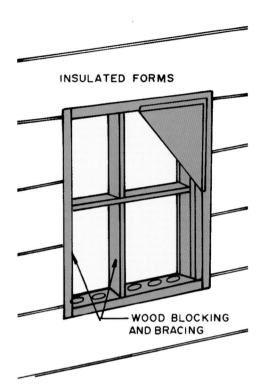

INSULATED FORMS

WOOD BLOCKING
AND BRACING

15-55 Openings for doors and windows are cut into the forms and framed with wood blocking and carefully braced. **Courtesy AMF R-Control**

15-56 After the forms are set and braced and the reinforcing bar has been installed the concrete is flowed into the cavity. **Courtesy Portland Cement Association**

15-57 This cast-in-place concrete house is weather-tight and ready for the exterior finish material to be installed. **Courtesy Portland Cement Association**

15-58 This large cast-in-place concrete home has the exterior finished with Portland cement stucco. **Courtesy Portland Cement Association**

Once all is set the cavity is filled with concrete and properly compacted **(15-56)**. The ICF's remain in place after the concrete has cured and serve as a thermal and acoustical insulation, an air and vapor barrier, and the exterior wall sheathing **(15-57)**.

The exterior can be finished with traditional siding materials such as brick veneer, stone veneer, stucco, or lap siding **(15-58)**. The roof is constructed with any of the commonly used wood or steel framing systems.

Steel Framing Systems

Steel framing has been used for constructing commercial buildings for many years. It has proven to be durable and reliable and an effective framing material. It is now finding increasing use in residential construction. Steel has the advantage of being noncombustible, termite resistant, strong, lightweight, dimensionally stable, has load carrying capabilities that can be established accurately for various structural member designs, is easy to install, and the cost is competitive with other types of materials.

A key to satisfactory installation is to have a skilled construction crew. While it is assembled in much the same manner as wood framing, the means of joining the members is different. It typically will use self-drilling screws, power-driven pins, bolts, and welded connections. Experienced construction workers can learn to assemble steel framing rather quickly. They will be using different tools than when they assembled wood framing. These include electric screw guns, pneumatically powered drivers, and various types of welders. There are special electric saws for cutting the steel and a number of hand-operated cutters and snips.

Structural Materials

A wide variety of steel structural members are manufactured **(15-59)**. The manufacturer provides detailed information about their strengths, and where and how they should be used and joined. The design of the structure should be made by a professional qualified to make the decisions necessary to produce a structure that will carry the loads and meet the codes. This includes the size of each member and the gauge of the steel used to make it. Steel gauges are indicated by a single number, as 20 gauge. The smaller the gauge number the thicker the steel. For example, exterior wall studs may be 20 gauge while the interior non-bearing studs used in partitions might be 25 gauge. Observe the recommendations of the manufacturer and consult designers who have experience with steel framing requirements.

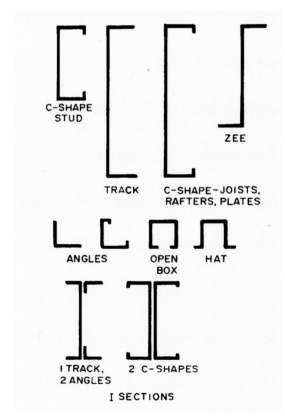

15-59 Commonly used lightweight structural steel shapes.

The Steel Frame

The steel frame of a house is much like that of a wood-framed house (15-60). The steel framing receives the load placed upon it and transfers it to other members and on down to the foundation. Both steel and wood framing systems use studs, headers, joists, rafters, trimmers, and cripples. As mentioned earlier, the major difference is the method of assembly and connections. These will be discussed in this chapter.

The items discussed and the examples shown in this book are typical of those recommended by various manufacturers. There are differences in design and connection recommendations so those presented are general examples. The actual decision on what to use requires the recommendation of experienced steel designers.

Typical Light-Gauge Steel Framing Members

Light gauge structural steel shapes are formed from flat cold-rolled pieces of car-

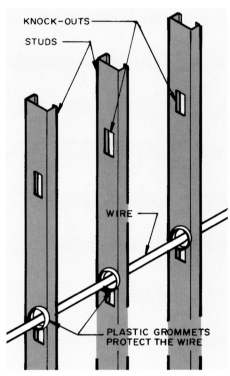

15-61 Steel studs have knock-outs through which electric wires and plumbing piping may be run. A plastic grommet is inserted to cover the sharp metal edges.

bon steel. Typically the gauge thickness runs from No. 12 to No. 20. Some are formed by folding a single steel sheet while others have several folded shapes welded together. They are available in nailable and non-mailable types and either galvanized or primed with zinc chromate. Typical structural shapes are shown in **15-59**. C-shaped members used as studs have openings referred to as knockouts through which plumbing and electrical wiring can be installed **(15-61)** parallel with the foundation construction.

Framing the Floor

The foundation is prepared in the same manner as explained for wood-framed floors.

15-60 This steel framed two-story residence looks much like a stick-built wood-framed structure.
Courtesy North American Steel Framing Alliance, www.steelframingalliance.com, and Schuler Homes, Inc.

15-62 *These tradesmen are laying in the floor joists and connecting them to the perimeter track.*
Courtesy North American Steel Framing Alliance, www.steelframingalliance.com, and Schuler Homes, Inc.

15-63 *This finished floor framing is ready to have the subfloor installed.*
Courtesy North American Steel Framing Alliance, www.steelframingalliance.com, and Schuler Homes, Inc.

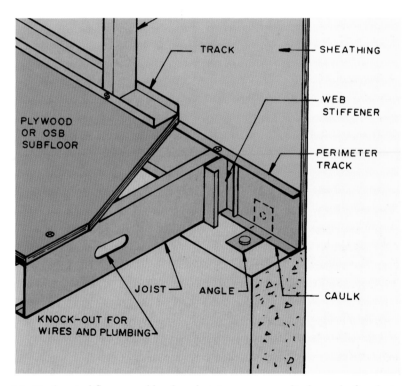

15-64 *A typical floor assembly when the joists run perpendicular to the foundation.*

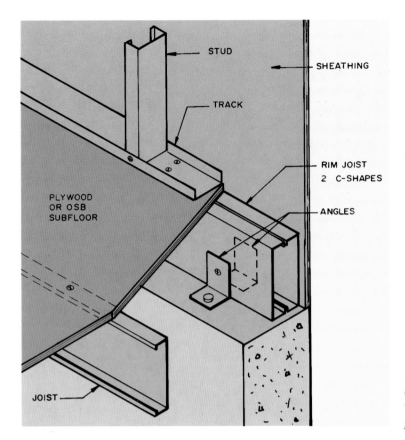

STUD

SHEATHING

TRACK

RIM JOIST
2 C-SHAPES

ANGLES

PLYWOOD
OR OSB
SUBFLOOR

JOIST

*15-65 A typical floor
assembly along the foundation
with which the floor joists are
parallel.*

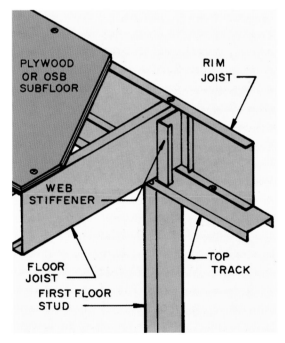

PLYWOOD
OR OSB
SUBFLOOR

RIM
JOIST

WEB
STIFFENER

FLOOR
JOIST

FIRST FLOOR
STUD

TOP
TRACK

*15-66 Typical framing for a second floor supported by
the exterior first floor stud wall.*

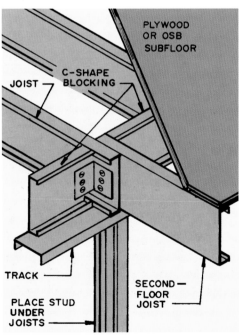

PLYWOOD
OR OSB
SUBFLOOR

C-SHAPE
BLOCKING

JOIST

TRACK

PLACE STUD
UNDER
JOISTS

SECOND—
FLOOR
JOIST

*15-67 This is typical framing for a second floor when
the joists are spliced over an interior load-bearing wall.*

15-68 *These steel floor joists have knockouts through which the electrical and plumbing systems can run wires and pipes. Notice the cross strapping on the partition. This helps prevent racking.*
Courtesy North American Steel Framing Alliance, www.steelframingalliance.com, and Schuler Homes, Inc.

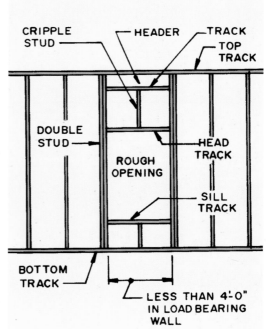

15-70 *Framing a window opening with a width of less than 4'-0" in a load-bearing wall.*

15-69 *A steel stud wall assembled with the top and bottom track. Notice the strap bracing.*
Courtesy North American Steel Framing Alliance, www.steelframingalliance.com, and Schuler Homes, Inc.

The floor joists run from the foundation to a beam when the span exceeds that capacity of the joist. See Fig. **15-62** and **15-63**.

A typical detail when the floor joists run perpendicular to the foundation is in **15-64**. The perimeter track is secured to the foundation with an angle. The joists are C-shaped members joined to the track with screws. A C-shaped web stiffener is installed between the flanges of the track.

Where the joists run parallel with the foundation construction like that in **15-65** is typical. In both examples notice the track for the wall studs is directly over the floor track or C-shaped rim joist.

If the house has a second floor the framing at the exterior wall could be like that shown in **15-66**. When the second floor joist is supported by a load-bearing interior partition construction as shown in **15-67** is typical. A view from below second floor

15-71 Typical headers used on small windows.
Courtesy North American Steel Framing Alliance,
www.steelframingalliance.com, and Schuler Homes, Inc.

15-72 Typical header and sill framing for a wide window.
Courtesy North American Steel Framing Alliance,
www.steelframingalliance.com and Schuler Homes, Inc.

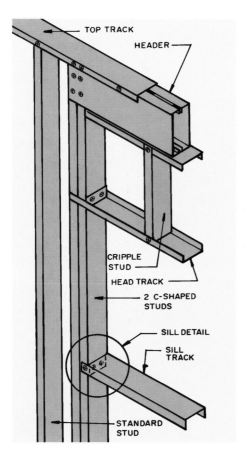

15-73 A typical framing detail for a header and sill.

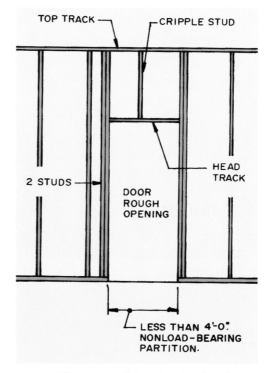

15-74 This is a typical framing plan for a door opening less than 4'-0" wide in a nonload-bearing partition.

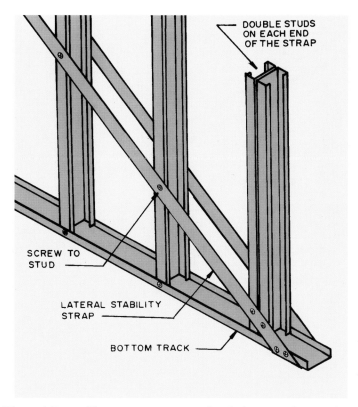

15-75 The steel diagonal bracing straps as screwed to the bottom and top tracks and each stud.

joists is in **15-68**. Notice the bridging running through one row of knockouts stabilizing the floor. They also serve as ceiling joists.

Framing the Walls

Steel studs are assembled in much the same way as wood studs **(15-69)**. The difference is the methods used to secure them to the bottom and top tracks.

The layout for a typical exterior wall with an opening is in **15-70**. This example is for windows with an opening less than four-feet wide. Sizing of members for this and larger door and window openings must be decided by an engineer knowledgeable in light steel structural framing. Notice the headers over the small windows in **15-71**.

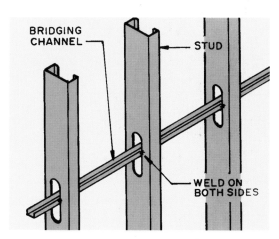

15-76 Bridging is installed to help prevent the studs from bending and control rotation of the flanges. This is only one type of bridging used.

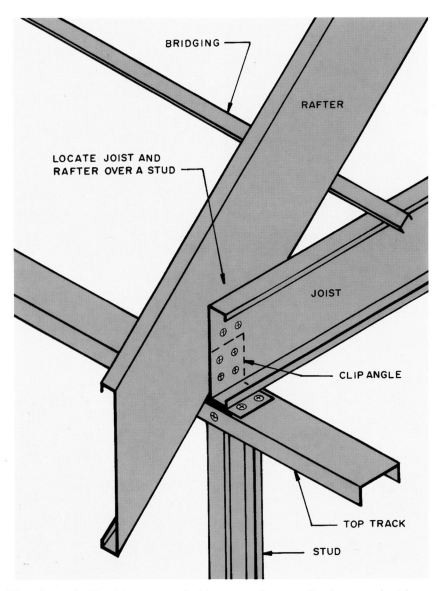

15-77 The rafter and ceiling joist are secured with screws and connected to the top track with a metal angle.

Openings in wide load-bearing walls require a header be installed **(15-72)**. Typical details for construction of the header and sill are in **15-73**. A typical framing plan for a door opening in a nonload-bearing interior partition is in **15-74**. In a load-bearing wall it would have a header shown for windows.

Exterior walls are braced with steel diagonal straps as shown in **15-71**. They run from the bottom track to the top wall track. A detail is in **15-75**. Bridging is installed about midway in the height of the stud wall. It provides lateral bracing, which prevents the studs from bending and restricts rotation of the flanges **(15-76)**.

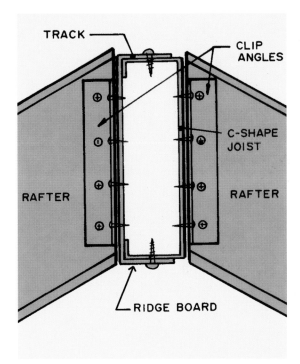

Framing the Roof

The roof may be framed with C-shaped members, such as rafters or a factory-assembled truss. A typical rafter detail at the top wall track is in **15-77**. The rafters can be secured to a ridge board made from a joist and track as shown in **15-78**. A typical installation is in **15-79**.

A typical king post truss is shown in **15-80**. The design must be prepared by a qualified structural engineer. It is often secured to the top wall track as shown in **15-81** and **15-82**.

15-78 One way to form the ridge is to assemble two sections of track. The rafters are connected to the ridge with angles.

15-79 This finisher rafter installation shows the rafters and ceiling joist screwed together and secured to the top track. **Courtesy North American Steel Framing Alliance, www.steelframingalliance.com, and Schuler Homes, Inc.**

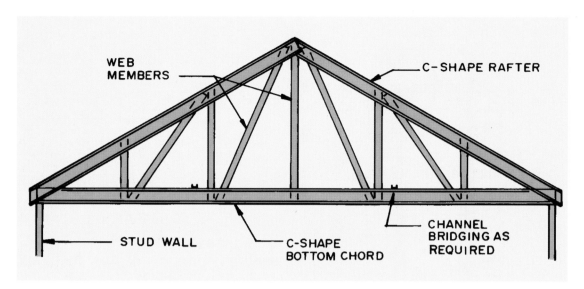

15-80 *A king post truss is often used with steel framing.*

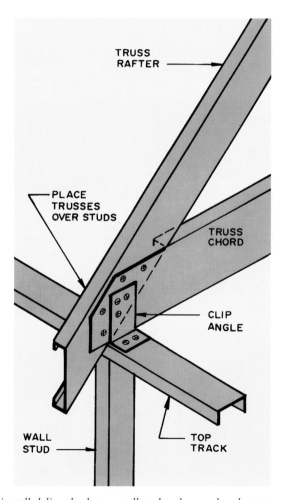

15-81 *Trusses are installed directly above a wall stud and secured to the top track with a clip angle.*

15-82 *This close-up view shows the assembly of steel framing members making up a roof truss.*
Courtesy North American Steel Framing Alliance, www.steelframingalliance.com, and Schuler Homes, Inc.

Sheathing the Walls & Finishing the Interior

Typical sheathing materials include plywood, oriented strand board, and gypsum sheathing. Plywood and oriented strand board are widely used because they add considerable structural strength to the wall. Gypsum sheathing increases the fire rating of the walls.

Sheathing is installed by screwing it to the studs, rafters, tracks, and columns. The sheathing should be flashed and sealed where it meets other surfaces. Masonry stucco and other commonly available exterior finish materials are applied as is customary.

Interior walls are usually finished by screwing gypsum wallboard panels to the studs. Other materials, such as wood or plywood paneling, are also used. Construction is similar to wood-framed houses.

ENERGY EFFICIENCY & GLAZING

Whether the homeowner has decided on wood-frame construction or another construction method, the energy efficiency of the home is a prime consideration. As plans are being drawn up for the design or remodeling of a house, any decisions that are made related to glazing for windows and doors will impact the energy efficiency of the home. Proper considerations of the glazing will not only save energy costs, but make the rooms more comfortable for the occupants in all seasons.

In the winters the glazing must reduce the heat loss to the exterior and, in the summer, reduce heat gain to the interior. In addition to windows, doors that have considerable glazing, such as patio or French doors **(16-1** and **16-2)**, are important to consider.

Types of Glass

There are a number of choices of glazing materials. Improvements in glazing materials have affected not only energy efficiency, but visible and ultraviolet light tranmittance as well as fire resistance. Standard doors and windows will have certain types of glazing specified. Some manufacturers will custom-build doors and windows and can then install glazing materials, such as spectrally selective or reflective glass. The advantages and disadvantages for the common types of glass should be considered as decisions are made. Following is information about the process of glass-making and the various common types of glass available, including float (annealed) glass, tempered glass, heat-treated glass, tinted glass, spectrally selective glass, and reflective glass.

16-1 These patio doors have a large glazed area that has energy-efficient glazing to reduce heat transfer through the glass. **Courtesy Therma-Tru Doors**

FLOAT (ANNEALED) GLASS

There are several types of glass manufactured. The type that is typically used in doors and windows—including insulating, reflective, and tinted glass—is a soda-lime-silica type. It is the least desirable because, when it is struck, it will shatter into sharp fragments, and it does not perform well under low temperatures or rapid temperature changes. It is not used in large pieces on doors and, in some cases, its use may be prohibited.

The type of glass used for windows and doors is float glass. It is made by floating the molten glass across a bath of molten tin. This produces a smooth, flat surface. It moves into an annealing lehr (oven) where the temperature is carefully lowered; it cools and rolls out in a long sheet, which is

16-2 French or patio doors should have adequate energy efficiency to minimize heat transfer through the large glass area. **Courtesy Weather Shield Manufacturing Company**

cut into the desired sizes. This process is called annealing, and float glass is often referred to as annealed glass.

TEMPERED & HEAT-TREATED GLASS

Tempered glass is used when standard annealed glass is not strong enough. Tempering involves raising the temperature of the glass almost to the softening point and then chilling it by blowing jets of cold air on both sides. Tempered glass is three to five times as resistant to damage as standard annealed glass. If it is broken, it falls in rounded, rather smooth pieces, reducing the danger of serious cuts.

Heat-treated glass is strengthened by heating and is then cooled as described for tempered glass. It has about the same strength as that of standard annealed glass.

TINTED GLASS

Glass is tinted by color-producing ingredients that are added to the molten glass in the glass-making furnace. The color is not a surface coating, but is consistent throughout the thickness of the glass. The color may vary some with the thickness of the glass. The degree of tint affects the solar-heat gain, light transmittance, and other properties. For each color and thickness of glass, the manufacturer provides specifications of such data.

The tint absorbs some the natural light and solar heat. In doing so, it reduces glare within the room from brilliant sunlight and reduces the transmission of solar heat.

Tinted glass has adequate transparency from the inside looking out. During the day it provides some privacy when viewed from the outside of the house. At night it is difficult to see outside from the inside and easier to see inside from the outside.

Tinted glass is made to absorb selected parts of, or all of the solar spectrum, and, therefore, to absorb heat. This heat develops within the glass, raising its temperature. A lot of this heat is radiated and then convected into the room, so that the amount of solar-heat reduction is not as great as with other types of glazing. It is much better at reducing glare than reducing heat.

SPECTRALLY SELECTIVE GLASS

Spectrally selective glass is a coated glass with optical properties that are transparent to selected wavelengths of energy and reflective to others. Such glass is transparent to visible light and reflective to shortwave and long-wave infrared radiation. Spectrally selective coatings filter out 40 to 70 percent of the heat that normally would be transmitted through clear glass, yet allow the full amount of natural light into the house.

REFLECTIVE GLASS

Reflective glass has one surface covered with thin transparent layers of metallic film. The film is placed on the inside surface of the glass on single-glazed lights and, on double-glazed lights, on the side of the inside glass that faces the exterior—thus, it is inside the airspace cavity.

Reflective glass reduces the amount of solar energy transmitted through the glass. Typically 85 to 90 percent of solar energy is reflected to the outside. Reflective coatings reduce invisible, as well as visible, light transmittance into the house. From the outside,

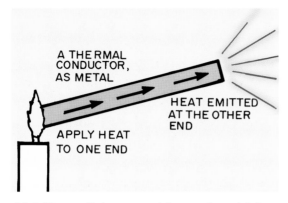

16-3 *Heat applied to a material moves through it by conduction.*

energy is transmitted particle to particle through the material without actual displacement of the particles **(16-3)**. Heat will pass through the door stiles, rails, panels, glazing, and frame by conduction. The greater the temperature difference between the exterior and interior air the faster the heat will be conducted.

Glass is a good thermal conductor, so it is especially important to use energy-efficient glazing to reduce heat-loss. A single glass pane may have only a few degrees difference between its outside surface temperature and the inside surface temperature. In cold weather this glass will conduct considerable heat out of the house and, in the summer, conduct heat inside **(16-4)**. This increases energy costs and occupant discomfort. You can control

doors with reflective glass appear to be mirrors because they reflect the light from outside in the same manner as a mirror.

Heat Transfer

Heat is transferred by conduction, radiation, convection, and air infiltration.

Thermal conduction is a process of heat transfer through a material in which kinetic

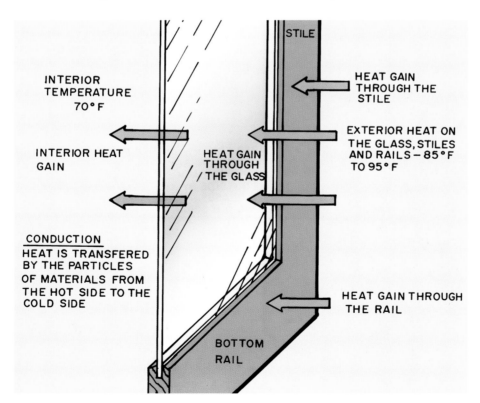

16-4 *Glass is a good conductor of heat. Heat is transferred through it by conduction.*

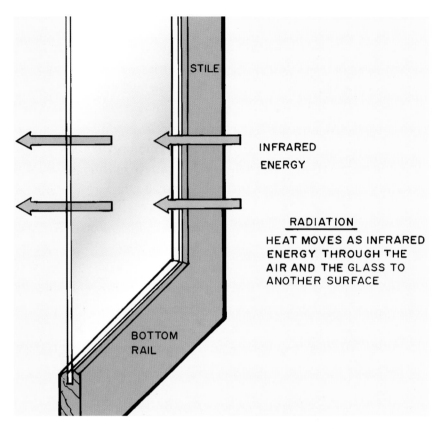

STILE

INFRARED
ENERGY

RADIATION
HEAT MOVES AS INFRARED
ENERGY THROUGH THE
AIR AND THE GLASS TO
ANOTHER SURFACE

BOTTOM
RAIL

*16-5 Glass absorbs
heat and radiates it to
the other side and on
into the room.*

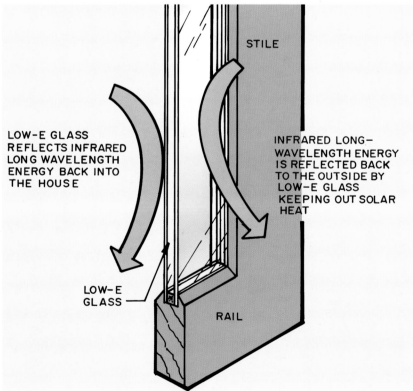

STILE

LOW-E GLASS
REFLECTS INFRARED
LONG WAVELENGTH
ENERGY BACK INTO
THE HOUSE

INFRARED LONG-
WAVELENGTH ENERGY
IS REFLECTED BACK
TO THE OUTSIDE BY
LOW-E GLASS
KEEPING OUT SOLAR
HEAT

LOW-E
GLASS

RAIL

*16-6 Low-E coatings
reflect long-wavelength
radiation, keeping out
solar heat and retaining
interior heat.*

conduction through glazing by using energy-efficient glazing. Storm doors can reduce heat loss and gain some, but more-efficient exterior doors are the best solution.

The doorframe exposes quite a few square inches to the exterior conditions. It can be a source of heat loss and gain. Wood and vinyl frames are more energy efficient than metal.

Radiation is the transfer of heat as infrared electromagnetic waves through the glass. It moves from a warmer source to a cooler surface (16-5). As radiation moves toward the cooler surface, it does not heat the air, but rather heats whatever it strikes, such as a chair or person. Glass absorbs heat and radiates it to the other side. If you sit near a door with a large glazed area, your body radiates heat to the colder glass, making you feel cold.

Part of the sun's energy is visible. The shorter wavelengths are beyond purple and are termed ultraviolet (UV), while the longer wavelengths which are beyond the red part of the visible spectrum of the sun's energy are termed infrared and are felt as heat. As the sun strikes the glass, heat, UV, and visible light enter the room. Here they may be absorbed and radiated into the room or reflected to other parts of the area.

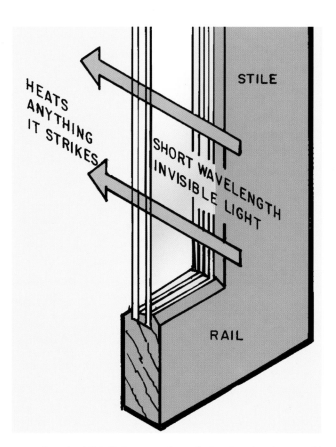

16-7 Short-wavelength visible light passes through the glass, heating anything it strikes.

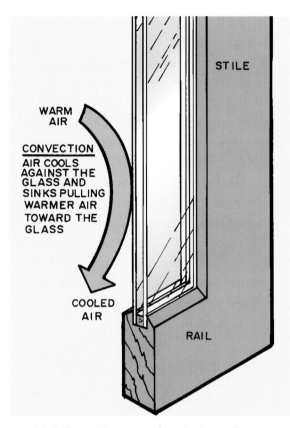

16-8 Convection occurs when air gives up heat to a cooler surface.

Long-wavelength radiant-heat loss or gain can be overcome somewhat by placing a low-E coating on the glass. This coating reflects the infrared wavelengths **(16-6).** Short-wavelength visible light that passes through the glass to the interior will be absorbed by interior surfaces that it strikes, and the heat that is gained will be radiated as heat **(16-7).** This heat gain can be reduced, if desired, by lowering blinds or closing draperies over the windows, blocking the visible light. However, such heat gain may be desirable in the winter, providing a source of solar heat as well as natural light.

Convection occurs when air gives up heat to a cooler surface, such as the door glazing **(16-8).** The cooler air sinks to the floor, pulling new warmer air against the cold glass or door interior and creating a draft within the room. If a person is seated near a door with considerable glass, this draft will be very noticeable and uncomfortable. This draft can be reduced somewhat by placing insulated draperies or shades over the door and by using energy-efficient glazing and insulated doors.

Infiltration is the leakage of air through poorly fitting door assemblies. The doorframe should be caulked around the edges where it butts against the walls **(16-9).** A very small gap, over a number of hours, will

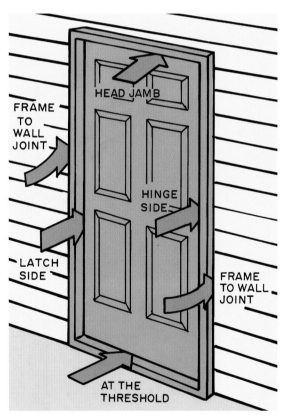

16-9 Air infiltration is a major source of heat loss and gain, and occurs around the edges of the door and the doorframe.

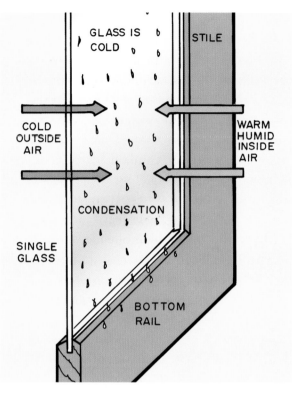

16-10 When the single glazing on door lights is cold, the humid inside air is likely to lead to condensation.

conditions the condensation can freeze on the interior of the glazing.

Manufacturers of glazing often have it tested to find its Condensation Resistance Factor (CRF). Areas where it is seasonally very cold require glazing with a CRF rating of 35. Warmer climates can use units with a lower value.

Performance Data

Some manufacturers have their doors tested by independent laboratories that certify that the doors are manufactured to the American Architectural Manufacturers Association (AAMA) and Window and Door Manufacturers Association (WDMA) specifi-

permit a large volume of air to enter the house. Quality doors and frames that will not bow or warp and that have adequate weatherstripping are required.

Condensation

Condensation is the formation of moisture on a surface. On doors this will be most apparent on the glazing **(16-10)**. Even energy-efficient glazing will, under certain conditions, be subject to having condensation form on it **(16-11).** This is due to the high humidity of the interior air, not necessarily a defect in the door glazing. The thing to do is reduce the level of humidity in the air in the house. About 30- to 50-percent relative humidity is recommended. Under certain

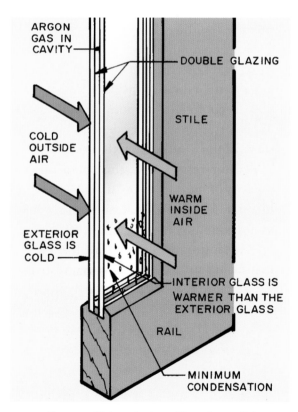

16-11 Energy-efficient glazing will, under conditions of high humidity, have some condensation form, but this is very unusual.

cations. Additional tests include air-infiltration rates, water penetration, and structural pressure in pounds per square foot (psf). Air-infiltration tests show that wood-framed doors are more efficient at blocking air leakage than metal-framed doors, because metal expands and contracts more than wood. Many metal doors are built with a wood frame, as shown earlier in Chapter 3.

Air leakage around a door produces a much larger heat loss than the heat loss through the material of the door itself. Weatherstripping systems are critical to the energy efficiency of a door assembly.

Air infiltration is measured under controlled conditions, at a specified pressure difference between the air inside and outside the building. Leakage is expressed in cubic feet per minute per square foot of the total area. Lower rating numbers indicate a more airtight door. Many doors test at 0.10- to 0.20-cubic-feet-per-minute infiltration. Air infiltration will vary depending on the speed of the wind striking the door.

Water-resistance ratings indicate the capacity of the door to resist the penetration of water. The rating is measured as the maximum pounds per square foot (psf) at which no penetration will occur. Typical ratings vary from 3 to 15 psf.

Structural testing reveals the pressure that a door can resist in pounds per square foot. Typical ratings run from 30 to 90 psf.

Performance standards for some types of door are available from the American Architectural Manufacturers Association (AAMA), the Window and Door Manufacturers Association (WDMA) and the American Society for Testing and Materials.

The energy efficiency of a door or window and its glazing is specified by its U-factor. The U-factor is a measure of the rate of heat flow through a material or an assembly of materials. It is the rate of nonsolar heat flow through the glazing and the stiles and rails, and core, for a door. The U-factor is expressed in British Thermal Units (BTU) per hour per square foot of surface per degree of Fahrenheit (F) or watts per square meter per degree Celsius (C) per degree difference between the inside and outside surfaces. Some doors have a U-factor rating that includes the frame, glazing, and door.

Energy-Efficient Glazing

Typical energy-efficient glazing is usually double-glazed. A comparison of the U-factor of single- and double-glazed window units is given in **Table 16-1**. Typical heat gains for these glazings are in **Table 16-2**.

Insulating Glass

Insulating glass is a glazing unit consisting of two or more layers of glass with an airspace between them. The edges are sealed so that the airspace is airtight. The edges of the glass are separated by an edge-spacer bonded to the glass. A sealant or glue is used around the perimeter to contain the glazing gas and ensure that the assembly is watertight. The spacer contains a desiccant material that absorbs any traces of moisture left in the airspace after the unit has been sealed. If the spacer is a metal gasket that touches the glass, heat and cold are convected through it reducing the efficiency at the edges of the glazing. To reduce this loss, manufacturers are using a variety of edge-

Table 16-1 Typical U-Factors for Single & Double Glazing

	Center of glass U-factor	Unit U-factor	Percent relative humidity when moisture forms at the center of the glass
Single glazing	1.10	0.80	14
Double glazimg	0.25	0.30	66

Table 16-2 Typical Heat Gains for Clear Glazing

Clear Heat gain glazing	(Btu/ft^2/hr)
Single pane ⅛"	214
Single pane ³⁄₁₆"	208
Double pane	186

spacers made from materials that have insulating value. One type uses a silicone foam spacer containing desiccant. It has adhesive on the edges to seal it to the glass **(16-12)**. Another uses a silicone rubber spacer. When metal spacers are used, they are separated from the glass with a sealant or the thermal break is placed in the center of the spacer.

The airspace is usually filled with argon or krypton gas. This provides a degree of insulation which reduces the transmission of heat and cold through the airspace.

In areas of high wind or unusually high temperatures that cause stress on the glass, insulating glass units are made that use heat-strengthened or tempered glass. They are available with tinted, reflective, laminated, and low-E glass.

Gas Fills

The efficiency of multiple-glazed windows is improved by replacing the air in the cavities with a gas that has a lower conductivity than air. The gases used are inert. Inert gases are a group of chemically stable, nonreactive gases that occur naturally in the atmosphere. If the window were broken and the gases released into the atmosphere, the gases would be harmless.

The most commonly used gas is argon. It is effective and inexpensive. Another gas

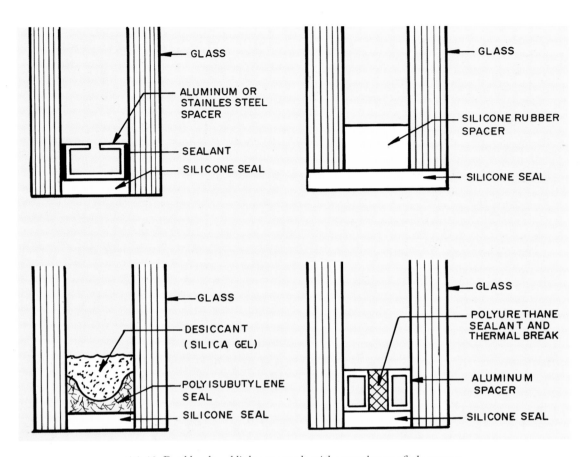

16-12 Double-glazed lights are made with several types of edge spacer.

used is krypton. Krypton is better for reducing heat loss than argon but is more expensive. Krypton is often used in triple- and quadruple-glazed units; because being more energy efficient, the width of the cavity can be reduced. Argon-filled glazing cavities are typically ½ inch. The gas does not affect visible light transmittance.

A well-made, properly sealed, multiple-glazed unit will retain the gas for many years. Some manufacturers use a dual seal around the edge of the unit. A dual seal is more likely to retain the gas in the unit longer that a single seal.

When argon or krypton gas fills the cavities of a multiglazed unit that has a low-E coating, the heat transmission by conduction and convection is greatly reduced. This reduces summer heat gain and winter loss. Since the interior glass is warmer, condensation is less likely to occur.

Low-E Coatings

The efficiency of the glazing can be improved by using glass with a low-E coating. Refer to **16-6.** This coating is a microscopically thin metal or metal oxide layer applied to the surface of the glass. This type of coating is almost invisible. Typical low-E coatings are transparent to the visible spectrum and also allow the transmission of shortwave infrared radiation. The low-E

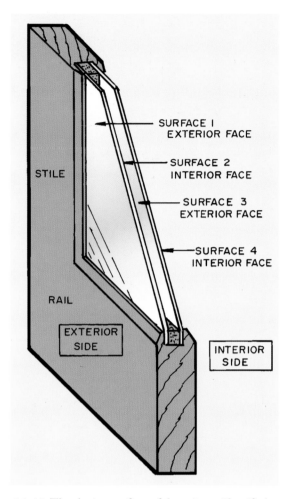

16-13 *The glazing surfaces of the unit are identified by number.*

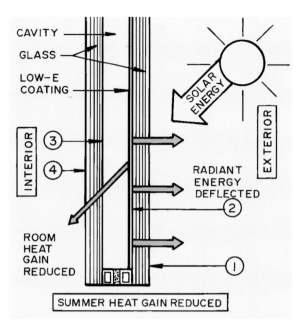

16-14 *In areas where air-conditioning is important, the low-E coating is placed on the inside of the exterior glass (surface 2) in double-glazed insulating units.*

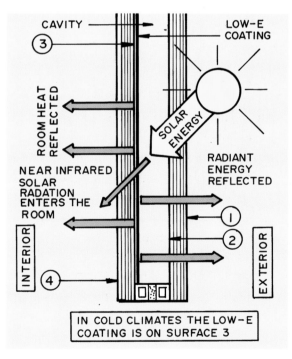

16-15 *Where heating is the major consideration, the low-E coating is placed on the inside of the interior glass (surface 3).*

coating, however, is effective at reflecting longwave infrared radiation and limiting the emission of radiant energy. This suppression of infrared radiation increases the energy efficiency of the glazing, thus giving a reduced value for the U-factor. This type of coating permits a high level of natural light transmission. These coatings are especially valuable on glass doors and doors with considerable glazing.

Low-E coatings can be applied to either of the interior surfaces of the glass in double-glazed units. The surfaces are numbered as shown in **16-13.** Because some shortwave energy is absorbed by a low-E coating whether it is on surface 2 or 3, this affects its performance. Where cooling the air is most important, the coating is placed on surface 2 **(16-14).** This lowers the solar-heat-gain rating and reduces solar energy gains. Where heating is most important, the coating is located on surface 3 **(16-15).** This permits solar energy to pass through the exterior glazing and the cavity, putting the absorbed solar energy on the room side glass and increasing solar-heat gain in the room.

Low-E coatings may be hard-coat (pyrolitic) or soft-coat (sputtered). Generally soft coats have lower emissivities, so have higher insulation values, but do not admit as much solar heat as hard coats. Soft coats are easily damaged and are used only on the interior surfaces of double-glazed units. Hard coats are more durable and can be used on exposed surfaces. While they are thicker than soft coats, they are still very thin.

There are several types of low-E coating and they absorb and transmit different amounts of solar energy. If you live in a northern climate, choose one that admits sufficient solar energy to be useful in the winter yet blocks come heat gain in the summer.

Heat-transmission low-E coatings are used in northern areas. They permit the transmission of near infrared solar radiation and reflect the far infrared radiation **(16-15).** This provides for solar-heat gain in the winter and reduces heat loss from the inside to the exterior.

16-16 This entryway is glazed with laminated glass that is more break-resistant than tempered glass. This provides security against storms and break-ins. It also has desirable sound-transmission properties.
Courtesy ODL

Selective-transmission low-E coatings are used on window glazing to be used in climates where both winter heating and summer cooling requirements are important. In the summer they admit natural light yet reduce solar infrared energy transmission. In the winter they reduce heat loss from the interior of the house. A typical example is shown in **16-14.**

Low-transmission low-E coatings are used in warm climates, allowing the smallest amount of solar-heat gain and reducing the amount of visible-light transmission to control glare.

Solar-control film is another product used to provide solar-heat control and ultraviolet-radiation control. The film is a polyester substrate with a special scratch-resistant coating on one side. It is applied to the interior surface of the glass, It reduces the transmittance of light and infrared heat through glass and has ultraviolet absorbers to reduce the amount of ultraviolet radiation transmitted through the glass. This product is placed on the glazing after the doors or windows are installed.

Safety & Acoustical Glazing

As discussed earlier in this chapter, tempered and heat-treated glass are much stronger than the float (annealed) glass commonly available. Doors, especially, are subject to considerable hard use and occasionally someone will walk into a glass door not realizing it is closed and blocking their path. Building codes typically require specific

16-17 The glass in the entry is a combination of crystalline glue-chip and clear beveled glass. Round brass caming is in the bevel, highlighting the geometric shapes. **Courtesy Therma-Tru Doors**

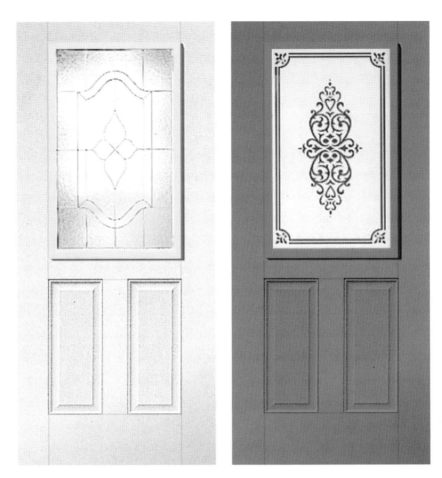

16-18 The door on the left has decorative beveled glass framed with caming. The door on the right has a double-paned safety glass that has a design outlined by a lightly frosted background.
Courtesy Therma-Tru Doors

types of glass in all exterior doors. Some additional products to consider are laminated glass, acoustical glass, and safety film.

LAMINATED GLASS

Laminated glass is used in areas where extra protection against breakage is needed. A hurricane-prone area is one place where this glass would help give protection against flying debris **(16-16)**. Laminated glass consists of the bonding of layers of float glass with interlayers of plasticized polyvinyl butyral

(PVB) resin or polycarbonate (PC) resin. The glass is chemically strengthened by immersion in a molten salt bath. Should it be broken, the polyvinyl butyral interlayer keeps the glass intact so that there is no interior damage. This glazing also reduces noise transfer and ultraviolet radiation into the room. Laminated glass also reduces the chance of an intruder breaking and entering the house though it. The frame used must be strong enough to resist the same damaging forces as the glass.

ACOUSTICAL GLASS

Acoustical glass is a form of laminated glass. It has a layer of sound-absorbing plastic bonded between layers of glass. The soft plastic inter-layer permits the glass panels to bend slightly in response to the pressure from sound waves. It is also available in multiglazed insulated units.

Two panes separated by an airspace are better than a single pane. The thicker the glass, the better it resists sound transmis-sion. Wider airspaces will have a greater sound-transmission loss. Some units use a glass pane and a plastic pane with an airspace. Of course, the door must be tightly sealed. Sound as well as air can filter in around a poorly fitting door. Generally a sound level for residences of 30 to 40 dBA (decibel scale) is recommended. The rating system used for describing the sound-transmission properties gives a single number that is identified as the Sound Transmission Class (STC).

16-19 This door light has a six-color image developed on it using a texture silk-screen process. Each design has colors offset by clear glass. **Courtesy ODL**

16-20 These lights are made by bonding acrylic colors to the glass to produce the appearance of stained glass.
Courtesy ODL

SAFETY FILM

Safety film is a thin plastic film that is applied to provide some protection when the glazing is shattered by holding the shards, preventing them from flying in the air. This is valuable in particular situations, such as during a storm in which objects can become projectiles blown against the glass, shattering it. The safety film does reduce visible light transmittance and may slightly obscure the view.

Decorative Glass

A number of manufacturers produce decorative glass lights. These are available as door lights and as sidelights. The fiberglass entry door in **16-17** has lights made from clear beveled glass and crystalline glue-chip glass. They are framed with a polished brass caming. Caming is a strip—such as lead, zinc, or brass—that is bonded to the glass, forming a decorative pattern. A door light with frosted glass is seen in **16-18.** A delicate pattern is formed on the glass by frosting the background and leaving the pattern on the clear glass. Another approach is shown in **16-19.** Here the glass has a six-color image developed on it using a texture silk-screen process. This enables the use of several colors to create an elegant entryway. Still another product bonds vibrant acrylic colors permanently to the glass **(16-20).** It appears much like a stained-glass window.

16-21 This decorative glazing places a center cluster of bevels and brass caming between two panes of safety-tempered, insulating glass. This provides energy efficiency and security.
Courtesy Therma-Tru Doors

16-22 Acrylic-block glazing units are used to glaze doors, sidelights, and transoms. They admit natural light yet provide privacy. **Courtesy Hi-Lite Products, Inc.**

16-23 *When standard doors are used, acrylic-block glazing can be used for sidelights and transoms. Considerable natural light is admitted into the foyer.* **Courtesy Hi-Lite Products, Inc.**

The light in **16-21** uses a swirled baroque glass. The design cluster has curved bevels and rounded brass caming. The design is sealed between two panes of safety-tempered, insulating glass.

Many other designs and assembly techniques are available from door and glass manufacturers.

Acrylic Blocks

Acrylic blocks appear much like glass blocks but are considerably lighter and can be used to glaze windows, door lights, sidelights, and transoms (**16-22** and **16-23**). They are available in scratch-resistant, high-quality acrylic units that will stand up against harsh weather and resist discoloration. Several surface patterns, such as a frosted finish and a clear, smooth surface, are available.

Acrylic blocks are made by hermetically sealing two cast pieces to create a cavity, providing an insulating airspace. The U-factor is about the same as for a typical double-glazed window.

HARDWARE & SECURITY

Choosing hardware is an important part of the process of selecting items that enhance the appearance of a home and maintain its security. The major entryway deserves an attractive, high-quality lockset that reflects the style of the house and is of a quality that will remain attractive and operate easily for years **(17-1).** Security considerations are equally important as appearance given the incidence of home break-ins. While many of these entries are through windows, secure doors deserve major consideration. Electronic sytems can be a critical to interior and exterior security as discussed in the section on

17-1 Quality entry locksets add to the overall impression of the front entrance and remain attractive and operate easily for many years.
Courtesy Baldwin Hardware Corporation

home security in Chapter 10, "Home Automation & Other Systems." Here the focus is on effective hardware and easy-to-install security devices, including devices typically used in both hard-wired and wireless alarm systems.

Locksets

There are a variety of locksets available. Some are designed for use on interior doors where security is not as important. Exterior locksets that are key operated are stronger and provide the needed security. The level of security varies with the type of lock and the quality of its construction.

There are two commonly used kinds of lockset available, bored and mortised. Bored locksets come in two types that are easy to install. They require only two holes to be bored in the door. The two types of bored lockset are tubular and cylindrical.

TUBULAR & CYLINDRICAL BORED LOCKSETS

The tubular-type lockset (17-2) has a spring-loaded latch bolt inside a tube. The knobs or lever handles mount on a spindle that passes through an opening in the latch-bolt tube (17-3). When the knob or lever is turned, the latch bolt moves back into the tube, permitting the door to be opened.

Locksets used on interior doors are tubular type. Tubular-type exterior locksets are also available. Those on interior doors, such as for bedrooms and bathrooms, will have a means for locking for privacy, but can be opened from the outside in an emergency. They will have a locking button on

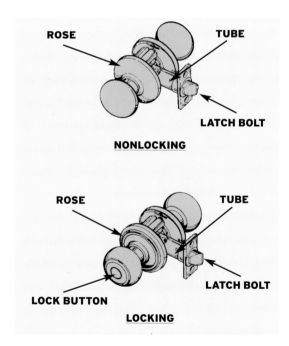

17-2 *Tubular-type interior locksets are available as locking and nonlocking types.*
Courtesy Arrow Lock Manufacturing Company

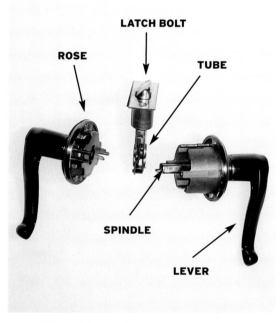

17-3 *The latch bolt in the tube is operated by the spindle that is turned by the knob or lever handle.*

17-4 *Dummy-lock knobs and levers are used on doors that do not need a latch bolt. They serve as a door pull. This one is on a bifold door.*

wire or nail can be inserted to unlock the door from outside the room. Other interior locksets will latch the door but cannot be locked. These are often referred to as passage locks. They are used for closets, storerooms, and other places where privacy is not required. Another type consists of just a knob or lever that is screwed to a door to serve as a pull **(17-4).** It is sometimes called a dummy lock. It is used on doors, such as bifolds, where a latch is not required. It is simply screwed to the face of the door. Generally the same style knob or lever is used on the other doors selected.

the inside knob or lever that is pushed in to lock the door. It is unlocked from the inside merely by turning the handle. The outside knob or lever has a small hole into which a

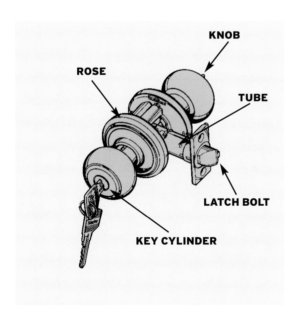

17-5 *This is a tubular-type exterior door lockset. It has a key cylinder in the outside knob and a lever to control the lock on the inside knob.*
Courtesy Arrow Lock Manufacturing Company

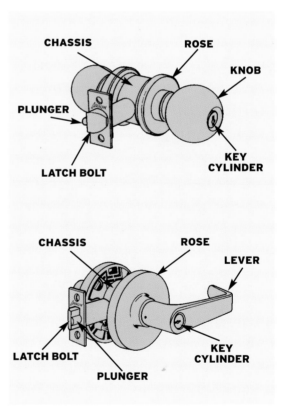

17-6 *Cylindrical locksets provide excellent security for exterior doors.*
Courtesy Arrow Lock Manufacturing Company

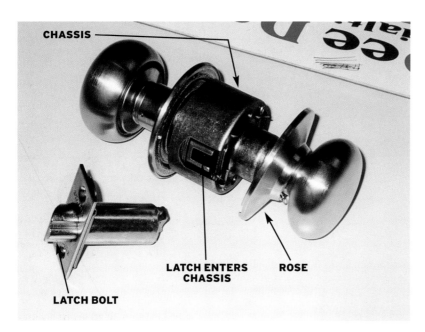

CHASSIS

LATCH ENTERS
CHASSIS

ROSE

LATCH BOLT

17-7 A typical cylindrical lockset.

Tubular-type locksets are also available for use on exterior doors. They have a key control on the outside knob and a lever on the inside to lock and unlock the door **(17-5).** They are not as secure as cylindrical locks, which are recommended for use on exterior doors.

A cylindrical lockset is shown in **17-6.** It is installed in the same general manner as the tubular-type; however, it provides greater security. This type of lockset has a large-diameter cylinder called the chassis **(17-7).** The latch is secured into the side of the cylinder. The key cylinder is installed in the knob. A lever or pushbutton on the inside knob is used to lock and unlock the door from the inside.

The cylindrical and tubular locksets are available with a wide variety of knobs and lever handles. The lever handles are

17-8 Quite a variety of levers are available. Choose one that fits the interior décor of the house

17-9 *These are a few examples of the many knobs available. When visiting the building supply dealer, be certain to view the total array of knobs.*

available in a straight shape and a variety of curved designs **(17-8)** and in a number of different finishes. The large variety of knob locksets also come in a number of different finishes **(17-9).** The lever-type handle has the advantage that it makes it easier to open the door. This is especially helpful for children and those who have some disability that makes turning a round knob difficult.

Another widely used lock is the dead bolt **(17-10).** It is much like the lockset just described. However, it has a single metal latch that can be moved only by a key from the outside **(17-11)** or by an inserted key or thumb turn on the inside of the door **(17-12).** Some entry

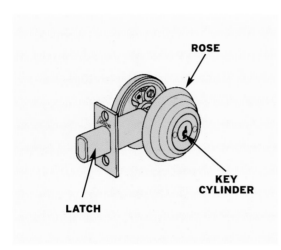

17-10 *A dead bolt provides additional security.*

locksets have a dead bolt included in addition to the latch used to hold the door closed **(17-13)**. A dead bolt is used to increase the security of the door. Some locksets with plungers can have the plunger pushed back with a plastic card, allowing the door to be opened. The dead bolt alongside the latch bolt prevents this from happening.

Single- and double-cylinder dead bolts are both available. A single-cylinder dead bolt has a key that operates it from outside and a thumb turn to operate it from the inside. This is quite adequate for residential

17-12 *This dead bolt has a thumb turn on the inside of the door.*

17-11 *The dead bolt is operated by a key on the outside of the door.*

use and, in some areas, it is the only type permitted by the local building code.

Double-cylinder dead bolts require a key to open or close the lock from either side of the door. This prevents an intruder who has entered some other way from opening the

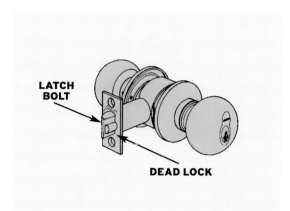

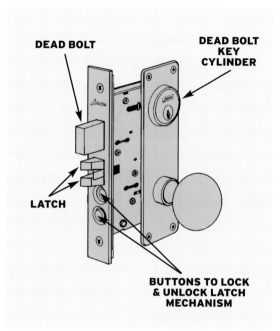

17-13 *A dead-bolt lock next to the latch bolt blocks attempts to slide the latch back with a plastic card.* **Courtesy Arrow Lock Manufacturing Company**

17-14 *This double-cylinder dead bolt requires that a key be used to unlock the door from the inside. It is usually mounted in tandem with a lever or knob lockset.*

17-15 *A mortise lock has a latch bolt and a dead bolt.* **Courtesy Arrow Lock Manufacturing Company**

door **(17-14).** Generally these locks are prohibited by local codes because, in an emergency, finding the key can be a problem and would keep the occupants from fleeing the building. Some want to use these to keep a potential intruder from opening the door by breaking the side glass or door light and reaching in to unlock the door, as could happen with a single-cylinder lock. It is better to provide security glazing over any glass than to use a double-cylinder lock.

Select a dead bolt that has a hardened steel bolt so that it cannot be cut through. The dead bolt should penetrate the door-jamb at least one inch and have and extra-strong strike plate that is secured with extra-long screws. It must be firm enough so that it cannot be torn away from the doorframe.

MORTISE LOCKSET

A mortise lock is a high-quality entryway lockset **(17-15).** It differs a great deal from bored locksets. It has an anti-friction latch

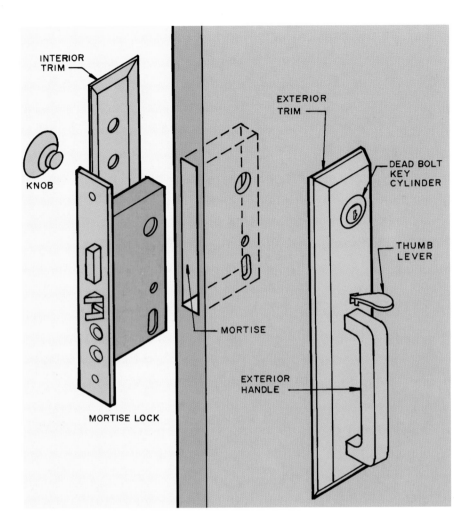

INTERIOR TRIM

KNOB

MORTISE LOCK

MORTISE

EXTERIOR TRIM

DEAD BOLT KEY CYLINDER

THUMB LEVER

EXTERIOR HANDLE

17-16 Mortise locks are set into a deep mortise pocket cut into the edge of the door.

and a hardened-steel saw-proof dead bolt. A mortise lock requires that a deep-pocket mortise be cut into the edge of the door to receive the mechanism. Then several holes are bored through the face of the door for the key cylinder, knob spindle, and other controls **(17-16** and **17-1).** Follow the manufacturer's instructions, since designs vary. A view of the interior mechanism is shown in **17-17.** This shows that the internal parts are fitted with clock like precision, giving long service, security, and trouble-free operation. Mortise locks are the very best units available.

The mortise lock also adds considerably to the overall appearance of the entryway. A variety of designs and finishes are available. One example is shown in **17-18.**

Other entryway locksets have separate dead bolts and a latching handle-set assembly **(17-19).** The dead bolt has a decorative rose behind the key cylinder. The handle-set assembly has a decorative escutcheon. Brass is a popular finish, though other finishes are available. Each is installed separately, much like the dead-bolt and bored-lockset installations shown in Chapter 7. The manufacturer supplies detailed installation instructions.

17-17 *A mortise lock has a complex, carefully crafted internal mechanism that enables it to function smoothly for a very long time.*
Courtesy Baldwin Hardware Corporation

17-18 *The exposed mortise trim plate sets the style of the entryway door and deserves major consideration as choices are considered.* **Courtesy Baldwin Hardware Corporation**

17-19 *A commonly used entryway lockset installation includes separate dead bolts and a latching handle set assembly.*

17-20 *Sliding-glass-door locks provide minimum security.*

The locking mechanism for sliding glass doors is built into the unit at the factory. It has a hooked lever that fits into a metal packet, latching the door. An interior lever controls the operation **(17-20)**. This is not very secure, and other security devices are needed to provide adequate protection.

Hardware Accessories

A door knocker is an attractive addition to the entryway door **(17-21)**. Various designs are available in brass and bronze and can be chosen to complement the style of the house. Since electric doorbells are almost always installed, these carryovers from an earlier time are mostly decorative.

Another accessory is a kick plate on the bottom edge of the door. This provides protection of the door, but, on residences, it is again mainly decorative **(17-22)**.

Door closers are part of the hardware that is received with a storm door **(17-23)**. They give protection from high winds by limiting the amount of outward swing, pulling the door closed, and cushioning the closing of the door. The hold-open washer permits the door to stand open when ventilation is wanted or an item needs to be moved through the entry and there is no hand free to hold the door.

Doorstops are used to keep the door from striking a wall or cabinet if opened too far. There are several types available **(17-24)**. The hinge-mounted stop is one of the most convenient doorstops because it does not stick out into the room.

17-21 *A door knocker adds a decorative touch to the entryway door. It should complement the door-lockset escutcheon design.*

17-22 *Brass kick plates protect the door but mainly serve as a decorative feature.*

17-23 *Door closers should be mounted on the top and bottom rails of storm doors.*

17-24 *Doorstops are used to keep a door from swinging back and striking the wall. The type that mounts on a hinge is especially nice because it is up out of the way.*
Courtesy Baldwin Hardware Corporation

17-25 *Butt hinges with rounded corners are used on interior doors.*

17-26 *Stylish square-corner butt hinges are often used on the exterior doors.*
Courtesy Baldwin Hardware Corporation

Hinges

While hinges on most types of door are not seen, their selection is important. Cheap hinges are a poor investment. They get frequent use and carry a heavy door. Many doors used today come pre-hung on a doorframe. Be certain the hinge supplied is a quality product.

The most commonly used hinge for exterior and interior doors is the butt hinge. The hinge with rounded corners is generally used on interior doors **(17-25)**. The one with the square corner leaves is used on some exterior and interior doors **(17-26)**. The hinge with one square corner and one round corner hinge is used on steel and fiberglass exterior doors **(17-27)**.

HINGE ON METAL DOOR

HINGE ON FIBERGLASS DOOR

17-27 *Steel and fiberglass doors are often hung with a hinge that has a round corner leaf mounted on the jamb and a square corner leaf on the door.*

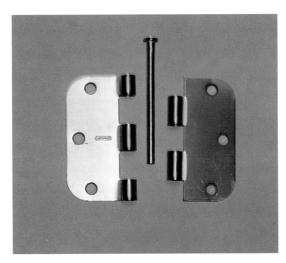

17-28 The pin on hinges used on interior doors can be removed, enabling the door to be removed.

Hinges mounted on an interior door have a loose pin that enables you to remove the door by pulling the pin **(17-28)**. Hinges on exterior doors should have the pin secured in place with another small pin inserted through the barrel into the pin. This prevents an intruder from removing the pin on exterior doors to gain access to the house. Heavy doors should have commercial-grade hinges or ball-bearing hinges. Heavy doors could have an extra hinge installed. Typical exterior and interior residential doors will have three hinges.

Hinges that are used on exterior and interior doors are swaged as shown in **17-29**. This reduces the size of the gap between the door and frame.

Hinges are specified by giving the length of the leaf parallel with the barrel and the width, which is measured when the hinge is open in a flat position **(17-30)**. The width of the hinge chosen depends upon the thickness of the door. The various sizes available and some recommendations for selecting hinges are given in Chapter 7.

A typical hinge that is used on bifold doors in shown in **17-31**. It is a small non-mortise hinge. Since one leaf fits into the opening in the other leaf, only a very small gap exists between the doors.

Doors can be hung without mortises using a nonmortise hinge **(17-32)**. The leaves are screwed to the edge of the door

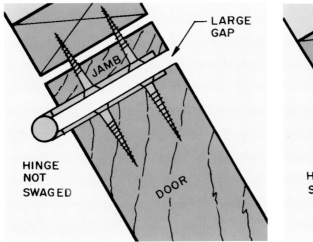

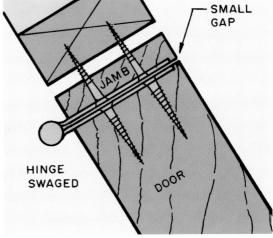

17-29 Door hinges are swaged, meaning the leaves are bent in such a way as to reduce the size of the space between the door and the jamb.

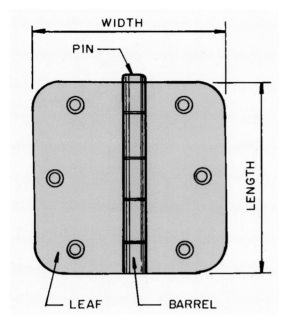

17-30 *The size of a hinge is indicated by specifying the length of the leaf and the width in a flat open position.*

and jamb, leaving a very narrow gap the width of the thickness of the hinge leaf. If the doors are heavy, check to see whether they will carry the weight.

Further Aspects of Security

As mentioned earlier, quality locks, dead bolts, and strong hinges with nonremovable pins are an essential element in creating good deterrents for unwelcome intruders. There are a number of other measures that can be taken to increase security specifically in relation to doors. A peephole set through the door is a simple way to allow you to have a view of who is at the door before you unlock and open it **(17-33)**. Even better is installing a video sentry system, as discussed in Chapter 10 in the section on home security.

17-31 *This hinge is used on bifold doors. It does not require a mortise and leaves a narrow crack.*

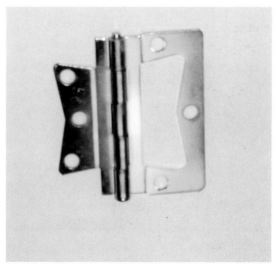

17-32 *This nonmortise hinge can be used to hang doors to the jamb. It leaves a very small crack between the door and jamb.*

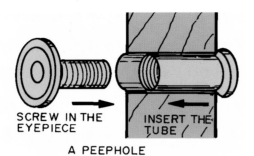

SCREW IN THE
EYEPIECE

INSERT THE
TUBE

A PEEPHOLE

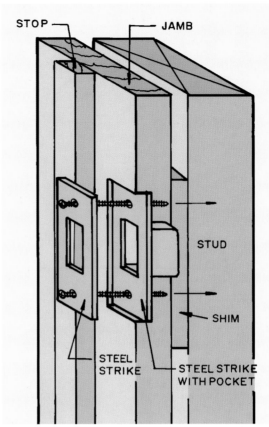

STOP

JAMB

STUD

SHIM

STEEL
STRIKE

STEEL STRIKE
WITH POCKET

17-34 Making sure that you install a steel strike that has a pocket as well as a flat strike plate will provide additional protection against the possibility of an intruder's being able to force open or even break in the door.

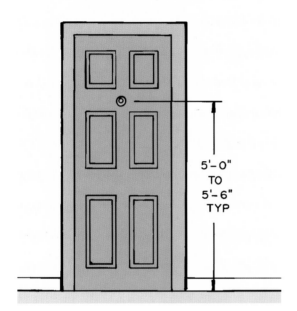

5'-0"
TO
5'-6"
TYP

17-33 A peephole installed through an entry door lets you see who is there outside before you open it

Another easy-to-install security device is a double-plate strike that replaces the single-thickness door strike. The double-strike back plate has a metal box into which the plunger from the door lockset fits **(17-34)**.

You can also replace the screws in the hinge on the doorframe with longer screws **(17-35)**. Use 3- or 3½-inch screws that will penetrate firmly into the stud behind the doorframe. If the door has sidelights, be careful that the length of the screws is not so great that they continue to into the stile and break the glass.

Garage doors are notoriously rather easy to force open and an intruder, once inside, is typically concealed from view. This makes it necessary that the door from the garage into the house be as secure as all the other exterior doors of the house.

Allowing your pets access to the outdoors can be a security concern. Careful thought should be given to the placement and accessibility of pet doors. Electronically or magnetically activated pet doors are widely available that can be set to lock after entry or exit of the animal.

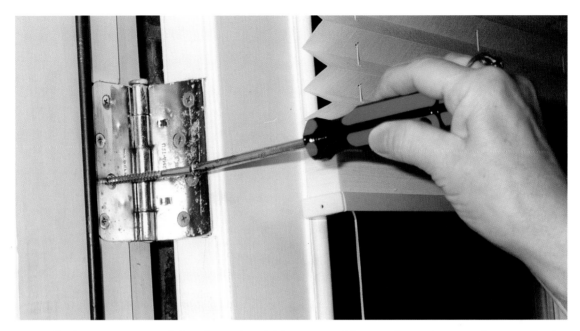

17-35 Replacing one or more of the ordinary-length hinge screws with screws that are long enough to enter firmly into the stud increases the security of the doo

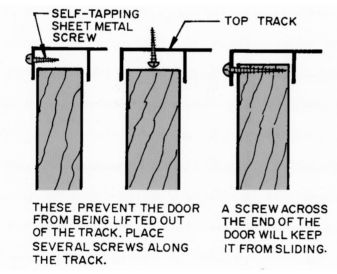

SELF-TAPPING SHEET METAL SCREW — TOP TRACK

THESE PREVENT THE DOOR FROM BEING LIFTED OUT OF THE TRACK. PLACE SEVERAL SCREWS ALONG THE TRACK.

A SCREW ACROSS THE END OF THE DOOR WILL KEEP IT FROM SLIDING.

17-36 Sliding glass doors can be made more secure by installing sheet-metal screws to prevent them from being lifted off the track.

Sliding glass doors can be a major security problem. To increase their security, some types have been designed so that the sliding door cannot be simply lifted off the track to give entrance to the house. If the sliding door is an older type, screws can be installed along the top of the doorframe, preventing the door from being lifted out **(17-36)**. A wood stick or metal bar can be placed in the track on the floor **(17-37)**. Pins can also be set through holes drilled in the frame at the floor, blocking the door from sliding open **(17-38)**. Commercial products are available, such as a long adjustable rod that is placed between the end of the door and the doorframe. A small clamp that is screwed to the frame at the floor is also available **(17-39)**. Another security tip is to place steel plates at the lockset to keep someone from slipping a plastic card in the gap and opening the plunger. If the

17-37 *A wood stick in the track, or a commercially available stop rod, will prevent a sliding door from being forced open.*

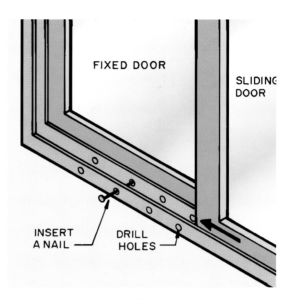

17-38 *A series of holes drilled in the track will limit the amount the sliding door can be opened. The door can be open a little for ventilation but not forced open enough to permit entry.*

17-39 *This is a commercially available clamp that locks on the track, blocking the movement of a sliding door.*

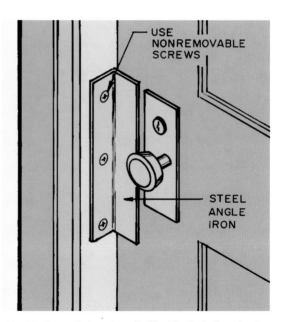

17-40 *An angle iron installed beside the lock makes it difficult for a potential intuder to get to the latch and force it open. This is used on doors that open into a house or an apartment.*

door opens into the house, an angle iron can be screwed to the doorframe with non-removable screws **(17-40).** If the door swings out, a steel plate can be bolted to the door, as shown in **17-41.** Use bolts with round heads or peen the end after the nut has been tightened to keep it from being unscrewed.

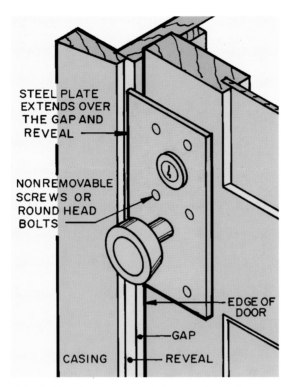

17-41 *If the door opens out, bolt a metal escutcheon plate over the area surrounding the lock. Use screws that cannot be removed or run bolts that have raised heads through the door.*

There are a number of door security devices that are secured to the inside of the door and connected to the doorframe (17-42). While these do not provide the protection given by a good lock, they do offer a deterrent.

Another simple technique that can be used to keep a door with loose-pin hinges from being removed after the pins have actually been pulled but while the door is closed is shown in 17-43.

Alarm Systems

Alarm systems are widely used to provide security for the home when occupied or unoccupied. Some send an alarm to the local police station or to a central monitoring site operated by the alarm company. They also can be set to just sound an alarm at the house and not notify authorities. The

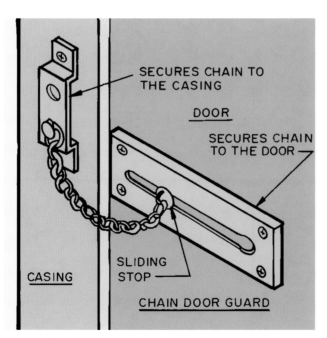

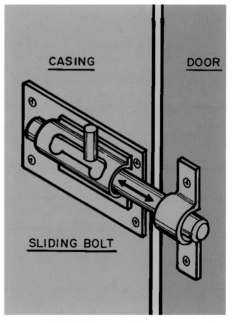

17-42 *These are two of the several types of door-security devices that are available. These provide some security but are not a substitute for a quality door lock.*

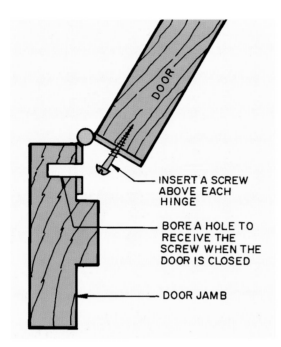

17-43 *This is an easy way to prevent the door from being lifted out when the hinge pin has been removed.*

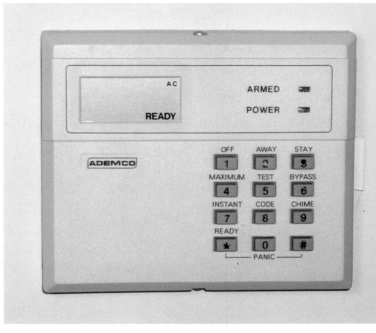

17-45 *This control pad is placed near the most frequently used exterior door and operates the system.*

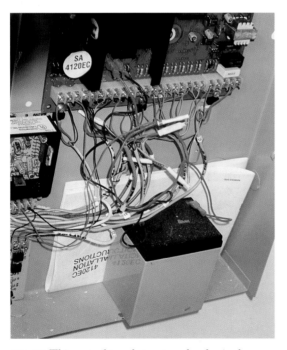

17-44 *This control panel operates a hard-wired security system. It is placed in a closet or other out-of-the-way location. A 120V transformer supplies 24V to the system.*

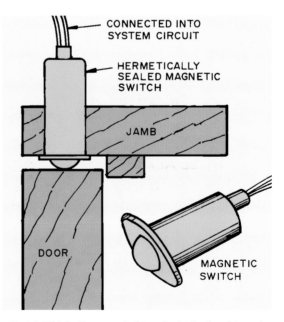

17-46 *This ball-type switching device is placed into the doorframe and activates the alarm when the door is opened.*

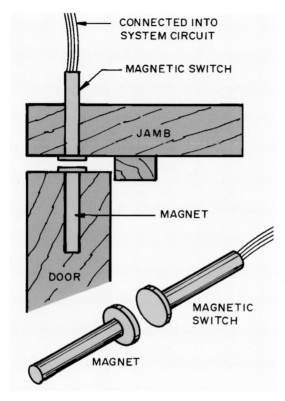

17-47 This sensing device consists of a concealed magnet switch in the jamb and a magnet inserted into the edge of the door.

entrance doors generally used, such as the front door and the door from the garage **(17-45)**. When you enter the house, the control typically has a 30-second delay before sounding the alarm, allowing you time to deactivate the system by punching in a code on the pad keys.

A mechanical switch that is sometimes used on swinging doors is much like that on a refrigerator door. Commonly they become unreliable due to corrosion. A better switch is a hermetically sealed unit with the switching device and magnet in one unit. The control ball on the end touches the edges of the door **(17-46)**.

Another concealed type of switch has a magnet inserted in the edge of the door and a magnetic switch recessed into the door frame **(17-47)**. A significant advantage of this type of switch is that the switch is not easily visible or noticeable, even when the door is open **(17-48)**.

systems available included hard-wired and wireless installations.

HARD-WIRED ALARM SYSTEMS

A hard-wired system has a control panel **(17-44)** that has a transformer operating on 120 volts that converts the current to a low voltage. Switches used on doors and sensors used on windows are connected to the panel. The system operates on a closed circuit. When it is turned on, a low-voltage current flows through the wires connected to the door switches and window sensors. When a door or window is opened, the circuit is broken and the alarm is activated. The system has a control pad near the

17-48 The concealed magnet is not noticeable even when the door is open.

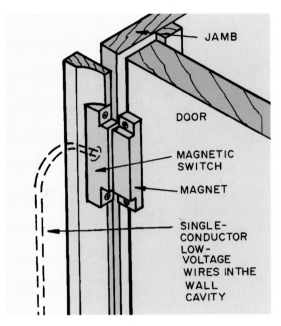

17-49 *Some older alarm systems use surface-mounted switches. They are not decorative and are best-hidden by draperies or shades whenever possible.*

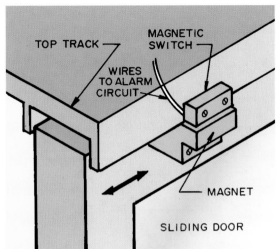

17-51 *Sliding doors may have a magnetic switch mounted on the track and a magnet on the sliding door.*

Surface-mounted sensors are sometimes used. The magnet is mounted on the door and the switch is on the doorframe **(17-49)**. The wires from the switch are run inside the wall. There are a number of sensors available for garage door installation. One is shown in **17-50**. Sliding glass doors also may be protected by surface-mounting a magnet on the door and the switch on the door-frame **(17-51)**.

There are sensors available for use on door glass so that they will detect any glass

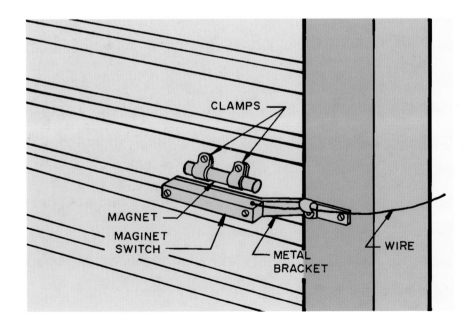

17-50 *This hard-wired alarm sensor is designed for use on a garage door.*

17-53 The central control station of a wireless security system. The transformer above the unit on the right supplies the 14 volts needed to operate the station.

17-52 For warning of, and protection against glass breakage, use a shock sensor on the glass that connects to a sending device triggering an alarm.

breakage. The sensor is mounted on the glass **(17-52).** The magnet and switch are mounted in the edge of the door and the door frame.

Hard-wired systems are installed at the same time as the house is built. The wires to doors and windows are run in the wall cavities in the same manner as the electric wiring is normally run. After the drywall has been put up, access to the wall cavities becomes greatly limited, and system installation becomes much more difficult.

17-54 The sensor is mounted on the door and is connected to the transmitter by a small wire. When the door is open, the sensor activates the transmitter that sends a signal through the air to the control station, thus activating the alarm.

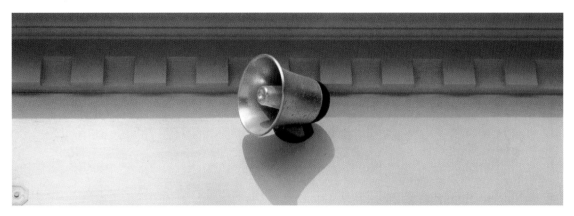

17-55 When the alarm is activated, an inside alarm and an outside siren sound a warning.

WIRELESS ALARM SYSTEMS

Wireless alarm systems typically operate on 14 volts from an ordinary 120-volt electricity outlet. The system has a central control station that has a transformer, which steps down the house current to the required 14 volts **(17-53)**. Remote sensors are mounted on the doors and windows **(17-54)**. These sensors are connected to a transmitter that is typically powered by a 9-volt battery. The alarm sytem is thus wireless since the transmitter needs no physical connection to the central control station.

As with the hard-wired system, the alarm can be connected to the local police station or can simply activate an alarm inside the house and, perhaps, a siren outside **(17-55)**. This system also can operate medical alarms, smoke monitors, and glass-breakage sensors. This system is installed after the house is built. The sensors are mounted on the door and window casing and the door and window stile **(17-54)**. Installation on sliding glass doors is shown

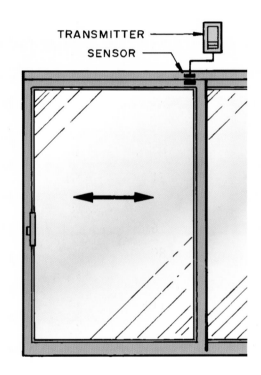

17-56 Sliding doors can be secured with the wireless-system sensor and transmitter.

in **17-56.** One transmitter can operate on two doors if they are reasonably close together.

Metric Equivalents

[to the nearest mm, 0.1cm, or 0.01m]

inches	mm	cm	inches	mm	cm
⅛	3	0.3	14	356	35.6
¼	6	0.6	15	381	38.1
⅜	10	1.0	16	406	40.6
½	13	1.3	17	432	43.2
⅝	16	1.6	18	457	45.7
¾	19	1.9	19	483	48.3
⅞	22	2.2	20	508	50.8
1	25	2.5	21	533	53.3
1¼	32	3.2	22	59	55.9
1½	38	3.8	23	584	58.4
1¾	44	4.4	24	610	61.0
2	51	5.1	25	635	63.5
2½	64	6.4	26	660	66.0
3	76	7.6	27	686	68.6
3½	89	8.9	28	711	71.1
4	102	10.2	29	737	73.7
4½	114	11.4	30	762	76.2
5	127	12.7	31	787	78.7
6	152	15.2	32	813	81.3
7	178	17.8	33	838	83.8
8	203	20.3	34	864	86.4
9	229	22.9	35	889	88.9
10	254	25.4	36	914	91.4
11	279	27.9	37	940	94.0
12	305	30.5	38	965	96.5
13	330	33.0	39	991	99.1

Metric Equivalents

[to the nearest mm, 0.1cm, or 0.01m]

inches	mm	cm	Conversion Factors
40	1016	101.6	**1 mm** = 0.039 inch
41	1041	104.1	**1 m** = 3.28 feet
42	1067	106.7	**1 m²** = 10.8 square feet
43	1092	109.2	
44	1118	111.8	**1 inch** = 25.4 mm
45	1143	114.3	**1 foot** = 304.8 mm
46	1168	116.8	**1 square foot** = 0.09 m²
47	1194	119.4	
48	1219	121.9	**mm** = millimeter
49	1245	124.5	**cm** = centimeter
50	1270	127.0	**m** = meter
			m² = square meter

inches	feet	m
12	1	0.31
24	2	0.61
36	3	0.91
48	4	1.22
60	5	1.52
72	6	1.83
84	7	2.13
96	8	2.44
108	9	2.74

INDEX

U-shaped kitchens, 24, 158–159
U-shaped offices, 138
U-shaped stairs, 223, 224
Utilities, 292, 357
Utility rooms, 188–189

Vacuum systems, central, 271 273
Vapor barriers, 335–336
Vaulted ceilings, 20, 38, 62, 65, 66
Veneer plaster, 341
Veneers, exterior, 320
Ventilation
    bathroom, 192, 329–330
    kitchen, 146, 164–165
    natural, 79, 178, 179
    power, 329–330
    utility room, 184, 189
    windows and, 79, 178, 179
Video, whole house, 253–256
Video entry system, 250–251
Views, 32, 127
Vinyl flooring, 123, 347

Wainscot, 341
Walls, exterior
    bracing, 312
    erecting, 311–313
    framing, 311–313, 360–362
    sheathing, 312–313
    SIP, 373–376
    steel framing system, 401–407
    thickness of, 289
Walls, interior
    ceramic tile, 341–342
    finish/texture, 339–340
    gypsum drywall, 131, 172, 337–340, 341–342

noise and, 192, 193
painting/papering, 343
plaster, veneer, 341
section drawings, 283
steel framing system, 407
water resistant, 341–342
wood paneling, 131, 340–341
Washer/dryer
    outlets, 184
    size/spacing, 182, 183
    venting, 184, 189
Waterfalls, 87
Water heater. See Utility rooms
Water resistant walls, 336, 339, 341–342
Water tables, 292–293
Weather stations, 273–274
Wheelchair access
    bathroom, 194, 196, 209
    grab bars and, 200, 201
    kitchen/countertop, 165–166
Whirlpool tubs, 69, 111, 204, 205, 208, 209
Window and Door Manufacturers Association (WDMA), 415, 416
Windows
    bedroom, 178–179
    energy efficiency and, 127–128, 408–426
    final plans, 289
    installing, 319
    kitchen, 150
    ventilation and, 178, 179
    See also Glass
Windows, examples
    circle, 91
    cottage home, 45, 47

double hung, 20
European/American country, 21
hoods over, 48
maintenance-free, 52, 65
roof, 109
sidelight, 105
transom, 105
ventilation and, 79
vinyl, 65
vinyl clad, 52
Windows, wall of
    contemporary, 32, 62
    eclectic country home, 71
    French country, 54
    golf course home, 101, 103
    log home, 39, 40
    mountain duplex, 110
    post/beam contemporary, 67, 68
Window wells, 138–141, 143
Wiring
    amps/wire size, typical, 323
    cabling systems, 246–248
    SIP construction, 378–380
    structured, 246–248
Wood-frame construction, 358–370. See also Building the house
    balloon framing, 363–364
    diagrams, typical, 362–367, 369–370
    floors, 309–311, 359–360
    overview, 358–359
    platform framing, 362, 363
    roofs, 314–-317, 364–370
    walls, 311–313, 360–362
Work triangle, 155–160

Zoning, noise, 285